G000155176

The State in Modern Society

Also by Roger King

Capital and Politics
The Middle Class (with J. Raynor)
Respectable Rebels (with N. Nugent)
The British Right (with N. Nugent)

The State in Modern Society

New Directions in Political Sociology

Roger King
with Chapter 8 by Graham Gibbs

MACMILLAN

© Roger King 1986
Chapter 8 © Graham Gibbs 1986

All rights reserved. No reproduction, copy or transmission of this publication may be made without written permission.

No paragraph of this publication may be reproduced, copied or transmitted save with written permission or in accordance with the provisions of the Copyright Act 1956 (as amended).

Any person who does any unauthorised act in relation to this publication may be liable to criminal prosecution and civil claims for damages.

First published 1986

Published by
MACMILLAN EDUCATION LTD
Houndmills, Basingstoke, Hampshire RG21 2XS
and London
Companies and representatives
throughout the world

Typeset by Wessex Typesetters
(Division of The Eastern Press, Ltd)
Frome, Somerset

Printed in Great Britain by
Anchor Brendon Ltd,
Tiptree, Essex

ISBN 0-333-36606-9 (hardcover)
ISBN 0-333-36607-7 (paperback)

For Sue, Helen, Tim and Vera

Contents

Acknowledgements

I am very grateful to colleagues over many years who have assisted me in my thinking about political sociology, particularly David Jary who introduced me to the subject and who has continued to be a source of illumination ever since. Steven Kennedy at Macmillan will also have to share some of the responsibility for what follows as he persuaded me that the book could and should be written, although other commitments appeared too daunting for me to even contemplate the effort of producing a political sociology text. However, I am extremely grateful to Graham Gibbs for his chapter on the state in an international context, not only for the valuable dimension that this brings to the book, but also for the relief that his agreement to do it afforded me at the time.

Finally, I must thank my wife, Sue, for helping to provide the conditions without which this book could not have been written.

Humberside College of Higher Education Roger King

The author and publishers wish to thank the following who have kindly given permission for the use of copyright material: Cambridge University Press for extracts from 'Urban Politics and Markets' by R. P. King from *British Journal of Political Science*, vol. 15; Longman Group Ltd. for extracts from *The Middle Class* by R. P. King and J. Raynor; Plenum Publishing Corporation for 'Sociological Accounts of Power and Political Processes' from *Behavioural Decision Making*, ed. G. Wright; The Politics Society for extract from 'Updating: Political Sociology' from *Teaching Politics*, vol. 11, no. 1, Jan. 1982. Every effort has been made to trace all the copyright-holders, but if any have been inadvertently overlooked the publishers will be pleased to make the necessary arrangement at the first opportunity.

Introduction

The last two decades in the social sciences have been characterised by change and rapid developments, and this is exemplified by political sociology. As a well-established area of study, with a recognised set of issues and approaches (democracy/non-democracy), it had in the early 1960s an air of orthodoxy, even complacency. Yet today no one is sure what political sociology is, or even whether it still exists. Earlier assumptions have been challenged, overturned and have occasionally re-emerged, often in a different guise. People who call themselves political sociologists, in contrast to their predecessors of twenty years or more ago, are more interested in state and economy than socialisation and culture, and the approaches employed are generally more critical and diverse.

Many political sociologists see this increased fragmentation as a sign of growth and openness, reflecting the liberalism and plurality of its major topic – democracy. It is preferred to what they regard as the palsied state of 'cold-war' political sociology that spanned the Atlantic in the 1950s and 1960s. Others, however, prefer a science with a firmer set of verities, with knowledge accumulating on the basis of a uniform and dominant model. Whichever, political sociology is very different now from what it was twenty years ago.

However, it would be easy, and mistaken to overlook the continuities with an earlier period in contemporary political sociology. The current concern with the state, for example, not only resonates with the dilemmas that also confronted the classical European sociologists at the turn of the century, but in its increased *rapprochement* between Marxism and Weberianism, also echoes the 'grand' social science of an earlier period. It perhaps brackets the post-1945 'orthodoxy', with its unconcern with the state and focus instead on politics and power, as the aberration rather than its more radical contemporary counterpart.

This book seeks to take stock of political sociology by examining the continuities as well as the breaks with an older political sociology. It starts with an examination in Chapter 1 of the traditional political sociology that has dominated in both the United States and Britain in recent years. Rooted in behaviouralism it is characterised largely by an unconcern with the state and with generating a pragmatic, 'realistic' response to participatory democratic theory. American behaviouralism was an especially significant force in the United States in the inter-war years and contrasted with the more speculative or 'macro' concerns of European political sociology by focusing on individuals, power and values. There was a concern with detailed and methodologically rigorous enquiry into the social psychological aspects of politics and the ways in which 'non-political' institutions such as the family and the media acted to create political attitudes. The focus was on the 'ordinary man' or the behaviour of the 'non-élite' rather than the élite, and explanations of voting patterns or other forms of political participation rested on the attitudes generated in wider socialisation and cultural processes. Power was regarded as voluntaristic and divorced from the state or class power and was conceived individualistically or atomistically as the ability of actors to control others in social relationships.

However, the 'sociology of democracy', which became the orthodoxy on both sides of the Atlantic in the post-1945 decades, was founded on the link between American behaviouralism and European democratic theory. It sought to revise classical assumptions of participatory democracy, the claimed benefits to both individuals and the political system gained through extensive involvement in decision making, by noting the relative disinterest in politics by most individuals found in election and other studies of political behaviour. Rather, democracy was best exemplified by stability and consensual values. The agenda for political sociology became characterised by two assumptions. First, that the liberal regimes in most of the western industrial nations were as democratic as one could reasonably expect and that the issue was to identify how such regimes could be stabilised and their example furthered elsewhere. Second, that social processes largely determined political arrangements, and that the answer to the issue of stabilising liberal democracy lay in establishing the social causes or requisites of democracy.

In Chapter 1 we examine recent critiques of the role of values in traditional political sociology, focusing especially on Britain as the alleged exemplar of a stable democracy. We also consider recent election studies which display a more critical approach to behaviouralism and a greater recognition of structured inequalities, not least by the state, as the basis for opposed political outlooks. However, the main theme of the book is to suggest that a major dissatisfaction with orthodox political sociology has been its neglect of the state. New approaches in political sociology have recognised the need to return to earlier concerns with the state as found in both Marxism and Weberianism. In contrast to classical interpretations, however, contemporary political sociology is characterised by a more sophisticated account of the relationship between state and economy than found in early Marxism, and recognises the state as a structured source of inequality and power, and not simply a reflection. Moreover, there is a less satisfied conception of the nation-state than found in early Weberianism and increased awareness of international and 'world' systems.

The chapters outlining the new political sociology begin with an historical account of the development of the modern state (Chapter 2) and the major dilemmas raised by the emergence of a liberal constitutional state. A number of particular issues for state–society relationships are identified. First, the emergence of a centralised structure of institutional authority entailing relations of command and obedience ('public'), distinct from the voluntary established associations of society in which relations are typically based on affinities and ideas. To what extent does the modern state become distinct and separated from society, in which its impersonal rules attain a certain degree of freedom from the constellations of social interests? A related issue is the relative power of the public and the private, and especially state and economy. Although the centralised state with its standing armies and large treasuries casts an increasingly large shadow from the sixteenth century onwards the development of capitalism provides a strength and influence to the private sphere that, for some, enables it not only to match rulers but to dominate them. Second, the state that emerged in the nineteenth century came to be understood also as founded on consent, in that the state's power must be legitimated and turned into authority. Modern states come to be regarded as 'built' or 'made' purposefully and operate with reference to some idea of popular will or goal to which it is instrumental. Thus the claim to supreme authority is no longer based upon the hereditary rank of a monarchical lineage but lies in the relationship between the rulers and the ruled. The key notion is that legitimate authority is based upon the consent of the ruled, although this raises the further question of how extensive and on what basis should be this consent. The issue of who 'belongs' to the political community in turn leads to a widening social basis for the state through an extension of civic, political and social rights.

In Chapter 3 the relationship of the individual to the state (sovereignty) is distinguished from the related problem of the relationship of state to private power. At the moral heart of a number of state–society questions is the issue of whether the state is regarded as the guarantor of liberty and equality, or as a threat. Socialists come to see the state as the purposeful builder of a more just and equal society, while liberals find its paternal and collectivist influence and the search for impersonal equality inherently dangerous. In this view individual liberty and social dynamism derive from the unfettered institutions of private property and the family. However, as we shall see, even Marxism has been characterised by an ambivalence towards the state. Is it an oppressive, authoritarian and essentially bourgeois creation that has to be smashed in the pursuit of a freer society, or an essential tool in the building of a socialist society free from material want and able to defend itself from hostile capitalist states? Chapter 3 examines the different interpretations of state–society relationships and considers the external face of the nation-state through notions of imperialism and state–state exploitation and rivalry.

In Chapter 4 we return to a more historical and empirically grounded analysis of the modern state, exploring particularly the development of more collectivist forms of state–economy organisation. Although the historical connection between capitalism and liberal democracy is less pronounced than is often acknowledged (as is testified by the cases of Germany and Japan), left and right traditionally connect the necessity of the former for the development of the latter. That is, while Marxists regard the liberal constitutional state as predicated upon the economic requirements of the competitive phase of capitalism (and as a political rebuttal to feudalism), market society theorists see capitalism and the liberal state as mutual guarantors of individual freedoms. However, the liberal state is not necessarily a liberal democratic state, and the development of democracy is regarded by some liberals as undermining liberty through the development of collectivism. State–society relationships in the twentieth century became increasingly characterised by a concertation between organised labour, business and the state, and modern societies, whatever their political coloration apparently converge around a more state-directed, organised form of socio-economic arrangement. In the West the emerging dilemmas for the state presented by the development of electoral democracy and organised labour are first, how does the state balance the often contradictory requirements for popular support and the need for capital accumulation, and second, does this require the incorporation or the submission of labour? In the East, the dilemmas for state socialism are rather different. One reflects the perpetual socialist ambivalence to the state as an organisational form – should it be 'smashed' as an inevitable instrument of bourgeois rule or used to ensure socialist advance? In the USSR the chaos of the immediate post-revolutionary period was in part occasioned by the Leninist embrace of the former interpretation, and was replaced by the view of the state as a guarantor of the building and maintenance of 'socialism in one country'. However, the drive to state-directed industrialisation raised the additional problem of the extent to which incentive and differential rewards, apparently necessary for material advance and military and economic defence, were compatible with socialism.

In Chapter 5 we examine more specifically the issue of corporatism and the apparent displacement of parliamentarism and pluralism by a concerted form of political decision making between the organised representatives of capital, labour and the state. In part corporatist theory may be seen as a response to the benign and 'state-free' view of interest groups found in orthodox political sociology in the 1950s and 1960s. The sociology of democracy conceived interest groups as voluntary associations of like-minded citizens who would coalesce around a particular issue, but which would generally not persist. The state was regarded as either a form of interest group, like any other, or as a rather passive switchboard between contending private interests. Effectively the state dissolved into society. Corporatism, however, reflects the crises and recessions of the late 1960s and subsequent years in which the overwhelming and undisciplined claims of interest groups are seen as a contributory cause. Rather, new forms of authoritative state–society intermediation are required to re-impose social order, limit popular expectations and safeguard the means for economic accumulation and competitiveness. It is a strategy that risks the extension of part of state authority to the leaders of major economic associations in exchange for controlling members and eliciting support for negotiated agreements. A feature of corporatism is that the state–society distinction (public/private) becomes blurred as representative and decisional functions are combined in a range of quasi-official, non-elected administrative bodies.

In Chapter 5 we note also that, in common with pluralism, corporatism is inimical to the notion of a centralised state. Rather state authority is partially 'franchised' to powerful economic groups, whose membership is structurally rather than voluntarily generated, and the state seeks to limit the extent of its involvement in the economy for fear of damaging the means of production and accumulation. Consequently corporatism may be regarded as inherently unstable, open both to capitalist disaffection with state interference and accommodation to labour, as well as subject to trade union (rank-and-file) hostility at wage and other controls. However, the question of who benefits from corporatist arrangements is not without dispute. Although Marxists and others regard them as a means to control labour in the interests of capitalist accumulation, the persistent disaffection with corporatism displayed by both capital and 'New Right' governments suggests that the benefits to capital may be more than outweighed by the concessions to labour.

In Chapter 6 we return more specifically to a major model within orthodox political sociology – its behavioural interpretation of power. We examine the extent to which it is useful to consider policy outcomes as the consequences of choice(s) made by autonomous individuals in conflict or co-operation with others. Particularly we consider more recent approaches to power that claim that the positivistic, behavioural and conflictful conceptions of power ignored the role of ideology in human affairs and that the result of such an exercise of power is not necessarily conflict but its absence, not action but inaction. It may be best, therefore, to assess the benefits and costs of power independently of the desires and preferences of the individuals concerned, and the extent to which such gains or losses are cumulative or patterned.

Most of the empirical work that has underpinned discussions of power is derived from analyses of power relations in American local communities. Until recently very few local power studies had been carried out in Britain, partly because of the view that, in contrast to the United States, local government in Britain is held to be both the formal and real source of power in local communities. In Chapter 7 therefore, we examine recent interpretations of the 'local state' found in the new urban political sociology. Continuing a number of themes raised in Chapter 5, we examine claims that the local state is specifically concerned with the politics of collective consumption (housing, transport) rather than production. The assumption is that we should move away from notions of a monolithic state to one which recognises different levels and functions. Dual state theories, for example, typically distinguish between the central state, which is concerned with production and is characterised by corporatist forms of decision making, and the local state, which is concerned with consumption issues and is characterised by a more open and competitive form of decision making.

Dual state theories make more problematical the answers to question of control and external influences over urban governments. The relative openness of local political processes and the functional specificity of local government in consumption allows for both left or right, capitalist or socialist, control. The local state cannot be regarded as either a simple reflection of the central state, nor as inevitably a means for advancing capitalist interests. In recent years in Britain at least, it would have been extremely difficult to regard metropolitan authorities such as Liverpool or the Greater London Council as simply agents of capital. However, there is an ambivalence on both left and right to local government, and interpretations of urban political processes (do they benefit capitalist or non-capitalist interests?) have shown a tendency to vary according to particular political circumstances.

Finally, in Chapter 8 we seek to consider the international context for the state and redress the emphasis generally given to 'internalist' accounts of the nation-state. The distinction between the internal and external determinants of state action is raised and the chapter explores the theoretical assumptions behind the earlier accounts of modernisation and political development found in the sociology of democracy. In these earlier accounts the state is regarded as the major agent of modernisation, seeking initially to remove the obstacles to economic transformation as the basis for social and political reforms. However, the emphasis is still primarily internal and generally ignores the past history of relations between third and first worlds.

In the 1970s, however, political sociology has witnessed a paradigm shift in which greater emphasis is given to external factors, such as imperialism and colonialism, and in which the 'modern/traditional' dichotomy of modernisation theory is rejected. Rather, it is argued that the spread of modern institutions to the third world will further underdevelop, not modernise, them and sustain the creation of metropolis/satellite relations in the world economy. Moreover, local bourgeoisies may use the state to further a policy of underdevelopment, indicating that independence from colonial domination only changes the mode of domination. Certainly there is little to support Lenin's view in believing that direct territorial control (colonialisation) is a permanent necessity. We must also beware the danger of assuming that under-development is a permanent condition for all so-called third world societies, as some countries such as Singapore and Korea have experienced considerable development. Similarly, relations between states and transnational corporations are complex and vary according to period and circumstance. States competitively respond to transnational corporations and seek to protect their own transnationals. In the third world a process of mediation takes place between state and corporations, and phases occur when corporations are strictly controlled, often by authoritarian regimes.

In conclusion the portrayal of political sociology that results in these chapters is different and less behavioural than it would have been in such a book written 15–20 years ago. There is a quite explicit concern with the state and, in concluding chapters, with approaches to state–society intermediation. There is no apology for devoting a chapter to corporatism, despite the dismissive claims of some, for it has led to a body of literature that has given much needed focus and discipline to the study of state–organisation relations, and generally more than found in some abstract accounts of the state. Similarly, the final two chapters seek to correct the imbalance in accounts of the state towards internal and central-level processes by returning to Marxian and Weberian state theories as applied to the local and international levels.

The picture of political sociology that emerges reflects the movement towards more radical and collective accounts of politics in modern society. However, the book emphasises the necessity in contemporary political sociology not to neglect the important contributions of the earlier orthodoxies, for to do so leads to a generally fruitless pursuit down theoretically false trails and a-historical blind alleys.

1

Behaviouralism and the Sociology of Democracy

Introduction

In recent years political sociologists have constantly bewailed what they regard as the subject's fragmentation and lack of focus. There has appeared little agreement about the topics to be covered or what constitutes the intellectual framework of the discipline. In large part this reflects the disintegration in the 1970s of the dominant orthodoxy that governed political sociology in the 1950s and 1960s, which we label 'the sociology of democracy', and the search by some for another all-embracing paradigm. But it also reflects a more persisting aspect of political sociology, the compounding of dissensus on scope and methods to be found in both sociology and political science. In Britain, for example, political sociology has generally possessed a schizophrenic institutional location, in some cases being taught within sociology departments and in others within political science departments (Dowse and Hughes, 1972, p. 2). This appears to make a difference to what is taught. Courses provided by political science departments are much more likely to pay attention to individual political behaviour, covering such topics as voting, participation, attitudes, socialisation and formal models of political systems and institutions, than those provided by sociology departments which tend to indicate an interest in large-scale socio-political change, the state and ideology.

To a large extent these differences reflect the two major traditions in political sociology. That is, the earliest sociologists, such as Marx, Weber and Michels, were political sociologists. The European tradition has concerned itself with grand theory or 'macro' issues, focusing particularly on the sources and effects of the great socio-economic and political changes, such as capitalism, the division of labour, and the development of the nation state. Its legacy to contemporary political sociology is the recognition that patterns of social stratification and the economic structures of society are crucial sources of political institutions, and its elaboration of key concepts such as 'class', 'élite' and 'bureaucracy'.

The American or behaviouralist tradition originates later and became especially influential in the United States in the 1930s and 1940s. It may be said to differ from the European in three particular ways: (1) whereas the Europeans emphasised the 'macro', Americans studied the 'micro', or the social psychological aspects of politics. Alongside this, Lazarsfeld (1948), Berelson (1954) and others pioneered techniques of participant observation, questionnaire survey, attitude tests, and generally sought methodological rigour; (2) instead of making assumptions about the psychological aspects of politics, the Americans factually researched it and questions about socialisation and culture were answered by detailed research into the ways in which institutions such as the family and the media acted to create attitudes; and (3) whereas the Europeans studied ruling classes or élites, American behaviouralists, such as Lasswell (1948) and Key (1961), focused on the 'ordinary man', and typical results that emerge from the case studies and surveys were descriptions of the range of factors that influenced ordinary voting decisions or affected political participation.

A general feature of political sociology in a lengthy period following the classical theorists was the absence of a concern with the state. In Europe, apart from Gramsci, there was little Marxist work on the state, and orthodox Marxism was characterised by an economism that rendered the state as a simple reflection of material forces. Despite the greater importance attached to the state within the Weberian tradition, most attention focused specifically on the bureaucratic dynamics of large political organisations, such as parties and trade unions. Weber's 'action' sociology also tended to attain greater prominence in both Europe and the United States in the 1950s and 1960s than his comparative, historical accounts of states and societies, largely as a result of Parsons' claimed synthesis of classical sociology within a general theory of action (Parsons, 1937). Weber's work thus contributes to the preoccupation with power relationships within American democratic studies, rather than facilitating an interest in the state. Power was conceived as voluntaristic and divorced from state or class power, with the focus on the ability of actors to control others in social relationships.

This 'narrowly purposive' Weberian notion of power contrasts with 'its pre-Hobbesian meaning as uniquely human developmental capacities' (Held and Kreiger, 1984, p. 12). By the middle of the twentieth century the classical emphasis on participation had become suspect in Anglo–American democratic theory. The rise of inter-war fascism with its relatively high levels of mass participation, and the post-war establishment of so-called totalitarian regimes based on, or at least claiming, mass participation sustained notions that too participatory a form of democracy could open the door for popular authoritarian leaderships. A more limited concept of democracy seemed a better safeguard for maintaining the stability of systems than the classical stress on the liberating potential of mass participation (Pateman, 1970, p. 2). Weber, and especially one of his major sociological exponents, Robert Michels, had earlier raised serious reservations about the possibilities and desirability of classical participatory democracy in increasingly complex and bureaucratised industrial societies. Michels (1915) argued that the very structure of an organised society gives rise inevitably to an élite. Even in organisations dedicated to preserving internal democracy, such as socialist parties, the necessity for technical expertise and efficiency eventually leads to greater leadership power and restrictions on membership participation in key policy making.

Weber, like Michels, accepted the necessity for many aspects of modern representative democracy, but primarily as a means for selecting able political leaders rather than a forum of direct popular rule. It was a view that received particular reinforcement in the USA with the publication of Schumpeter's *Capitalism, Socialism and Democracy* (1943). Schumpeter eschewed 'classical doctrines' of democracy as in need of drastic revision to make them more realistic and compatible with the modern world. The notion that democracy was associated with particular ideals or ends, as incorporating specific values concerning political participation and the relationship between political rulers and the people, was rejected. Rather, Schumpeter conceived democracy as 'a political *method*, that is to say, a certain type of institutional arrangement for arriving at political, legislative and administrative decisions'

(p. 242). In so far as one supported democracy it was because it enabled the furtherance of other ideals, such as liberty or justice.

Schumpeter's chief objection to 'classical theory' was that the emphasis on the central participatory role of the people was empirically unfeasible. Democracy was more soundly redefined if greater recognition was given to the inevitability and desirability of political leadership, but exposed to periodic competition for popular support. Thus, 'the democratic method is that institutional arrangement for arriving at political decisions in which individuals acquire the power to decide by means of a competitive struggle for the people's vote' (p. 269). It is the competition for leadership that is the particular feature of democratic society and which distinguishes it from non-democratic methods or systems. The analogy is made with the economic sphere. Schumpeter not only refers to the historical relation between the development of capitalism and the development of democracy, but regards political parties as similar to companies engaged competitively to increase their share of the market. Voters, like consumers, choose between the policies (products) offered by competing political entrepreneurs in which power is the index of profitability.

Pateman (1970, p. 14) notes that Schumpeter paid some attention to the necessary conditions for the operation of the democratic method, such as civil liberties and tolerance, which are not necessarily generated by the democratic method itself, but that participation has no special or central role. All that is required for effective democracy is sufficient individual participation to keep the electoral arrangements in working order. Schumpeter's emphasis is distinctly élitist. The individual citizen is restricted to periodic voting and discussion, and the minority of leaders carry the responsibility for decision making. It is an approach that was enormously influential for later theorists of democracy, especially in the United States. Importantly it provided the American behaviouralist movement in political science with a theoretical framework within which could be located more empirical and attitudinal accounts of the ordinary citizenry. The narrowing notion of democracy as a method for the selection of political leaders also crucially influenced political scientists to regard elections and voting behaviour as providing key political data.

Political behaviour and American political sociology

Behaviouralism was largely associated with the Americanisation of political science in the post-1945 period and represented a critical reaction to the two dominant approaches in traditional political science: political theory, and the study of formal political institutions and constitutions (Kavanagh, 1983, p. 1). Political theory was primarily prescriptive and concerned with preferred forms of government, often as formulated by the ancient philosophers. It rested on taken-for granted assumptions about human nature and lacked a theoretical and systematic corpus of knowledge that integrated new data and generated causal explanations. On the other hand, the formal or institutional approach tended to ignore informal individual and social processes in political practices and was open to the charge of confusing prescribed rules and formal powers with reality, and with overlooking non-governmental bodies such as political parties, pressure groups and the mass media. A call for a more empirical political science, based upon observable data and testable hypotheses, and which would incorporate developments in concepts and methods from the other social sciences, especially social psychology, was always likely to be generated within an American context. As Kavanagh (1983, p. 7) points out, American political history displayed an Enlightenment belief in a progressive science of politics and a sympathy to pragmatism. 'A general regard for an engineering approach to society was joined to an optimism that new techniques and forms of knowledge could be applied for the improvement of society.' Although influential political scientists such as Charles Merriam (1925) believed that a more scientific and behavioural approach to politics could enhance social order and help build a democratic society, later theorists were more disposed to insist that a sharp distinction be drawn between an ethically neutral political science and political prescription (e.g. Easton, 1965).

The best account of the development of the behavioural approach in American political science is provided by Kavanagh (1983). He suggests that it is primarily an orientation to collect and evaluate data according to the methods of research generally found in the natural sciences. This involved utilising new research techniques, such as surveys and statistical analyses, and the focus on behaviour is largely because it is observable. Thus institutions are examined through the actual behaviour of individuals in those institutions, using operational indicators (attitudes, orientations) for higher-level concepts (culture, alienation) that allow empirical tests of hypotheses. A feature of the behaviouralist approach has been the substantive focus on electoral behaviour, in part because voting decisions lend themselves to survey and other quantifiable research techniques. Moreover, the findings of the early voting studies provided an important empirical referent for democratic theorising within the context of issues raised by Schumpeter (1943). Studies by Lazarsfeld *et al*. (1948) and Berelson (1954) in particular challenged many traditional assumptions about the discerning, rational voter found in democratic theory. The conventional portrait of the typical citizen as open-minded, deliberative, knowledgeable and given to weighing the basic issues, was severely dented by these studies. Findings revealed that most voters decided on their choice well before the campaign and that they were often unaware of issues or evaluated them on the basis of an already-formed partisanship, while their views were often contradictory and comprised no coherent scheme. These early voting studies also raised considerable doubts about claims made for the influence of the mass media. Contrary to initial expectations, for example, Lazarsfeld *et al*. found few changes in voting intentions that could be explained by media influence. Voters were selective in exposure to political information, and generally sought reinforcement for their existing positions. Moreover, the surveys revealed widespread disinterest in political affairs and little evidence of sympathy for liberal and democratic principles.

Consequently, many behavioural students of politics took issue with classic participatory notions of democracy and the view that participation was to be encouraged as a means of securing good, consensual decisions, and also as an end in its own right that would promote individual development and efficacy. Rather, the informed and interested citizens comprised only a small minority, and behaviouralists and others argued that democratic theory needed to be revised along more realistic and élitist lines to take account of the findings of the electoral studies. Mass participation in political decision making was to be avoided as endangering the stability of the system, and policy was best entrusted to political leaders who were more likely to display the civility and tolerance associated with the democratic temper (Almond and Verba, 1963). Berelson, for example, in a chapter in *Voting* (1954), examined the implications for 'classical' democratic theory of the empirical evidence outlined in the rest of the book. He argued that classical theory focused on the individual citizen and largely ignored the political system. It overlooked the possibility that the needs of the political system may require a degree of disinterest among its citizens to allow for systematic flexibility and order, even if these characteristics appear 'less desirable' when measured against individual needs. Thus, limited popular participation, even apathy, can have a positive function for the whole system by reducing intensity of conflict and enabling the system to change with stability. The position is that:

> high levels of participation and interest are required from a minority of citizens only . . . [while] the apathy and disinterest of the majority play a valuable role in maintaining the stability of the system as a whole . . . [and] the amount of participation that actually obtains is just about the amount that is required for a stable system of democracy. (Pateman, 1970, p. 7)

The implications for democratic theory raised by Berelson and the findings of the election studies were examined systematically by Robert Dahl in *A Preface to Democratic Theory* (1956). Dahl also regarded earlier theories of participatory democracy as inadequate for the modern world, advancing an alternative concept of polyarchy, or the rule of multiple minorities. Following Schumpeter, democracy is conceived as a method, a set of 'institutional arrangements' that are based on the electoral process. Elections are a central democratic mechanism that allows the non-élite to exercise influence over leaders and constrains the latter. In Dahl's view there is little sense in advancing a theory of democracy that requires extensive participation from citizens when we know that most people are generally disinterested in politics. Inevitably, in modern, complex and large-scale societies only a few individuals are involved in political decision making. The test of democracy is provided not by the extent of participation in actual policy making, but by the periodic competition between leaders for the people's vote.

Dahl is also concerned with the conditions for the maintenance of democratic systems, and points to a basic agreement on values, especially among leaders, as a vital prerequisite. This concern with the social conditions of democracy was taken up by the major political sociologists in the 1950s and 1960s. It enabled the American and European traditions to come together in a mutually complementary way that gave political sociology an agenda and an orthodoxy that endured for over twenty years. It was based on the assumed acceptability of existing liberal democracies and a search for their stabilisation, and brought together the micro, empirical concerns of the behaviouralists and the theoretical and speculative notions of the Europeans. The outcome was a convergence in what we may term a 'sociology of democracy', and was based on a resolution to the long-standing tension in political sociology arising from competing conceptions of democracy, in favour of democratic élitism. Originating in European élite theory, democratic élitism provided a key link, particularly through the work of Schumpeter, between the European and American traditions as it became a strong influence within the behaviouralist approach. As with the classical élitism of Mosca, Pareto and Michels (Parry, 1969), the democratic élitists considered themselves as seeking a more realistic and scientific account of politics.

The sociology of democracy: Almond and Verba, Lipset

From the mid-1950s political sociology on both sides of the Atlantic became marked by an academic orthodoxy which was characterised by two main assumptions. First, that the liberal regimes in most of the western industrial nations were as democratic as one could reasonably expect and that the issue was to identify how such regimes could be stabilised and their example furthered elsewhere. Secondly, that social processes largely determine political arrangements and that the answer to the issue of stabilising liberal democracy lay in establishing the social causes or requisites of democracy. Two works of crucial influence were Almond and Verba's *The Civil Culture* (1963), which sought to demonstrate through cross-national surveys that democratic regimes were sustained by a 'civic culture', operationalised as a mix of participatory/deferential attitudes in its citizens, and Lipset's *Political Man* (1960), which additionally connected stable liberal democracies with industrial advance which, it was claimed, provided the resources and wealth to sustain regime legitimacy. A feature of both approaches, however, was the élitist version of democracy adopted. It seemed to set the main task for political sociology as the search for the causes of stability, rather than democracy *per se*, and in demonstrating how élite rule can be made acceptable to largely non-participatory masses.

Dowse and Hughes (1972, p. 228) note that the development of the concept political culture is aimed at closing the gap between psychological interpretations of political action, found in behaviouralism, and macro-sociological analysis. There was a need to relate the individual act to the social aggregate to avoid the danger of ignoring the political community as a collective entity. Almond (1980) adds two further reasons for the systematic use of the concept political culture from the 1950s. First, the reception of classical European sociology, particularly the work of Weber, Pareto and Durkheim, in the United States through Talcott Parsons' influential *The Structure of Social Action* (1937), which emphasised the role of social norms and values in these writers' accounts as the foundation for a more general theory of social action. Secondly, the development of survey research which enabled moves beyond what had been largely speculative statements about culture to the collection of data about attitudes or orientations to politics. Culture became operationalised through notions of attitudes that could be elicited from individuals in a systematic way, and then re-aggregated into statements about a nation's political culture. A further step was to examine the congruence between a nation's political culture and its political system. Almond and Verba (1963), for example, suggest that a participatory political culture best 'fits' a liberal democratic regime, while a 'subject' or 'passive' culture is more closely associated with authoritarian regimes.

Almond and Verba's massive comparative survey of five countries – the USA, Britain, Italy, Mexico and West Germany – used a similar questionnaire on all respondents (over 5000) to elicit combinations of psychological orientations that enabled them to draw up profiles of national political cultures. Of particular interest were the mixed political cultures that are most likely to be found in the real world (Dowse and Hughes, 1972, pp. 230–1):

1. *The parochial-subject* In this cultural system, although the individual relinquishes purely local political attachments and

develops allegiances towards more specialised government institutions, a sense of self as a political force is still relatively weak and political parties and pressure groups are relatively poorly defined.

2. *The subject-participant* Examples of such cultures are found in contemporary France, Germany and Italy, where the citizens tend to be divided into a significant number of politically aware and active people and others who are relatively passive.

3. *The parochial-participant* Here the input institutions are relatively local – tribal or caste associations – while the national output institutions are fairly well-developed. However, both the input and the output organisations may be taken over by 'parochial' interests.

4. *The civic culture* This includes the notion of participation in structures widely regarded as legitimate but in which, for the majority, life offers a range of opportunities for commitment to parochial and a-political institutions, a commitment which helps to develop both a sense of potential personal competence and a sense of trusting other people. The sense of competence and trust allows the citizen to feel at ease with the government and that it is not necessary to oppose the government on all issues. However, individuals feel competent to associate in opposing it on issues which are felt to be important. Moreover, although participation may be a relatively rare occurrence, the fact that potentially it may be deployed as the occasion warrants, serves as an effective constraint on government abusing its freedom to act. Both the United States and the United Kingdom are regarded as approximating to the civic culture with widespread participatory norms. However, in contrast to the United States, the British political culture is seen as having a strong deferential element which allows leaders greater freedom of action. Cultures are therefore linked to the structural features of society. For example, the suspicion of active government in America is associated by Almond and Verba to the lack of political leadership found in its political system, while the ingredient of deference in Britain is causally related to a tradition of strong and stable rule. This mixture of participant and passive attitudes in the civic culture was regarded by Almond and Verba as the best cultural 'fit' for a stable democracy.

There are a number of well-remarked difficulties with Almond and Verba's comparative study, to which we briefly allude. One is the suggested causal connections between the political culture and the operation of the political system. As Kavanagh (1983, p. 63) notes, 'it is not clear that any research design can actually demonstrate that a change in the culture produces a change in structure/performance, or vice versa.' Additionally, satisfaction or dissatisfaction with a particular government or set of leaders may be confused by respondents with attitudes to the system as a whole, and these are responses which may vary independently. There are also technical and conceptual difficulties in such a massive cross-national survey of attitudes, especially involving standardisation and comparability. Finally, those interviewed may not be the politically important section of the population, or they may be confined to those able to cope with interview schedules, thus ignoring the 'social periphery' or marginalised sectors of society (Dowse and Hughes, 1970, p. 234).

A rather different approach to establishing the social bases of democracy was advanced by Lipset, who sought to provide an alternative socio-economic explanation to that of Marxism of both the origins and the maintenance of liberal democracy. In *Political Man* (1960), Lipset tests the proposition that democracy is related to levels of economic development. Distinguishing between stable and unstable democracies/dictatorships in terms of periodic changes of government, and taking wealth, industrialisation, education and urbanisation as indices of economic development, Lipset argues that in every case the average level of economic development is higher in the more democratic countries. The theoretical interpretation of these correlations is that increased income and better education lead to a less radical and evolutionary perspective amongst the lower classes, creates a middle class which acts as a buffer between the upper and lower classes, thus reducing class conflict, and generates a range of intermediary associatons between government and citizen. Finally, Lipset suggests that there are two sources of support for a regime: a belief in its efficiency and a belief in its legitimacy. Although these are independent variables they tend to be causally related as an efficient regime is likely to engender feelings of legitimacy and is able to 'buy off' potential disruption. Moreover, consensus and minimal levels of class conflict are conditions that are likely to produce efficient government, which enables a large accumulation of national resources to be available for distribution, which, in turn, adds to the regime's popular support.

There are also difficulties with Lipset's approach, however. As Barry (1970, p. 66) notes, there is no attempt to consider necessary or sufficient conditions for stable democracy. It would appear that either legitimacy or effectiveness is a sufficient condition of stability, although neither is a necessary condition. Moreover, Lipset's socio-economic reductionism ignored major differences between political systems, particularly the way in which political variables have influenced system outcomes in different societies. However, a subsequent work by Lipset and Rokkan, *Party Systems and Voter Alignments* (1967), sought to account for variations in European party systems (and, by implication, political systems) by referring them back to the historical conflicts and cleavages faced by all advanced European societies, i.e. subject versus dominant cultures, churches versus secular governments, rural versus urban, and workers versus employers. The two fundamental questions that concerned Lipset and Rokkan were: (1) how, and in what way, do the cleavages and supports of wider stratification systems get translated into party and political forms? and (2) can party systems themselves be seen as an independent force over and above social and economic systems? The overarching concern, however, was to explain how a viable system of political decision making is achieved in the face of the fissures and divisions of interest produced by industrialisation, with a crucial factor identified as the 'non-cumulation' and resolution of essentially non-bargainable cleavages – those centred on religion, language and culture – before these have the opportunity to overlay the essentially secular and bargainable cleavages between workers and employers over the distribution of goods in advanced capitalism. A feature of this work, reflecting the influence of American behaviouralism, was its methodological sophistication, particularly the multivariate analysis of voting statistics.

This emphasis on political parties reflected a crucial ingredient of the democratic élitist approach. In confronting the problem of accountability and control in modern democracies, the 'new democracy' regarded political parties as both more identifiable by, and responsive to, the people than were the special interest groups. Supported by a large proportion of the electorate, political parties combined the goals of less influential groups in programmatic platforms which were then put to the electorate and if successful, implemented. Moreover, as Margolis (1983, p. 121) observes, 'at the same time the socialisation of successful party candidates to the values associated with their government positions was likely to cause them to take account of interests broader than those of their party alone'.

However, revised theories of democracy also placed considerable emphasis on the active role of groups in politics. In 1951, for example, Truman had claimed that the open, pluralistic competition among different interest groups ensured that American society was not dominated by a single ruling élite. Although individuals may be generally apathetic about politics, or unable to make their individual voices felt, the relevant interest groups would guard their interests. Interest groups articulated different issues and fed them into the decision-making process and, in negotiating with other groups, including government, generally adopted norms of toleration and accommodation.

This view of the role of interest groups received powerful reinforcement from mass society theory, which attained a post-1945 explanatory attractiveness as a result of the excesses of Nazism and Stalinism in the 1930s and 1940s. Kornhauser (1960), in *The Politics of Mass Society*, regarded pluralism and an array of interest groups as safeguards against authoritarian intrusions by the masses into the political arena. Pluralist democracy and its established élites he regarded as threatened by the rise of mass society, which generates an increased potential for popular counter-élites, unrestrained and unattached to prevailing values. In this view the traditional élites are committed to the civilised values of an open, democratic system, but require a degree of autonomy and insulation from the populace in order to discharge their protective responsibilities. A strong system of intermediary interest groups, however, filters out popular demands on political rulers and acts as a buffer between mass and élite.

In contrast to pluralist democracy is totalitarian society, the term used to describe, particularly, the Nazi and Stalinist regimes. Despite major ideological differences between the two regimes, the notion totalitarian reflected a view that both regimes shared similar basic characteristics, and, in the post-1945 period, it became part of the language of the cold war. The concept was most clearly delineated by Friedrich and Brzezinski (1956) who outlined six characteristics of, it was claimed, all totalitarian dictatorships. There were (1) an all-embracing official ideology, (2) a single mass party to be led by an authoritarian leader, (3) a secret terror police, (4) party control over the system of mass communications, (5) monopoly control of armed force, and (6) central bureaucratic control of the economy. Friedrich and Brzezinski lay particular emphasis on terror as a basic characteristic of totalitarianism, which they apply to all communist societies. However, following the Stalin period, real terror was much less a feature of the Soviet Union's internal affairs, and even less apparent in some other communist states. The blanket description 'totalitarian' not only obscures important differences between fascist and communist regimes but also major differences among communist regimes (Brown, 1974, p. 38). However, it did serve to emphasise the pluralist, competitive conception of liberal democracy at the other end of the political continuum and the apparent necessity in democratic societies for a strong system of interest groups. For theorists such as Dahl democracy was conceived as governance by multiple minorities, or polyarchy, and the state was confined to responding to different demands and seeking the means for their orderly reconciliation and compromise. There was little notion of state leadership or a collective national interest apart from the continuous reproduction and affirmation of democratic values.

A large part of American political sociology largely ignored the subject of the state in its consideration of Anglo–American society, and focused instead on behaviourally-based notions of social power. The state was conceived as either one group of actors among others, or simply as a switchboard for transmitting different social demands. However, despite the general neglect of the state by political scientists, there emerged in the 1960s in American sociology a renewed interest in the state from the perspective of functionalism. The functionalist model of the state, as found in the works of Smelser (1963), Eisenstadt (1966), Parsons (1966) and Bendix (1964), for example, rested on the view of an increasing differentiation of the sphere of public authority from that of private social relations. The state is seen as directing authority relations in the public sphere, promulgating conditions for citizenship, institutionalising authoritative relationships, and claiming the primary allegiance of citizens over local and private groups. As

Badie and Birnbaum (1983, p. 27) observe of the model, 'historically, the state is one aspect of the rationalising process that takes place in all societies undergoing modernisation . . . and the welfare state is the end result toward which political development leads in all societies'.

A crucial concept in the functionalist account of the state is differentiation. Authority structures, as with other increasingly specialised and autonomous social roles and organisations, become differentiated from other structures, and the state becomes a crucial co-ordinating element in the new division of labour (Durkheim, 1933). A key figure in this approach was Talcott Parsons (1966) who, after largely ignoring the state in his early writings, in the 1960s constructed an evolutionary theory of social development in which the state emerges historically as a solution to the problem of overall social integration in a liberal democratic, constitutional form which is indispensable to the full differentiation of the political system from the other social subsystems. By freeing power from its association with old social hierarchies and distributing it among newly autonomous social groups, power does not become monopolised by any one group, thus paving the way for political competition and pluralist democracy (Eisenstadt, 1966). In some functionalist accounts, however, the state becomes the prime source of social harmony, developing new institutions for securing equilibrium and order, especially in the economic sphere. A concern with economic development, especially in the Third World but also in some non-Anglo–American societies, encouraged a more favourable view amongst functionalists of a strong state as a means for capitalist/industrial take-off (Smelser, 1963; Huntingdon, 1968). Nonetheless, the functionalist emphasis on the autonomy of political structures implies that the resources from which power derive must be differentiated and widely available. One source of power should not outweigh all others.

This tension in functionalist thinking on the state between a view of the necessity for a strong, modernising, central co-ordinator on the one hand, and a relatively equal distribution of social powers on the other, reflects the cross-pulls from two allegedly functional pre-requisites: the need for autonomy and the need for integration. As Badie and Birnbaum (1983, p. 41) observe, 'it is not clear that the need for integration is not, in some respects at least, opposed to the need for autonomy and universality'. There is also an ethnocentric tendency in functionalism to regard the Western nation-state as the single, evolutionary model of state-building. Moreover, as an autonomous source of power, the state is also a stake in political conflict, rather than merely a means of reconciling conflicting interests. Thus,

> Neofunctionalist sociologists err in arguing that the nation-state is a perfect functional substitute for vanished community solidarities and traditional forms of spontaneous accord . . . [for] once the state becomes an autonomous power centre, with access to previously unavailable sources of power, it becomes a target for political action . . . (Badie and Birnbaum, 1983, p. 56)

Consequently the state may add to social conflict, rather than lessen it, and become an extra source of dispute.

Critiques of behaviouralist accounts of democracy

Numerous critiques have been advanced of the 'new realism' in democratic theory. Although the scientific and empirical methods of a more behavioural political science, along with a pluralist interpretation of American society as 'the good society', had become well-established in the United States by the mid-1960s, plural-élite theories of democracy subsequently became 'tarnished by events and battered by philosophical critiques penned by theorists well-versed in scientific methods' (Margolis, 1983, p. 125). By the late 1960s many of the empirical weaknesses of plural élitism had become apparent. The description of the USA as a relatively open and competitive political system, allowing every interest group an opportunity to mobilise and advance its claims, looked increasingly misconceived in the face of the persisting inequalities in life chances that both demonstrated and served as barriers to effective participation for many social groups. Events such as the Watergate affair cast doubt on the claim that élites were necessarily better guardians of democratic ideals than the mass of the people, and in the 1970s political distrust and cynicism appeared to become endemic among even the better-educated.

An early critic of plural-élite theories of democracy was C. Wright Mills, who focused his sights on many of the central assumptions of democratic élitism. Mills regarded power as institutionalised and structured in modern society, with a 'power élite' drawn from leading positions in the strategic hierarchies. Mills argued that in the USA there is sufficient cohesiveness between the leading positions in the institutional hierarchies, facilitated by personal interchanges (between government and business, for example), to indicate the existence of a military–industrial–governmental complex that dominates the non-élite through the means of mass persuasion (Mills, 1956). In contrast to the democratic élitists' claims of open, competitive decision making, Mills saw the means for exercising power as more narrowly concentrated among a small group than ever before in the United States. Alongside this concentration of power in the hands of the military chiefs, executives of the large corporations, and top government officials, the typically atomised and privatised mass is incapable of mounting effective political challenges. The result is a heightened risk of foreign, imperial warfare with all the attendant nuclear horrors of the modern age.

Mills' critique of plural élitism was often disregarded because it was couched in a 'non-scientific', discursive style of an earlier period, while many Marxists and radicals were critical of what they saw as Mills' failure to develop a class analysis of western capitalism, such as his reluctance to consider 'the power élite' as a ruling class and his preference for a 'mass' rather than 'class' description of the non-élite. Nonetheless, his analyses became increasingly attractive with the revelations of corruption and non-accountable power in USA administrations in the 1960s and 1970s, and they helped to recall that much of the 'new science' of democracy was itself heavily normative and contained an implicit satisfaction with the existing state of political affairs. It was also recognised that a continuity existed between the 'new realism' and an older liberal tradition which also placed limits on popular participation (Pateman, 1970; 1980). The notion that 'classical democratic theory' comprised a uniform set of participatory ideals is largely mythical, while the fear of the mass and the alleged dangers of mass politics was also a well-established feature of much classical sociology. Both classical traditions shared with the revised theories of democracy a concern more with the stability of systems than with the developmental gains for individuals that were presumed to accrue from extensive participation in decision making. However, this raises the question of the relationship between an 'ought' and an 'is', or that between prescription and description. The democratic élitists derived their prescription or model of a democratic society from a general satisfaction with an existing political system, while participatory democratic theorists generally advance a model as a goal or ideal for attainment on the grounds that it is both achievable and desirable (Duncan and Lukes, 1963).

Values and the sociology of democracy

Prime determinants of the stability of liberal democracies, according to the post-war sociology of democracy theorists, are the legitimacy of prevailing institutional arrangements and agreement on basic democratic values. The emphasis is on the importance of internalised normative constraints which form part of a political culture and are acquired through a process of political socialisation. However, a number of criticisms have been levelled at the centrality of values in explanations of stable democracy, largely for underplaying coercive, economic and other material factors. One set of criticisms, associated with the work of Downs (1957), questions the assumption that any significant shared interest is likely to give rise to a pressure group whose influence will reflect the overall strength of the interests affected. A second set of criticisms focuses on empirical evidence of the inconsistencies which exist between a person's approval of general values and their specific applications.

1. *Values and interest groups*

As we have noted, the pluralist approach stresses the way in which all spheres of public office are subject to shared rules, a cohesive web of conventions that assures that all actors in the social system are regarded as essentially equal. Interest groups are formed by individuals seeking to join with their like-minded peers in the pursuit of group goals. This formation is based upon distinct social interests and its continuance is assured by the maintenance of an agreed set of political goals and values. Olson (1965), in *The Logic of Collective Action*, however, questioned the contention that group goals take the form of 'collective goods' that are non-excludable. Any political gains that a particular group makes are not exclusive to that group, but are also available to the population in general. Olson argues that if this is the case an agreement on group goals is generally not a sufficiently good motive for an individual to join. A rational self-interested individual will not act to achieve group goals for two major reasons. First, the individual will see that the cost incurred in joining the group will far outweigh the benefits that might accrue from such membership. Secondly, the individual will be motivated not to co-operate because it will be apparent that his contribution to the group will at best be marginal, while he will still benefit from any 'collective goods' whether he is a member or not. Olson argues that interest groups overcome such difficulties by offering what he calls 'selective incentives', benefits that are exclusive to members of the group, and which are offered by the group to outweigh the marginal costs of membership. Olson argues that 'selective benefits' are the main incentive for joining a group and that any lobbying activity is merely a by-product of such incentives.

A major weakness of the Olson model seems to be that its behavioural expectations are taken from a very restrictive set of assumptions about the way that individual choice is made. The logic of collective action approach fails to show why people should join an interest group for reasons other than economic gain, such as social acceptance, friendship, status, and business involvement, and 'purposive' reasons such as ideology, moral or religious principles. Nonetheless, the simplicity and elegance of Olson's model is still attractive, and it has proved a valuable corrective to an over-reliance on 'value' models. For example, revised versions of Olson's model have been advanced that attempt to accommodate both 'solidary' and 'purposive' incentives. Moe (1981), for example, argues that factors such as ideological commitment to a group's collective goals can shape the individual's evaluation of 'collective goods' and that the benefit from such action may outweigh any personal economic gain. In addition to this, the individual believing in group goals may well gain a sense of satisfaction from just contributing to these goals and such satisfactions may be classed as 'selective incentives'.

2. *Legitimacy and power*

Britain was generally regarded within the sociology of democracy as epitomising in the 1950s and 1960s a political system whose stability was guaranteed by a high level of social integration and value consensus. *The Civic Culture*, for example, indicated that the British, with a mixture of deferential and activist attitudes, were generally trustful of their political system and its leaders and were attached to norms of tolerance and moderation, and this was interpreted as indicating that Britain's political institutions were legitimated. However, there are a number of difficulties with this approach (Held, 1984).

To begin, this concept of legitimacy fails to distinguish between different grounds for obeying a command, observing a rule or consenting to particular decisions. For example, such actions may be the result of apathy, coercion, unthinking tradition, resigned acquiescence, instrumental acceptance or normative agreement. Moreover, Held (1984), Mann (1970) and Pateman (1980) are amongst those that suggest that Almond and Verba misinterpret their own data, which show that not only is the degree of common value commitment in Britain generally low but it varies by social class, with working-class people often exhibiting high levels of distrust and alienation. Mann's survey of empirical material of the 1950s and 1960s revealed that the middle class generally display greater trust and confidence in the political system than the working class, and that if there is a common value agreement amongst the working class, it is generally hostile to the system rather than supportive. Held (1984, p. 308) suggests that if there was a common value system amongst the working class in the immediate post-war years, 'it seems better interpreted in terms of "instrumental consent" . . . general compliance to dominant political and economic institutions linked directly to an expectation of a qualitatively new and more egalitarian life.' Rising standards of living and higher levels of economic growth and public expenditure gave substance to these attitudes, although the fiscal and political difficulties that followed in the late 1960s and 1970s, and reactions to them, testify to the conditionality of the consent of the earlier period. In contrast to 'overload' and 'legitimation crises' interpretations of the problems experienced in Britain as in most advanced industrial societies in the 1970s, Held (1984, p. 330) suggests that 'there is no clear empirical evidence to support the claim of a progressively worsening crisis of the state's authority and legitimacy'. Rather, legitimacy has never been high and the limited or instrumental consent amongst the working- and some sections of the middle-class in the earlier post-1945 period 'has given way to greater expression of dissent as, among other things, comforts diminish and/or the promise of future benefits appear even less meaningful and/or the pains of acquiescence increase' (ibid.). Even more importantly, perhaps, rather than state power diminishing with economic and legitimation crises, there is strong evidence that state capabilities and resources, especially within the state's police and military apparatuses, have actually increased (see also, Dearlove and Saunders, 1984, Chapter 6).

Abercrombie *et al.* (1980) also argue that there is little historical evidence to sustain a 'common value system' interpretation of British society. They regard expropriation and economic necessity as more important sources of lower class compliance than agreement with bourgeois or liberal values. Like Mann, Abercrombie *et al.* question the existence or the necessity of a coherent value system among the working class, in contrast to political leaders who require a reasonably high level of value integration for effective rule. Therefore, contemporary political attitudes in Britain, and elsewhere, are marked less by a decline in legitimacy than in the reduced availability of material and other rewards that help offset long-standing distrust. However, the coercive resources of the state develop to ensure that political outcomes are not straightforwardly a consequence of economic processes.

Electoral alignment and de-alignment in Britain

Kavanagh (1971) too has argued that the description of the British political system as sustained by a 'civic culture' is not supported by empirical evidence, and that 'no great popular confidence exists' in its political institutions. In contrast to Held, however, Kavanagh suggests that this state of affairs is relatively recent and is reflected in an increased volatility of electoral voting patterns. In his view a declining stability and predictability between class and electoral partisanship indicates that people's commitment to political institutions is increasingly instrumental and dependent upon effective economic and political policies.

Consideration of patterns of voting behaviour in Britain over the last two decades usually involves discussion of two major processes: 'class de-alignment', or the dissolution of strong correlations between people's occupational class positions and their party preference; and 'partisan de-alignment', or the lessening of the compatibility between people's choice of party and their positions on particular issues.

a. Class de-alignment

Voting behaviour in Britain has long been regarded as primarily reflecting class position which in turn is held to be signified by occupation. Butler and Stokes (1971, pp. 90–104), noting that 'in contemporary interpretations of British voting behaviour class is accorded the leading role', and although detecting a diminution in the class–party relationship, agreed with the general consensus following their trawl of the forces shaping electoral choice in Britain in the 1960s. Their evidence revealed that 'occupation is the most important of the elements that characterise the classes in the public's mind', and that there is a 'continuous fall of Conservative strength down the occupational scale'. Comparative surveys of electoral behaviour have shown that the influence of occupational class on voting behaviour was generally higher in Britain than elsewhere, such as the USA (Alford, 1963). Westergaard and Resler's more recent study of class in Britain, *Class in a Capitalist Society*, published in 1975, does not challenge these earlier interpretations, for they conclude that 'support for rival political parties is divided on class lines' and argue that all other influences on voting are 'of a very secondary kind' (p. 352).

These studies supported the familiar picture of British electoral politics as consisting of two major parties, Labour and Conservative, divided on manual/non-manual lines, but with just enough 'deviant' class voters to ensure that governments regularly change party hands. Voting on class lines is regarded as quite rational; the two major parties pursue different class policies, the Labour Party advancing working-class interests and the Conservative Party those of the middle class, and individuals thus vote on rational self-interested grounds for their class party.

Moreover, it was an interpretation that fitted well with the view advanced by Lipset and Rokkan that the party systems in western democracies were largely a reflection of social cleavages that had become established by the early years of this century (1967, p. 50).

Unlike the cataclysms expected by Marx the strong relation between class and political identity has been regarded by many non-Marxists as having a benign influence on the British political system. Lipset, for example, in *Political Man*, published in 1960, suggested that class issues are essentially economistic and bargainable; they involve competing claims on national economic resources which are resolved by regular adjustments. Class bargaining and compromise reinforce both the legitimacy and the effectiveness of capitalist societies, thus enabling working-class demands to be met out of increasing productivity. In contrast, 'traditional' conflicts between, say, religious or linguistic or ethnic communities involve clashes of 'ideology', or world views which are characterised by moral intensity. Such conflicts demand either complete victory or total defeat if they are to be resolved, rather than accommodation and pragmatism.

Whatever the merits of this approach the inability of Britain's economy in the last two decades to sustain the growth required to 'buy off' working-class demands has ensured that class conflict cannot be considered as somehow functional for the economic and political systems but may lead to them being severely disrupted. Furthermore, the relationship between occupational class and party alignment is shakier in the 1970s and 1980s than it was in the 1950s and 1960s. The 'troubles' in Northern Ireland and the development of nationalisms in Scotland and Wales have emphasised the 'Englishness' of class-related party loyalties and highlighted a tendency for some political scientists to equate Britain with only part of the United Kingdom. But even in England the association between occupational class and voting behaviour is declining. Although it has long been recognised that around one-third of manual workers vote Conservative (thus preventing a succession of Labour governments) an increasing tendency for the middle class to vote Labour has led a number of writers to describe British electoral behaviour in terms of its declining partisanship. Rose, for example, notes that in the two general elections of 1974 'the parties that saw their vote rise – the Liberals and Nationalists – drew their support from approximately a cross section of the electorate' and concludes that the relationship between occupational class and party allegiance, always 'significant but limited', may be declining further.

Crewe *et al.* (1977, pp. 129–31) also point to the 'accelerating refusal of the electorate to cast a ballot for either of the two governing parties'. They calculate that while the Conservatives were taking 47.8 per cent of the votes cast in 1951, this had declined to 36.7 per cent by October, 1974. In the same period Labour's share also fell, from 48.3 per cent to 40.3 per cent. Crewe *et al.* suggest that the combined drop in support for the two class-based political parties, from 96.1 to 77 per cent, is associated with a diminution in class alignment. Using the ratio of Conservative to Labour Party identifiers within manual and non-manual occupational categories as their measures they show that class alignment (the percentage of non-manual Conservatives minus the percentage of manual Conservatives) declined from 43 to 22 over the decade 1964–74. Furthermore, despite a return by politicians in the 1970s to the language of class conflict the proportion of respondents prepared to assign themselves (even after being pressed) to a social class 'fell sharply' (from around 50 per cent to just over 40 per cent). Crewe *et al.* propose that their findings reflect an improvement in standards of living, reduced occupational inequalities and a consequent 'blurring' of class lines.

Dunleavy (1983, p. 32) distinguishes two possible ways in which alignments can change. *Re*-alignment occurs when a new social cleavage replaces a previous one as the prime influences on people's voting. *De*-alignment occurs when an existing pattern of voting is not replaced, but simply declines. Many accounts of the decline in the long-established association between occupational class and partisanship in Britain fall into the de-alignment category. However, many do not seriously question the primacy of class-related electoral behaviour. Rather, the weakening of class differences in party alignment is thought to reflect changes in class structure, the blurring of class divisions or the fragmentation of class identities. There is little suggestion of new cleavages that may replace the salience of occupational class. Instead, Rose (1976) for example, looks to social influences other than occupation, such as housing or trade union membership, as a means of identifying 'pure' or 'core' classes – those with a high level of class-specific attributes – to provide greater predictiveness for class explanations of voting behaviour. Thus, non-manual workers with good academic qualifications who do not belong to trade unions and who own their house are more likely to vote Conservative than non-manual employees without these characteristics. Subjective class identification is similarly helpful in improving prediction as 'the higher the self-rating a person gives himself, e.g. upper middle class rather than middle class, the more likely he is to favour the Conservatives' (Rose, 1976, p. 217).

Dunleavy (1983, p. 33) points out that 'most commentators suggest that the association between occupational class and party support has simply faded away'. The different occupational classes are now much closer in partisan terms, while support for the major parties is socially much more similar. There appear to have been two distinct periods in the process of class de-alignment. Up to 1974 class de-alignment was largely the consequence of the erosion of middle-class Conservative support rather than manual disaffection with Labour, and middle-class Labour voting generally increased. In the late 1970s and 1980s, however, Conservative voting grew substantially amongst the skilled working class and in the 1979 general election it was only the managerial/professional groups that increased their support for Labour. Despite the declining association between occupational class and partisanship, however, most studies suggest that class-related influences on voting remain, such as trade union membership and housing tenure.

b. Partisan de-alignment

Partisan de-alignment refers to the declining relationship between party identification and political issues. Early electoral studies emphasised the durability of party identification, formed through an accumulation of social contacts and experiences. The propensity for voters was to adjust views on individual issues to fit with party loyalties rather than to come to a decision on party identification after a rational and balanced appraisal of parties' policies. Crewe and his fellow researchers (1977), however, argue that partisan de-alignment is now a marked feature of contemporary British electoral behaviour. The growth of third-party voting reflects the increasing conditionality of people's party loyalties while new issues have developed which are less easily accommodated within the pre-existing framework of the two-party debate. For example, the loss of Labour support amongst manual workers from the mid-1970s was traced to major differences on policy between the Labour Party and many of its potential voters. Voters appear more likely to take a more rational and critical view of party policies than before and to evaluate issues on their merits, which is explained, in part at least, by the inabilities of governments to arrest a declining British economy, rising levels of education, and more extensive mass media coverage of political issues.

Explanations of class de-alignment, however, focus less on political issues than on changes in British society. For example, explanations for the increase in middle-class left voting usually start from the recognition of two distinct types of middle-class Labour identifier, the 'proletarian' and the 'altruist', who are held to support the party on different grounds. The 'proletarian' Labour voter is drawn from the 'marginal' middle class and is so described because he possesses an employment status and level of rewards similar to those of manual workers and tends to subjectively identify with the working class. Left voting is hardly 'deviant' for this section of the middle class as the 'underdog' appeal of the Labour Party fits well with their own low status. The increase in middle-class Labour voting, therefore, may be regarded as a reflection of the increasing proletarianisation of routine non-manual occupations. A rather different interpretation attaches more explanatory weight to social background than work experience. Goldthorpe *et al.* (1978), for example, suggest that with the expansion of non-manual positions there is an increase in the number of upwardly mobile individuals from manual families, and these have a tendency to retain their original Labour sympathies.

The 'altruistic' type of middle-class Labour voter is found among the 'lower professionals' or the established middle class, especially in public sector jobs such as teaching and social work. They tend to be highly educated with a principled, well-articulated radicalism. This image derives primarily from Parkin's study of those involved in the Campaign for Nuclear Disarmament in the late 1950s and early 1960s, who exhibited these characteristics (1968). They are described as 'altruistic' because of their disinterest in the material rewards of political success in comparison with the psychic satisfaction to be derived from 'expressive politics'.

However, there are dangers in drawing general conclusions about established middle-class support for the Labour Party from a study of a rather special pressure group. The Labour Party periodically forms a government with attendant powers to change patterns of resource distribution and its comparatively stronger commitment to public expenditure than the Conservatives serves well the career prospects of that section of the middle class working in the public sector. Labour voting by them may be considered 'altruistic' only if we slavishly follow the class–party axis and ignore that pattern of partisanship constituted by cleavages between public and private sector employment.

The implications for the political system of a swelling in middle-class Labour support are the object of two contrasting interpretations. One, associated with Marxism, asserts a definite shift to the left in the political centre of gravity as a result of a twofold process: first, as a consequence of the increasing 'proletarianisation' of the 'intermediate classes', manifested in loss of authority, job security, income and status; secondly, a heightening radicalism by well-paid professional and intellectual employees whose opposition to existing patterns of power is engendered by the dissemination of critical thinking in higher education and the growth of public service occupations which foster hostile attitudes to the market individualism of competitive capitalism (see Habermas, 1976; and Gouldner, 1979). A contrasting interpretation, put forward by Lipset (1960), and by Crewe *et al.* (1977), posits a more benign possibility for liberal democracy. An increase in middle-class Labour voting is regarded as symptomatic of a general erosion of partisanship which may lead to a less ideological form of politics in which electoral behaviour is characterised by increasing 'instrumentality' and the political parties judged in terms of their efficiency and effectiveness, particularly on economic issues.

Class de-alignment approaches have been counterposed directly by a theory of re-alignment advanced by Dunleavy (1979) who argues that a new line of cleavage has developed which cross-cuts occupational class divisions. This new cleavage is based upon conflicts of interest between the public and private sectors, in both employment and consumption. For example, public sector employees are much more likely to belong to trade unions and support the Labour Party than those working in the private sector. In the sphere of consumption, Dunleavy distinguishes between individualised and collective forms in his account of the influence of housing and transport locations on political alignment from an analysis of data drawn from February 1974 Gallup surveys. Individualised forms of consumption (purchases in shops and stores, for example) are directly determined by market forces and involve the commercial or private organisation of goods. Location in these consumption processes is determined by the amount of income earned by a household in employment, and, consequently, political struggles over individualised consumption tend to be expressed in bargaining over wages and salaries at the workplace. In contrast, collective consumption processes usually refer to state-provided services, such as housing, education or transport, and usually reflect demands for governmental intervention following the inability of the market to provide these services. Collective consumption processes are inevitably 'politicised' by the assumption of state responsibility for them in a way that does not occur with the control exercised over individual commodity consumption by the 'invisible market'. This is reinforced by the large-scale provision and management of state services which creates favourable conditions for the emergence of collective consciousness and action. Finally, because location in collective consumption processes is less directly determined by market forces, and thus by income and work position, they 'constitute an independent basis for the development of social cleavages, standing outside those originating in production relations'.

Although the idea that some consumption locations are relatively independent of occupational class position is well established in Marxist urban sociology, an additional element in Dunleavy's formulation is the notion of 'consumption sectors' which refers to those areas where consumption processes are fragmented between individual and collective modes. For example, the existence of an individual/commodity/private mode alongside a collective/service/public mode in housing and transportation provides the basis for the constitution of electoral cleavages that are relatively independent of occupational class locations. Thus, voters involved in collective modes of consumption are aligned to the left, while those involved in individualised modes are aligned to the right, relative to the underlying alignment of their social class locations. As a result, in areas like housing there should be salient political cleavages between home-owners and public housing tenants.

Dunleavy is insistent that cleavages in consumption patterns cannot be regarded as simply mediated aspects of occupational class, for his survey data indicate that half of skilled manual workers are owner–occupiers, while a similar proportion of all manual workers have access to a car. This is not to underestimate the fundamental importance of occupational class interests, but to suggest that consumption influences, such as housing or transport, may be more 'immediate' and 'visible' to individuals and thus provide a vital influence on political alignment.

Conclusions

The work of Dunleavy, Held, Abercrombie *et al.*, Kavanagh and others considered above provide a powerful critique of the role of values in traditional political sociology in which Britain was regarded as the model of a stable democracy characterised by a consensual civic culture. Similarly, recent British electoral studies have displayed a more critical approach to behaviouralism and a greater recognition of structured inequalities as the basis for opposed political outlooks than earlier interpretations. Particularly there is increased awareness of the dissensus and instabilities in the political system and the role of the state in both generating and seeking to cope with social turbulence. Of special interest is the heightened political salience of public and private locations, not only in production but also in consumption sectors, and the awareness of a more fragmentary class system with a more complex relationship to political and ideological phenomena than perceived in the sociology of democracy.

In the 1950s and 1960s, political sociology in both Europe and the USA was characterised by a convergence on a model of democracy that basically accepted existing practices in existing liberal democracies and which brought together the empirical methods of the behaviouralists with European grand theory. In the late 1960s and 1970s, the limitations of the sociology of democracy were exposed by the eruption in the West of more conflictual political events than assumed by the model and the consequent scrutiny by more radical, often Marxist critiques that became more influential in the social sciences. This result was a greater eclecticism in political sociology in the 1970s and 1980s which reflects a continuing recognition of the advances made by the dominant orthodoxy as well as the stimulation and theoretical sophistication of the 'the new political sociology'.

A central feature is a renewed concern with the state, particularly relationships with socio-economic forces, which had generally been lost in the sociology of democracy. One of the exceptions had been the work of Bendix (1964) who had been concerned with examining the creation of national political communities through an extension of citizenship rights to the lower classes in exchange for their acceptance of the liberal democratic state. However, and in comparison with recent 'corporatist' theories, the incorporation of the masses was viewed only as positive, as stabilising regimes, and the constraints on political action by the disadvantaged that was also entailed were largely ignored. Furthermore, the implications of this work for theories of state power were never pursued and during this period political sociology generally turned away from a concern with the state. In so doing it ignored increasing state interventions in modern society, particularly the economy, and was unprepared both for those social movements in the late 1960s that challenged state regulations and existing political arrangements, and for the theoretical assaults on the dominant orthodoxy that followed.

In the following chapters we outline what we term 'the new political sociology' which is characterised by a renewed interest in the state. We shall examine the historical development of the modern nation-state and the emerging distinction that is created between public and private spheres. Subsequently we move on to consider classical interpretations of the modern state as well as provide some empirical and comparative discussion of selected developments. Of particular interest are recent corporatist and Marxist critiques of pluralism and liberalism although we are concerned to examine deficiencies in these approaches too. Finally, we move to a consideration of the state at the local and international levels.

2

The Development of the Modern Nation-State

Introduction

This chapter examines the development over time of the modern western state. Specifically it looks at the emergence of a more impersonal and public system of rule over territorially circumscribed societies, exercised through a complex set of institutional arrangements and offices, which is distinguished from the largely localised and particularistic forms of power which preceded it. At one level of abstraction the general structural contours of the emergent modern state will be outlined, whilst recognising that this may hide considerable diversity in practises and historical trajectories at the level of particular societies. We shall see that a major issue is raised by the development of a liberal constitutional state and the claim that legitimate authority is based upon the concept of the ruled. The claim to supreme authority becomes increasingly to rest less on hereditary rank or divine or godly sanction than on the relationship between the ruler and the ruled.

The idea or concept of the state lacks precision and significance in American and British experience in comparison with that of continental Europe. The view of the composite and pluralistic character of public authority, the separation and balance of different powers and interests, found in the 'stateless' English-speaking societies contrasts strongly with that of the integrated 'public power' of continental Europe, which is often defended in highly abstract and impersonal terms. As Dyson (1980) has emphasised, there is a symbiotic relationship between historical experience in which the state was not recognised as a living entity, and the empiricist or pragmatist intellectual outlooks in America and Britain which see the world as a mass of discrete, directly observable facts and has little patience with abstract political ideas or legal concepts, such as 'the state', which are outside immediate 'felt' experience. In continental Europe the consciousness of institutions is developed and closely associated with the state. Rationalistic and idealistic philosophical methods give recognition to the holistic, normative nature of public authority and the creative and unifying role of state institutions.

The focus in this chapter, therefore, will be on the major western powers, not because of any overall similarity in their state-building traditions, but because the revolutions in politics, civil society and science that shaped the development of much of the modern world are to be initially located in a few western societies. In the fifteenth and sixteenth centuries, for example, we see the decisive emergence of what Wallerstein (1974) describes as a 'European world economy' and the beginnings of an industrial heartland in its north-western parts, which led to the triumph of capitalism as a world economy. The growth of the Absolutist State, which introduced such features of the modern state as large standing armies, bureaucracy and codified law, provided a significant break from medieval society. As Weber (1968) insisted, the absolutist rulers played a significant role in the rise of capitalism in dismantling the normative framework of medievalism, as much as did the growth of the independence and wealth of the 'bourgeois' towns. Moreover, the development of the new sciences and their impact on modern western social and political thought relegated other forms of knowledge. As Gamble (1981a) underlines, the systematic application of rational techniques to find the best means for achieving ends had an undermining effect on established social institutions. The new sciences increasingly supplied both the practical knowledge and information that a capitalist market economy demanded, as well as providing legitimations for its political arrangements. However, to properly comprehend the development of the modern nation-state we need to consider forms of political power that preceded it.

Feudalism, patrimonialism and the Standestaat

The distinction between state and society found in most accounts of modern political communities rests in part on the analytical separation of two ideal-typical forms of social relations to be found in the respective spheres. Following Weber, the state is held typically to entail relations of command and obedience in which individual actions are guided by a belief in the existence of a legitimate order of authority. Identifiable persons, such as political leaders and officials, maintain that order through the exercise of authority and this order endures as long as the conception of its legitimacy is shared by those who exercise authority and by those who are subject to it. In the customarily and voluntary established associations of society, however, relations are typically based on affinities of ideas and interests. They may, for example, be based on considerations of material advantage or be prompted by a sense of familial or professional solidarity with others. Although authority and social relations are relatively autonomous spheres of action in all societies, the separation has been greatest in modern western societies. Access to positions of public authority has gradually become separated from kinship ties, property interests and inherited privileges, at least in a formal sense. Decision making at the legislative, judicial and administrative levels became subject to impersonal rules and attained a certain degree of freedom from the constellations of social interests.

The potentialities and beginnings of these changes in the West are discernible as early as the medieval era where the exercise of authority was associated with what Weber describes as the competing structures of patrimonialism and feudalism. In effect, it refers to the struggles between kings and landed nobles over the kind and extent of limitations to be placed on the former's power. Patrimonialism refers to the organisation of the royal household and its domains, which is in the hands of the king's personal servants, and develops as a structure of authority with the territorial expansion of royal jurisdiction. The king's authority derives from three conjoined statuses: territorial ruler, large landowner, and patriarchal overlord of his household. While this generates absolute authority 'on earth', however, the king's will is constrained by religious norms and institutions. The king's capriciousness in ruling his subjects is tempered by the recognition that such rule is exercised under God, a matter made manifest by the consecration of his succession to the throne, and which requires him to protect his subjects and their welfare. To flout these divine limitations would be to raise doubts about the king's own position. Nor are these simply moral bounds. A distinguishing characteristic of western European kingship from other types of patrimonial rule, is that it had to face considerable organisational resources possessed by the Christian church, which would be used against the absolute claims of secular rulers by submitting them to stringent legal, canonical enquiry. Consequently, 'democratic' notions of the 'consent of the people', of a reciprocal obligation between ruler and ruled, are at least nascent in medieval political practice and provide the foundations for their later, more formally legalistic, consolidation.

Rulers also ran up against the problems of what Giddens (1981) has termed 'time–space distantiation' – the difficulties of maintaining adequate surveillance with the extension of authority over a territory beyond their domain. The visible and direct nature of the king's rule in the latter, conveyed by the presence and immediateness of his commands, is stretched and replaced by temporary and spatially weakened forms of control. Rulers necessarily relied on either directly-appointed agents in far-flung jurisdictions, charging them with increased responsibility and, inevitably, added autonomy, or on local notables whose property and local authority enabled them to aid the ruler financially and militarily, but which also could result in increased independence for such notables. Feudal relationships, based on reciprocal obligation, tended to develop where a territorial ruler was unable to devise ways of securing the economic and personal dependence of the landed aristocrats on him. The result tended to be a more 'balanced' exchange of powers and responsibilities centred on the lord–vassal relationship, which is the heart of the feudal system of rule. In it, a vassal swore an oath of fealty to his ruler and thus acknowledged his obligation to serve him. In return, the ruler granted his vassal a fief or protectorate, usually lands and rights which included a guaranteed 'immunity' by which the vassal is entitled to exercise certain judicial and administrative powers.

A typology of medieval polities, therefore, would need to include a fundamental patrimonial–feudal axis along which regimes could be placed to the extent to which either the king or landed aristocracy were in the ascendancy. In effect, patrimonial and feudal domains competed and co-existed within particular political structures. Where patrimonialism was the stronger influence, the fiefdoms enjoyed by local notables were much more firmly embedded within the royal jurisdiction, and less subject to 'sub-contracting', the devolving or parcelling out of parts of the fief, or the establishment in them of proprietorial or familial rights. Where feudalism was the stronger in western Europe it became characterised by an explicit ideology of 'rights'. The relations between a ruler and his vassals was consecrated though an affirmation of rights and duties under oath and before God which reinforced the autonomy of feudal jurisdictions. In effect, however, in medieval polities the tugs and pulls between the patrimonial and feudal principle of authority resulted in a system of divided and overlapping jurisdictions competing for power and influence.

Consequently, the system of political authority in medieval society lacked integration and density. It was generally predicated upon personal relationships rather than general laws, with the majority of the population excluded as participants. As Duby (1962) has recounted, the feudal period was marked by an increasing fragmentation of each large system of rule into many smaller and autonomous systems, differing widely in their practices, and with no direct relation between top and bottom. The particularised fief, rather than the office, characterised relations between the king and the lords. Only in England, following the Norman invasion, was the king considered as the apex of lord–vassal relationships, and whose overarching authority was not diminished by the sub-division of fiefs by notables to their vassals. In other places it became increasingly difficult to distinguish between powers that derived from the proprietorial possession of land, and those that had a more 'state-like' origin. Poggi (1978) notes that the jurisdictional–political and the proprietory–economic prerogatives of fief-holders were fused in such a way that the purely patrimonial component became uppermost. The landed estate itself came to be seen as the inherent carrier of semi-political and formerly public prerogatives. Almost inevitably, the king lacked a monopoly of legitimate physical coercion, relying for order and the redress of grievances on the self-interested duals and conflicts of the landed nobles.

Given the layered, hierarchical and particularised nature of medieval society, it is not surprising that there was no form of plebiscitarian political participation – a direct relationship between individuals and the state. Individuals lacked particular legal recognition as individuals in the exercise of rights and duties.

Instead these followed from an individual's status, which was defined either by heredity (e.g. nobles) or membership in an organisation possessing certain immunities or liberties (e.g. municipal corporations). Similarly peasants' rights and duties were enjoyed as the result of a fealty relation to a lord, or through membership in an association or corporation possessing a more or less autonomous jurisdiction. Thus each community of peasants belonged to the jurisdiction of its lord, and each group of craftsmen to the jurisdiction of its town and guild. Feudal relations represented a unity of the economic and the political in which economic exploitation was fused with political–legal coercion at the molecular level of the village (Anderson, 1974).

It is this cellular nature of pre-Absolutist medieval society, in which economic and political relations comprised a series of tiny modules, which leads Giddens (1981) to suggest that although at the local level the 'economy' is embedded in the institutional framework of community life, in a certain sense production relations are much more distinct from the 'political' – in the form of the state – than they are in capitalist societies. Moreover, this segmentalised character inevitably involved a normative distance between centre and periphery, in which the power of those who needed to coercively extract taxation or other forms of tribute or services from populations subject to their rule did not penetrate many aspects of daily life. In such societies with high 'presence-availability' social integration is largely coterminous with societal integration as a whole, for societal power was usually legitimised through the mechanisms and traditional practices of community where kinship was the significant medium of collectivity organisation. The ruler was less dependent upon the normative allegiance of his subjects at large than upon the loyalty of the administrative and military apparatus. This is unlike contemporary totalitarianism, which is much more extensive in the level of authoritative command over a subject population and utilises modern surveillance and information processing techniques.

Nonetheless, the 'anarchy' of the feudal system of rule must not be overstated. Although the official structure of rule based on the territorial monarchs and their households lacked effectiveness, distinctiveness and abstract generality as a consequence of feudal indentation, it is still possible to discern some of the earliest glimmers of the modern state. As Poggi (1978) notes, feudalism in the twelfth and thirteenth centuries constituted a first attempt to impose a firm and workable framework of rule on lands that had suffered much devastation and insecurity. It also settled on the land a nomadically-inclined warrior class who progressively learned to consider criteria of equity and justice, and to exercise responsibility and protection. Furthermore feudalism established a more discursive and civilised basis for the determination of justice, as well as maintaining a set of protections against tyrannical rulers that became a particular feature of western judicial codes. It challenged, too, theocratic notions of kingship, in which all power was located in God and delegated to his secular officers, and which seemed to allow only for the passive obedience of the king's subjects (Dyson, 1980). In contrast, feudalism rested on the notion of a contract which created a legal bond between lord and vassal and made it possible to conceive of the king as a member of the feudal community and subject to that community's agreed or 'common' law. However, the importance of these ideas varied: in France the theocratic idea remained ascendant, whereas in England the feudal impulse was strongest and sufficiently malleable to incorporate notions of increased popular participation.

Over time, however, feudal patterns were replaced in the fifteenth and sixteenth centuries by a system of absolutist rule in which there was a displacement of political legal coercion upwards towards a centralised, militarised apparatus of royal power. The king exercised certain nationwide powers through his appointed officials, while other important judicial and administrative powers were pre-empted on a hereditary basis by privileged estates and the constituted bodies in which they were represented. Even England, where feudal practices continued with remarkable vigour long after their influence had been lost in some other European societies, experienced a period of Tudor absolutism before the Cromwellian 'revolution' severely reduced monarchical powers. Elsewhere, the introduction of money rents for dues and the elimination of serfdom broke apart the fused economic and political repression of the peasantry and threatened the power of the feudal lord, thus facilitating absolutist developments. However, in considering the factors which led to the emergence of European Absolutism in the sixteenth century, we need to examine the period of the Standestaat, or 'the polity of the Estates', for the part played by the towns in the change from feudalism.

The Standestaat

The Standestaat as a system of political rule was widespread in Europe by the thirteenth century, and is characterised by a more pronounced patrimonial influence than in the predominantly feudal order found in England. Indeed, British and French historians have generally failed to recognise the significance and staying-power of the Standestaat, largely because England did not see the consolidation of distinct legal privileges for the estates found in most of continental Europe, whilst the French Standestaat declined dramatically in the seventeenth and eighteenth centuries with the failure to meet of the Estates-General between 1614 and 1789 (Myers, 1975). However, in the German states, the Netherlands, and Sweden, for example, the Standestaat proved an enduring system of rule. It was characterised by the influence of Roman notions of justice and legal definition and the elaboration of canon law. It differed from the feudal order in being more legalistic, institutionalised and territorial in its reference and was based on a partnership of king and estates in the rule of a territory that produced a 'dualism' between two relatively autonomous centres of power not found in the modern, unitary state (Dyson, 1980; Poggi, 1978).

The Standestaat also marked the resurgence of the influence of the towns which, in a quite novel manner, became areas of independent and collective political action. Here we find one of the earliest examples of expanding economic activity running up against the administrative restrictions and legal–political fetters of the feudal system. The towns sought greater political freedom as a means of reducing feudal restrictions on trade, although the increasing trans-local nature of such trade also inclined the towns to welcome the wider system of rule provided by the territorial rulers. As Poggi (1978) notes, the Stande or Estates were devised to provide structures that would not only provide the towns with political autonomy but also the right to participate in a wider system of rule. Thus, the Estates or Stande were constituted bodies that were distinctive, not because they comprised assemblies of corporate groups, which had a long history, but because they were formed to specifically associate with the territorial ruler in those aspects of rule that were understood as characteristically public and general. In comparison, feudal assemblies were usually comprised of individual lords that lacked a territorial representative function against the king, but rather congregated around him. However, the Stande tended to debilitate the vassal–lord relationship between feudal elements and the rulers through the gradual inclusion of the former, alongside the urban interests, within its more institutionalised and territorial system of representation.

The towns also generated new political and administrative arrangements that strongly influenced wider territorial rule, including elected representative bodies that governed by enacting statutes, and by establishing systems of differentiated offices or roles, conceived as separate from the person, and which were gradually filled by a new type of political–administrative personnel such as secular-educated lawyers and literati. Political life also became more discursive, civilised and business-like, in which the process and style of law sustained the notion of an increasingly 'public' domain. Gradually, the ruler exercised authority as a public figure rather than as a feudal lord or property-owner, with a household that became the basis of an increased administrative system that was staffed by individuals in a more directly dependent relationship to the king than was the case with feudal vassalage. The result was a significant step towards the modern nation-state leading to absolutist systems of rule in most European societies, but with a rather different outcome in England.

The Absolute State

In the long run, as Weber (1968) suggests, a feudal landowning class is less well-placed than a prebendal or stipendiary land-controlling class to resist the growth of a truly centralised monarchy. The feudal value system could be used by the king to secure himself at the top of its hierarchical system of relationships, where loyalty is addressed to him as 'feudal lord-in-chief' and from which the personal element is then discarded. Loyalty is then to the nation of which the king is the manifestation. However, it was crisis and instability in international affairs that, alongside dynastic ambition, encouraged the territorial consolidation and centralising pressures that reinforced the patrimonial impulse. The fifteenth and sixteenth centuries saw the arrival of the great restorers of internal order in western Europe, who were given a strong impetus by the various crises of the late fourteenth century – war, disease, economic stagnation – which considerably weakened the lords of the manor. An additional factor which led to the creation of relatively strong state machineries in what would become the core-states of the capitalist world economy (Wallerstein, 1974), is located as much within the system of states that was emerging in Europe, as in the internal changes within each separate state. Both economic and political competition generated power struggles between states respectively defining themselves as territorially sovereign. External challenges and forays made it imperative for territorial rulers to centralise and organise power internally. Most importantly, the ruler could count on at least the tacit support of urban commercial interests, as a strong state provided not only opportunities for the opening up of foreign trade, but also protected the domestic market and provided a general framework of order and stability necessary for entrepreneurial enterprise. Moreover, the increasing trans-local division of labour facilitated the towns' acceptance of the weakening of the powers of representative bodies at both local and higher levels. Corporative restrictions on trade and the alienability of labour in the towns forfeited the interest of the commercial classes in local political autonomy, which was replaced by the more compelling desire to pursue profit.

Paralleling these developments, the economic and political position of the landed aristocracy, outside the special case of England, was gradually gnawed away by the commercialisation of the economy. The influx of bullion, as a result of exploration, and regular debasements of the coinage had inflationary consequences that debilitated the fixed revenues of the landed classes. Almost perpetual warfare in the fifteenth and sixteenth centuries within the system of emerging states resulted in increased taxation, heavy feudal dues, liquidity crises and stagnation, all of which weakened the landed estates whilst strengthening the monarchy. As Wallerstein (1974, pp. 29–30) notes, taxation was the key issue. Territorial rulers were seeking to become part of an upward cycle in which increases in state administration, rather than becoming a 'drag' on liquidity, were more than paid for from increased revenue drawn from an expanding economy. Accomplishing this 'take-off' however, harmed both the financial and political strength of the nobility. Furthermore, the feudal element largely lost its military significance and one of its original political tasks as the evolution of military technology made obsolete the medieval knight and strengthened the hand of central authorities increasingly requiring large standing armies.

As a result, the territorial ruler grew stronger with the acquisition of a body of permanent and dependable officials, although unlike modern state bureaucracies monarchs had to rely on the practice of selling offices ('venality of office') to achieve both loyal executives and much needed revenue. Whilst this practice helped meet the high costs of state building and created a 'fourth' estate of office-holders whose interests were allied to the ruler, it could contain the seeds of its own destruction by proving to be not only very expensive, but by creating a new hierarchy of offices which posed a threat to the status of traditionally powerful families. In France, however, venality of office allowed the state to incorporate both landed and newly urban classes within its machinery, thus making possible the relative supremacy of the state system. Nevertheless, as Dyson (1980) points out, the sale of offices in France encouraged an exploitation of office for personal gain, in terms of both clientelism and profit, which contrasts with modern bureaucracy. Only during the eighteenth century was the idea of a personal, private relationship to the prince replaced by the concept of a professional relationship to a permanent impersonal state. Yet the absolutist rulers' household was no longer a private, or familial affair, but a highly distinctive and expressive sign of his increasingly unchallenged power. It was complemented instrumentally by councils of government each linked to the king's administrators, and all responsive to the ruler's command. In addition, the influence of Italian humanism and the more complicated effects of the Reformation strengthened the power of the secular authority against that of the Church. The religious unity of the Christian community was fragmented, the theocratic basis of the Holy Roman Empire was undermined, and the idea of the charitable role of the secular authorities was established. Religious upheaval in the sixteenth and seventeenth centuries sustained princely power and encouraged the notion of a neutral public power which gave priority to the secular purposes of protecting life and maintaining order rather than the imposition of one religious truth. Secularisation, not just a rising bourgeoisie, played its part in the development of a public, state authority (Dyson, 1980, p. 30).

A consequence of such upheavals in ideology was the inadequacy of static conceptions of the ruler as the judge of traditional rights. Through the influential writings of Bodin, there emerged the idea that the ruler could will new law and was an 'absolute' legislator with respect to civil law. This novel conception transformed law into an instrument rather than a framework for rule (Poggi, 1978). Moreover, it was general law that applied directly to all within a territorially-delimited area, thus helping to depersonalise state authority from that of the ruler, and providing the basis for abstract rights and duties conceived separately from historically-accumulated, distinct prerogatives and rights.

The centralised monarchies that emerged in the course of the sixteenth century represented a decisive rupture with the pyramidal, parcellised sovereignty of the medieval social formations. They were characterised by the introduction of standing armies, a permanent bureaucracy, public taxation, a codified law, and the beginnings of a unified market. An important element in this was the so-called 'reception' of Roman law in continental Europe, whose rediscovery was consonant with the spirit of absolutism (Dyson, 1980, pp. 114–15). It was the decisive contribution of Roman law that established the idea that there existed in the community (people or prince, or both) a supreme will that could alter laws to suit changing social conditions. This provided juristic justification for overriding traditional, feudal rights, and with crediting the political community with characteristics that were previously regarded as belonging to the Church. As well as its traditions of equity, rational canons of evidence, and emphasis on a professional judiciary, which met not only the requirements of the centralising monarchies but also enabled codification of the practices sustaining commodity production and exchange, Roman law conferred on the continental European state the distinction between public and private (civil) affairs. A separate domain of public law, which pertained to the impersonal abstract character of the state, emerged with its own principles to guide legislation and administration, and with a distinct system of administrative courts, distinguishable from the civil law which applied to relations of private individuals. This distinctively legal basis to the identification of the state was, however, absent in England. There, a relatively cohesive political community had already developed, through its feudal institutions, the idea of making law through statute, while Roman law's association with autocratic government appeared incompatible with feudalism's tradition of a limited monarchy.

The development of capitalism and parliamentarism

The western absolutist state was clearly of fundamental importance in providing the legal and political framework for the development of both the modern nation-state and capitalist economies. Specifically it was associated with the growth of a new form of surplus appropriation, described by Wallerstein (1974, p. 16) as a 'capitalist world economy'. It was based not on the direct appropriation of agricultural surplus in the form either of tribute (e.g. world empires) or of feudal rents (e.g. European feudalism), but on more efficient and expanded productivity, first in agriculture, and later industry. This is achieved by means of a world market mechanism with the non-market help of state machineries, none of which controlled the world market in its entirety. Wallerstein (1974, p. 37) argues that three factors were essential in the establishment of this capitalist world economy: the territorial expansion of Europe, the development of variegated methods of labour control for different products and zones of the world economy, and the creation of relatively strong state machineries in what would become the core-states of this capitalist world economy. The distinctiveness of this new world system was that as an economic entity it was larger than any juridicially-defined political unit. Its accumulative potential in large measure derived from the changed economic role of the state which became less the central economic enterprise than the means of assuring certain terms of trade. This contrasted with the waste and primitive means of economic domination in political empires, for example, where complex administrative and military apparatuses devoured profits and physical resources that could be invested in capitalist development.

The north-western states became the economic heartland of the European world economy when, towards the second half of the sixteenth century, an emergent industrial sector began to locate in certain core-states. The pace-setter was England, where the thrust of export trade was in textiles. England had political as well as economic advantages over commercial competitors by this time – it was exceptionally unified, administratively and fiscally efficient, politically stable, with no overseas possessions requiring defence or administration, possessed a strong capital city acting as a cultural and economic unifying force and had no standing army which required resourcing through high taxation and a bureaucracy. Moreover, the confiscation and selling of Church land by Henry VIII dramatically expanded the amount of land available on the market and accelerated the extension of capitalist modes of production. The critical element, however, in the commercialising of English life was that the elimination of the peasant farmer made land fully alienable and helped the creation of a labour surplus. This, alongside quite special political practices, helped conduce 'the first capitalist society'.

A particular emphasis on the role played by economic processes in accounting for the historical variations in both the development of capitalism and democracy is found in Moore (1968), although Moore does not employ, as does Wallerstein, the notion of a capitalist world economy. Rather, Moore seeks to explain why the processes of industrialisation in England culminated in the establishment of a relatively free society in which the toleration displayed by landowning classes is a significant element. Crucially, and ironically, it derived from the 'legalised violence' of the enclosing landlord which finally destroyed the whole structure of English peasant society embodied in the traditional village and eliminated the peasantry as a factor from English political life. It removed a huge reservoir of conservative and reactionary forces of the kind which continued to exist in Prussia and France, and provided the basis for a successful agrarian capitalism that obviated the need for the landed classes to rely, as did the Prussian Junkers, for example, on repressive political action to sustain a declining and outmoded agricultural economy.

However, the political as well as the economic preconditions for the commercialisation of agriculture in England were also decisively important, particularly the limitations on royal power. Yet in the early sixteenth century, England's monarchy appeared to share many of the absolutist characteristics of those in continental Europe. The War of the Roses (1455–85) had weakened the landed aristocracy and, with the continuing stimulus of the wool trade, the Tudor dynasty successfully consolidated royal power. The Tudors pioneered a new renaissance state and produced great administrators such as Wolsey, Cromwell and the Cecils (Dyson, 1980). Yet 'Tudor discipline', peace and wool were a combination that occurred in a specific way. Unlike France, commercialisation in both towns and countryside advanced relatively autonomously and generally without royal patronage. With no standing army and little risk of maritime invasion, and in the context of the veto powers of the Commons, the English crown was unable to construct an effective administrative, financial and military base of its own that could have forced its will on the countryside and prevented the Civil War in the seventeenth century. Furthermore, the sale of confiscated monastery land, which strengthened the position of the gentry lost for the monarchy the one great chance of English Absolutism building up a firm economic base independent of parliamentary taxation. The Civil War was precipitated in the mid-seventeenth century by a crisis between the Crown and the increasingly powerful gentry, who regarded royal monopolies and judicial protection of the peasants as barriers to commercial ambition.

Through breaking the power of the king, the Civil War swept away the main barrier to the enclosing landlord (Moore, 1968, p. 9). Perhaps more importantly it strengthened Parliament as the locus of landlord power at the expense of the king. Moreover, it was a national single parliament with territorial representation which lacked the 'estate' divisions found elsewhere. The result was a flexible institution which constituted both an arena into which new social elements could be drawn as their demands arose and an institutional mechanism for settling peacefully conflicts of interest among these groups. Although the landed classes may have kept political control until the twentieth century, the connection between the enclosing landlord and the industrial bourgeoisie was close, for both the capitalist principle and parliamentary democracy were directly opposed to religiously-based authority in politics, and against production for use rather than for individual profit in the economy.

Consequently, from the seventeenth century onwards England's political development differed from the rest of Europe in that it remained remarkably well-nourished from its feudal roots. The political system was based on a complex process of negotiation between the monarch and the large landowners while the crown's authority was limited, not least because the monarch was conceived as part of a wider community. The revolution of 1688 succeeded in protecting the traditional rights and privileges of Parliament, the courts and local communities against the assertions of a centralising crown. Public action became subject to parliamentary control, legitimated by the notion that sovereignty resided in crown-in-parliament, not by reference to the notion of an autonomous state acting to realise certain inherent purposes (Dyson, 1980, p. 117). There was a gradual movement to the view that executive power was an effusion of parliament, although parliament was not regarded as representative of 'the people', which would have been too radical a notion. Rather, constitutional arrangements, unlike continental absolutism and its aftermath, encouraged neither an active role for the people nor an activist conception of the state.

In comparison, the French nobility achieved little independence from the king and continued to possess a more definite legal status than in England and an economic dependence on peasant dues. It lacked an economic base, such as that provided by the commercialised wool trade in England, and consequently relied on royal absolutism to extract surplus from an increasingly unproductive and traditional system. As economic and military pressures intensified from more successfully commercialising states, the French agrarian economy could not produce a sufficient return to remunerate its office holders in a way that would ensure their real dependence on the king. 'Venality of office' was the alternative method for consolidating royal power, but it imparted feudal characteristics to a bourgeoisie that became rigid defenders of local privileges, especially in the parliaments, and tied an uncommercial nobility into a singularly unproductive style of conspicuous consumption, war and general indolence within the royal household.

The value of Wallerstein's (1974) theoretical perspective of an emerging capitalist world economy is that it is possible to account for the variations in political and economic practice described above in terms of international constraints and opportunities, not simply as the consequence of discrete or domestically isolated factors internal to states. Wallerstein argues, for example, that it was England's position in the world economy that enabled it to become the first industrial nation, with a political accommodation between traditional and rising economic elements. It experienced the specific conjuncture of commercial opportunity (mainly textiles) and the absence of external threat or imperial obligations. The result was a state machinery just strong enough to provide external security, but sufficiently weak not to favour either the landed nobility or the new state administrators, so that neither were able to totally consume the surplus of the most productive forces.

Wallerstein's thesis is that capitalism was able to flourish because the world economy had within its bounds not one but a multiplicity of political systems. This provides capitalists with a freedom of manœuvre that is structurally based. The creation of a strong state machinery in territorially-limited societies served as a mechanism to protect disparities that arise in the world system. From the standpoint of the world system not all states can be equally strong, for this blocks the effective operation of transnational economic agencies in their ability to move most effectively between states as circumstances dictate, as well as providing a useful inter-state competitive edge to economic development. Moreover, some strong state machines are essential to protect capitalist interests and property rights. Thus, from the sixteenth century, the world economy developed a pattern where the state structures became relatively strong in the core economic areas, and relatively weak at the periphery.

The French state and social revolution

The emphasis placed by both Moore (1966) and Wallerstein (1974) on economic factors in explaining developments in political structures may underestimate the independent effects of changes in state organisation as an important determinant in such developments. The French Revolution in 1789 and its aftermath illustrates this. Skocpol (1979) has convincingly argued that to explain it, it is necessary to conceive of states as administrative and coercive organisations that are potentially autonomous from, although conditioned by, socio-economic interests and structures. Nation-states do not simply reflect dominant economic interests, but primarily are organisations securing internal control of a particular space and its people and potentially or actually engaging in warfare with other states in an international system. Such factors as state administrative efficiency, political capacities for mass mobilisation, and international geographical position may be as relevant as the condition of domestic economies or international economic positions in accounting for the comparative strengths and weaknesses of states. Modern social revolutions provide particularly good examples of this, for defeats in war, threats of invasion, and struggles over colonial controls have directly contributed to revolutions by undermining existing state authority, thus providing opportunities for successful social revolts 'from below'. More generally, state organisations, rather than merely reflecting dominant economic interests, may run counter to them. They may consume more resources, perhaps in military adventures, than dominant interests feel is compatible with the need for re-investment.

Revolutionary crises tend to happen when old-regime states fail to meet the economic and/or military challenge of more developed states, and lack the capacity to carry through political reform in the face of entrenched landed interests more concerned with preventing increased taxation or in using possession of state offices to procure revenue in a manner that maintained the domestic status quo. The dilemmas for rulers faced with intensifying military competition from nation-states with greater power based on capitalist 'breakthrough' were huge and required the rapid marshalling of immense social resources to carry out major reforms. The 'revolutions from above' in Prussia and Japan showed that such a task was not impossible, although it needed authoritarian political rule to extract more from a declining economic base. At a later stage in such 'revolutions', and with the support of a weak commercial bourgeoisie allied with the landed upper classes, the state directly supports capitalist development in several important ways, not least as an engine of accumulation through the introduction of armaments and heavy industrial needs. The political result is a regime with an authoritarian military ethic unfavourable to democracy.

In France, however, the old regime was unable to overcome the dilemma, and it succumbed to the opposition of politically powerful landed upper classes, which resisted the king's efforts at reform. Its origins lie in the inability of the royal household in the seventeenth century to eliminate medieval institutions, such as seigneurial domains and provincial estates. France remained predominantly an agricultural society in the seventeenth and eighteenth centuries, with an economy sluggishly characterised by a miasma of property interests that prevented any quick switch to capitalist agriculture or industrialism, and which retained a large peasant sector. A distinctive dominant class, neither feudal nor capitalist, appropriated surplus from this predominantly peasant-based agriculture through a complex pattern of rents and dues enforced in part by landlord-dominated juridical institutions, but with royal absolutism as the final back-up. This situation of dependence for proprietorial privilege on the state engendered a dominant class with a vested interest in opposing reform. When the system's economic foundations collapsed, the inability to secure reform against landed resistance led to the collapse of the royal administration and paved the way for social revolution (Skocpol, 1979, p. 64).

The calling of the estates general, as the dominant classes demanded a representative body to advise the king and give consent to any new taxes, set the revolution in train. It is instructive to contrast the nature and function of this 'corporatist' body with England's territorially-based Parliament. The latter was an established representative institution, already functioning to mediate diverse interests within the dominant class, whereas the calling of the estates general simply raised questions about the structure of government. Moreover, leaders from the dominant class in France encouraged increased political participation by appealing to urban groups for support in their struggle for 'liberty'. The central social thrust, however, was provided by the peasants revolting against heavy rents and dues, which finally forced the deputies in the constituent assembly to sweep away feudal rights and the privileges of medievalism. The removal of the institutional power bases of the landed upper classes eliminated the major obstacles to reform and, in so doing, highlighted the limitations on 'absolutist' power within the old regimes. The term 'absolutism' is a misnomer, for it did not involve untrammelled despotism, as the description implies, but rather claims to power. Absolutist states lacked the organisational capacity in the sixteenth and seventeenth centuries to clearly monopolise the means of violence within their borders, or to obtain the resources, or command the allegiance of their peoples, that would warrant their description. As Giddens (1981, p. 170) has noted, absolutist states lacked the capacity for surveillance and control based upon the information processing techniques of the modern state. Rather, absolutism corresponded to Bodin's theory of it – as doubly limited by the persistence of traditional bodies below it and the presence of an overarching moral law above (Anderson, 1974). In practice, too, banditry persisted, not as a form of traditional feudal opposition to state authority but as the consequence of the inadequate growth of state authority. It followed from the inability of the state to compensate for the dislocations caused by economic and social turbulence, and its unwillingness to ensure greater equalisation in the distribution of resources in times of inflation, population growth and food shortages. Furthermore, the state may be said to have contributed to banditry by depriving some peasants of their produce to feed the new bureaucracies and by creating a larger concentration of wealth so that it became tempting to seize it (Hobsbawm, 1969).

Under absolutism, the legitimation of the regime involved not the masses but state officials, and political stability depended upon state officials convincing local powers that it was in their interests, and in line with their values, that the regime continue to function without major disturbance. However, particularly with the development of bourgeois political claims, the notion of a wider community as properly influencing state policy became more acknowledged. This wider 'constituency' is not simply *ruled* but is *represented* and participates in rule. Moreover, the state was increasingly regarded as a new element of society: a structure of authority and a mechanical organisation of society. On the continent Prussia was seen as the paradigm of the modern state, particularly its concept of 'office', which served to objectify the state, after the accession of Frederick the Great in 1740. There emerges the idea of the impersonal, abstract state, which controls a consolidated territory and possesses a system of offices that is differentiated from that of other organisations operating in the same territory. The new constitutional design that develops reflects the aims of both bourgeoisie and state politico–administrators for general and abstract laws that would not only protect the autonomy of the market, and the privileges of the propertied, but also articulate the idea of the state, with categories that provided coherence and consistency in the exercise of power and the maintenance of social order.

The liberal constitutional state

The state that emerged in the nineteenth century came to be understood in terms of two central ideas: a centralised power that attempts to overawe all other powers in a given territory through the use of various agencies, force, etc; and as founded on consent, in that the state's power must be legitimated and turned into authority (Gamble, 1981a, p. 49).

1. *State as centralised power*

As we have seen the conception of the state that slowly emerges is that of a public power that is humanly created and distinct from other social powers and particular office-holders, including the king. It is characterised by authority, entailing relations of command and obedience, rather than utility and affinity ('state and society'), and involves at least some subordination of private to public interest, although in exchange for certain public rights ('citizenship'). Clear territorial boundaries mark out the administrative province of the nation-state, which previously had been indefinite and fluctuating, and which is associated with the formation of national police forces. The determination of very precise administrative boundaries, not 'nationalism', integrates the nation-state, each of which operates in its own territory as the exclusive source of rule. In contrast with the 'dualism' of the Standestaat, the nineteenth-century constitutional state is characterised by a unitary sovereignty which becomes manifest in a single currency, a unified legal system, and an expanding state educational system employing a single 'national' language. A literary tradition in this 'national' language erodes cultural particularism, and a system of national military conscription, which replaced the local recruitment of ancient military units, also tends to overcome 'peripheral' or localist identities. Moreover, this increasing monopoly of the means of violence by centralising states is sustained by the extension of the capitalist mode of production. It is associated with the extrusion of control of violent sanctions from the exploitative class relations involved in the capitalist commitment to freedom of contract. The increasing formal separation of the economic realm from the political should be regarded as based in the capital–labour contract, which involves, unlike pre-capitalist relationships, no immediate control of the means of violence by employers. Workers are denied authority at work but given distinct (thereby limited) political rights outside (Giddens, 1981, p. 176).

Modern states are also distinctive in that they are 'built' or 'made' purposefully and operate with reference to some idea of an end to which they are instrumental. This is a particular connotation of post-revolutionary regimes. Political leaderships involved in revolutions must be regarded as actors struggling to assert and make good their claims to state sovereignty, not simply as representatives of socio-economic interests but as claimants for state power (Skocpol, 1979, p. 164). The social and occupational backgrounds of such leaders is conducive to a view of them as 'state-builders' rather than as representatives of classes, for they tend to come from the ranks of relatively highly-educated groups oriented to state activities or employments and somewhat marginal to the dominant classes and government élites under the old regimes. The French revolution, for example, resulted in a professional–bureaucratic state rather than a 'bourgeois' or 'capitalist' state. While the simplification of property rights and the reduction of trade barriers certainly facilitated capitalism, the most marked developments were in state organisation which became more centralised and which introduced nationwide systems of law, customs and taxation. State finances under Napoleon, for example, became more a form of public administration than private capitalism, with the growth of a Treasury and full annual accounts of the nation's finances. The government took control of education, making it more selective, centralised and élitist, and providing a reservoir of talent from which state administrators and experts could be recruited. They were needed, too, as the number of bureaucrats multiplied during the revolution (from 50 000 to 250 000) with the emergence of a stronger and more autonomous state. Bureaucratisation and 'democratisation' were exemplified in the professionalisation of the officer corps and the emergence of a national army, processes symptomatic of the influence of warfare in the later stages of the revolution on structures of government. The pressures on the French revolutionary leaders after 1791 to mobilise for wars on the continent, even as they fought counter-revolutionaries at home, contrasts with the absence of invasions from major military powers in England (Skocpol, 1979, p. 181). If anything, a centralised, interventionalist state hindered capitalist industrialisation as much as it facilitated it, and the leading commercial interests would have preferred a more liberal, parliamentary outcome than the bureaucratic state form which developed. The nineteenth-century French state indicates one particular form that the emerging western nation state took as it centralised and legitimated its powers. Abstractly, it was not untypical, for the state generally became structured as a formal complex organisation, with offices hierarchically arranged and with an organic division of administrative tasks guided by general laws that 'depersonalise' decision making. Following Poggi (1978, pp. 108–12), we can outline five particularly distinctive characteristics of this developing 'machinery'.

a. Civility Although states come to possess technically more sophisticated and formidable means of coercion, this becomes differentiated from other aspects of the internal political process. The military and the police become subject to a higher-order 'civil' or 'political' control. While states are capable of violent aggression externally and repression internally, punishments for crimes generally become less draconian and public business takes on a more discursive, rational and peaceable ('parliamentary') air.

b. Plurality of foci The political process becomes correspondingly differentiated as the state comprises many different offices and agencies, with distinct scopes and functions.

c. Open-endedness Political business is a continuous process, publicly transacted less by reference to traditional prerogatives than to open-ended discussion and legal elaboration, indicating that the state is intrinsically changeable and purposeful.

d. Controversy Constitutional arenas, such as parliamentary assemblies, allow for the articulation of freely-expressed differences, and serve as constraints on executives.

e. Centrality of representative institutions Parliamentary assemblies help both to distinguish and to connect 'state' and 'society' as separate realms, roles and relationships.

This last feature takes us to a consideration of the second major characteristic of the nineteenth-century liberal constitutional state – the 'representative' nature of its claims to legitimation.

2. *The legitimation of the liberal constitutional state*

With the development of the modern state the claim to supreme authority is no longer based upon the hereditary rank of a monarchical lineage but lies in the nature of the relationship between the rulers and the ruled. More particularly, it comes to be seen as founded on consent, which raised the question of how extensive and on what basis should be this consent. The issue of who 'belongs' to the political community in turn leads to a widening social basis for the state through an extension of civic, political and social rights.

It is useful to distinguish the concern with sovereignty, or the relation of the individual to the state, from the related problem of the relation of state power to civil society, or political economy (Gamble, 1981a, p. 54). The latter is prompted by the apparent separation of society and the state with the development of a new market economy, particularly the new freedoms of civil society. One approach, associated with the economic individualism of Adam Smith and the British School of political economy was to seek to restrict the state to a specific role, that of enforcing the general rules that govern civil society. This by no means implies a weak state for the state may require considerable powers to enforce such rules. But it does imply a 'restrained' role which precludes detailed interference in civil society.

The legitimacy or authority of state power that derives from such conceptions finds expression in the early 'social contract' theorists and their speculation on the limits of state power. For Hobbes the limitations were more implied than explicit: individuals had a moral obligation to obey the state's commands and laws so long as the state preserved their security. For later theorists such as Locke and Montesquieu these limits were more pronounced, for they regarded the state as only one of the associations of individuals, and one without any extensive claims over them. Constitutions, it was argued, should seek to prevent accumulations of power preferably through provision for institutional checks and balances, or by a confederation of states (Macpherson, 1966). These essentially negative concepts of government complemented the view that it was civil society that was the sphere of individual liberties and that governments should limit themselves to promoting the conditions of, particularly, economic liberty. In contrast, a continental European tradition associated with Hegel and Rousseau, regarded the state as a higher moral community, an end in itself, which should actively seek to counter the harmful effects of civil society (Dyson, 1980). German Hegelianism, in its concern for the spiritual life, was especially conscious of the state as a basis of community and altruistic commitment.

As we have seen, however, early English liberalism is distinguished from that which occurred in France and the USA in its peculiarly feudalistic connotations which preserved the notion of the traditional accumulation of specific rights or 'immunities', rather than couching them in terms of universal rational or legal principles. They were established as unwritten constitutional conventions so that the legal privileges of the landed nobility, if not the king, would not be jeopardised. Thus, despite the emphasis on consent and civil liberty (originally aimed at the arbitrary powers of the king), political participation was restricted to the propertied class. As Gamble (1981a) notes, once the notion of rights is formulated in universalistic terms, it becomes logically difficult to impose limits on political participation, especially as the legitimacy of the state is apparently founded on the voluntary consent of all citizens and its purpose is to safeguard their natural rights. As a consequence, the ideal of liberty – the freedom from state intervention in the sphere of private life in civil society – was qualified by the ideal of democracy, in which the notion of equality was uppermost, and which, in its absence, could require remedial action by the state. As Gamble (1981a, p. 89) indicates, this is but a short step to arguing that liberty and equality could only be realised if the inequalities in civil society were abolished, particularly the inequality that stemmed from ownership of property.

In the nineteenth century, therefore, liberal constitutionalism was broadened to include a notion of representation that was more compatible with that of democracy, although liberty – the safeguarding of the private sphere from arbitrary government – remained paramount. An inherent tension between individualism and rationalism continued to infuse nineteenth-century liberalism, generated by the not ill-founded fear that moral liberty or freedom could threaten traditional normative or authority contexts (the family, work or church) which provided the orderly basis for property rights and capitalist accumulation. Moreover, in its commitment to the efficacy of rationalism and science, liberalism inevitably recoiled from the idea that the simple majoritarian principles of democracy provided 'sound' or technically-informed decisions. However, some liberals, such as J. S. Mill, took a more optimistic view about the individual educative benefits of more democratic participation – as informing citizens and inclining them to endorse basic liberal values (Ryan, 1974). Moreover, liberalism was more than merely economic individualism, but moral and social freedom as well. Individuals had the right to question traditional values and established institutions, although Mill believed that individual autonomy encouraged a more thoroughgoing responsibility and social restraint. More radically, however, forms of continental liberalism, associated with German idealism and the ideas of Rousseau and the French revolution, challenged the notion that the state simply existed to serve individual ends. Rather, civil society was the source of distortion and alienation, characterised by the pursuit of self-interest that compared poorly with the state's higher moral purpose and rule by the general will. The state's sovereignty, in this view, rested on the equality of all its citizens. This was not simply the formal equality of liberalism, but involved substantive equality and overcoming the large inequalities of civil society. As Gamble (1981a) notes, the principles of liberty and rationalism proved more important to most liberals than the idealisation of democracy, and this was a weakness within liberal ideology which socialism was to exploit.

The juxtaposition of legal equality and social and economic inequalities generated discussion as to which inequalities were intolerable. It was gradually established that equality is not sufficiently provided by freedom of contract alone, but requires social and political rights as well. Civil rights, however, are not only compatible with, but necessary to, a competitive market economy. The law in effect accorded rights of participation and association to those who owned property or had assured sources of income. However, the abstract principle of equality underlying the legal and ideological recognition of the independent individual often accentuated inequalities. Workers, for example, were denied the right to combine, as in England, on the grounds that this conflicted with individual autonomy. Moreover, medievalist conceptions of 'estates' or 'intermediate powers' were directly confronted by the extension of plebiscitarian principles of political participation which emphasised the necessity of direct state–citizen relations. In France the promulgation of the famous Loi le Chapelier in 1791 sought to destroy all powers intervening between the individual and the state, such as estates or corporations, so that all citizens as individuals possess equal rights before the national sovereign authority. Plebiscitarianism thus contrasts with the medieval notion of functional representation which, in modern form, designates group-specific rights and duties, rather than the direct vote by all qualified electors (Bendix, 1964).

A major indicator of the growth of the 'national' orientation of plebiscitarianism, in which individuals qua individuals come into direct relation with the state (rather than as a consequence of economic or other statuses), is the replacement of religious control of education by that of the state. This is less easy to achieve in predominantly Catholic countries, where the clergy is under an authority separate from that of the state, and where defence of the 'corporate' or 'functional' principle was partly successful. The developing requirements of capitalism also undermined the spread of plebiscitarianism and engendered strain between the two principles of representation. The attribution of a 'legal personality' to business organisations seeking limited liability in an era of expanding investment in the late nineteenth century, broke not only with strict plebiscitarianism but also checked that radical individualism involved in the notion of strictly formal equality before the law. The movement of civil rights from the representation of individuals to that of communities is also exemplified by the rise of trade unions, chambers of commerce and professional bodies.

Conclusion

The liberal state is characterised by an apparently sharp differentiation between the realms of state and society, with the former characterised by binding commands and the rights and duties of citizenship, and the latter as a voluntary realm of affinities of interests and ideas. Public action on economic matters consisted largely of the construction and management of legal fiscal monetary and financial frameworks for the land, labour and capital markets. The state played a positive but relatively unobtrusive role in the accumulation of capital and the reproduction of labour, including the provision of infrastructure (e.g. land for the railway companies), managing trade and fiscal regulations, and backing colonial and other foreign ventures.

The liberal state was thus responsive to the requirements of capital, and property owners generally benefited from assertions and support of individual rights. However, the form of the liberal state was also consequent on other than bourgeois interests. As Poggi (1978) notes, the state–society distinction had earlier found expression in the disentanglement of the western state from the religious authorities. Ideological and philosophical reflection played a significant role in the growth of the secular state. Yet the expansion of capitalism gave the sphere of 'society' a power in comparison with the state that was previously lacking. However, as we shall see in Chapter 4, the apparent separation of state and society gradually came under intensifying pressure with increased international competition between the major western economies in the latter part of the nineteenth century, and led to a greater interpenetration than the classical constitutional model envisaged.

To sum up, therefore, we have identified a number of issues for state–society relationships generated by the development of the modern state. One is the emergence of a centralised structure of institutional authority which is formally distinct as a public sphere from the private relationships of interest and affinity found in the wider society. A question to be explored in the next chapter is the extent to which the impersonality and legal-rationality of the modern state is not only distinct but relatively free from societal influences and interests. Similarly, does the development of capitalism and the force that it provides to the private sphere become such as to dominate even an increasingly centralised and extending public authority?

3

Interpretations of the Development of the Modern State

Introduction

The nature of state power and its relationships to society was a central theme in nineteenth- and early twentieth-century classical sociology. In particular the impersonal and public character of legally regulated state power, apparently quite distinct from the self-interested or communal forms of action in civil society, generated controversy as to its neutrality or partiality for different social interests. A related issue was whether the modern state was judged to be beneficial for society or rather a parasitic, alienating and ultimately dislocating force.

Despite the different analyses of the state to be found in classical political sociology, generally they shared a scepticism of many of the claims for the modern constitutional state that contrasts with the favourable and optimistic interpretations advanced within liberalism and liberal democracy. However, the extent of the critique of liberalism varied considerably. The mildest is found in Durkheim who, although aware of the possibilities of pathological state forms, exhibited a tempered optimism in the functionality of a modern secular state for securing social order and rationality. More ambivalent, however, was Weber who feared the stultifying effects of state bureaucracy on political leadership and national dynamism, yet recognised the inevitability and technical superiority of bureaucratic organisation as well as the advantages of representative democracy for keeping officials in their place. However, the most thoroughgoing critique of the liberal democratic state was offered by Marx and Engels who charged the 'public' character of state institutions in capitalism as being an illusion and basically a means for securing the interests of the dominant capitalist class.

Durkheim: the state and the division of labour

A major feature of Durkheim's account of the development of industrial society is the extension of a complex division of labour which generated novel institutions and sources of power, including the modern state. Moreover, the more advanced a society, the more extensive becomes the state as it undertakes more tasks and subjects their fulfilment to centralised and homogenised co-ordination. In contrast with pre-industrial societies where social control and stability are established 'mechanically' through strong external cultural constraints, in industrial society the functional deployment of tasks through the division of labour provides an 'organic solidarity' as a result of social interdependency. Moreover, as traditional, collective and rather repressive cultural values lose their hold, the state is enabled to develop as a separate and identifiable structure and become the brain or guiding intelligence for society (Durkheim, 1933).

Inevitably these metaphorical allusions to the function of the state as an agency of rationalisation and centralisation dispose Durkheim to a favourable view of its development, particularly in France where a secular, 'scientific' state gained influence over education, communication and surveillance from traditional religious control. Durkheim places great store in the facilitative and emancipatory function of the state for individuals, who become freed from the bright social glare of social customs and groups. In similar vein to Hegel, Durkheim underlines the necessity for an autonomous bureaucracy to develop to secure the institutionalisation of the state. Its officials assume responsibility for rationally advancing the 'universal interest' with an impersonality that distinguishes their behaviour from the rest of society. In this view Durkheim clearly differs from Marx and Engels, who regarded the division of labour as alienating, bureaucracy as parasitic, and the state as under the control of the dominant class and not as an autonomous entity. However, Durkheim was also aware of the potential dangers to individual liberty from too powerful a state. In 'pathological' forms of modern society, state despotism is sustained by the absence of intermediary groups or associations that could limit state power in an increasingly atomised or mass society. Moreover, social inequality becomes so disproportionate and deep-rooted that efficient meritocracy and the competent discharge of functions is undermined.

Unfortunately Durkheim's account is incomplete for he does not explore the character of the state in 'abnormal' societies, nor does he explain satisfactorily its causes, apart from occasional references to obstacles to rising talents. Rather, Durkheim's analysis tends to be categorical, a-historical and mechanically evolutionary. He thus assumes that all states develop from the division of labour according to the same laws. As Badie and Birnbaum (1983, p. 12) observe, 'He does not see that, depending on the historical circumstances, some societies may develop a political centre different from what he understands by the notion of the state.' Nor does Durkheim appear to recognise the difficulties in talking abstractly about 'the state', although there have been many types of state with different combinations of institutions and relationships. There are, for example, considerable differences between the relatively 'stateless' Anglo–American societies and the more 'statist' France and Germany, and which are explained in terms of particular historical developments and alliances (Moore, 1968; Skocpol, 1979). However, the state lacks a less important location in Durkheim's account of the development of modern society than it does either in the work of Marx and Engels, or, more particularly, in that of Max Weber.

Marx, Engels and Lenin

Liberal democracy, conceived as universal suffrage and citizenship rights, did not become fully established in most western democracies until well into the twentieth century (Therborn, 1977). None of the great bourgeois revolutions of the nineteenth century directly established liberal democracy and it took the national mobilisations for world war and the popular struggles of the present century for it to become generally consolidated in the West. Not surprisingly, therefore, in considering nineteenth- and early twentieth-century interpretations of the liberal democratic state, we find critics of bourgeois democracy from within liberal democracy. John Stuart Mill, for example, although no advocate of social and political equality, regarded the potential for participatory representative democracy as likely to remain largely unfulfilled unless the extensive social and economic inequalities of capitalism were mitigated substantially (see Chapter 4).

However, advocates such as Mill of constitutional liberal democracy and the extension of citizenship rights took the individual and his interests as the touchstone for democracy. 'The people' were less a collectivity than a collection of unique individuals who required the means to pursue their free choices with as little interference from the state as was compatible with a well-ordered, property-owning national community. However, the basis of Marx and Engels' theory of the modern state is a rejection of the notion that one starts from an analysis of the individual and his or her relation to the state. As Held (1983, p. 25) observes of their position, 'It is not the single isolated individual who is active in historical and political processes, but rather human beings who live in definite relations with others and whose nature is defined through these relations.'

For Marx and Engels the social nature of people's activities is located in class differences which, in capitalism, refers to the exploitative and inherently conflictful relationship between the owners and controllers of production on the one hand, and producers or wage-labourers on the other. The proletariat, which is the latter group, does not own or control productive property and is forced to sell its only 'commodity', its labour power, to those that do. Owners control the work process and possess or legally own all that is produced. Part of the time worked by the worker for the owner, however, is 'surplus' to the cost of production and is expropriated and turned into profit by the owner. Value is produced only by proletarian 'productive' labour, yet the creator of value receives only that which enables him to reproduce himself and his family socially. The picture is of endemic class conflict arising from the need of owners constantly to accumulate capital, to maintain and improve profitability, and to keep costs (including wages) as low as possible.

In this view economic dominance generates, and becomes sustained by, social and political dominance. The state, in its defence of private property, becomes inextricably fixed to particular economic interests, although it takes on an appearance of an autonomous and neutral structure acting on behalf of the public. Marx and Engels' critique of liberalism and liberal democracy is aimed at the view of the state as the defender of a communal and national interest that contrasts with the particularism and egoism of private behaviour. Not only is the state's claim to impartiality incorrect, for it serves the interests of capital, but Marx and Engels also argue that the claim for the state as a distinct and autonomous public realm, separate from society, has the ideological effect of defining class power as a-political and not an issue for public decision. Economic inequalities are regarded as the natural or spontaneous consequence of the markets for capital and labour, governed by the impersonal laws of supply and demand and encapsulated in individual agreements freely concluded, not the result of authoritative political rule.

It is now commonplace to recognise that the accounts of the state in capitalist society advanced by Marx and Engels were incomplete and not especially consistent. As Jessop (1982, p. 4) remarks, 'they offered a variety of theoretical perspectives which co-exist in an uneasy and unstable relationship . . . [and] it remains ill-formulated and inconsistent throughout its development'. We can distinguish, however, two major and generally contrary emphases in Marx and Engels' analysis of the relationship between the state and political action. First, the *economic or class reductionist approach* which is found in *The German Ideology* (1846) and *The Communist Manifesto* (1848). Here the state is seen as the form, or set of institutions, by which the bourgeoisie asserts its common interests. As an 'executive committee' of the economically dominant class, the state is seen as directly reflecting class power. It is 'independent' only so far as differences between the various branches of capital must be overcome, or the competing pressures resolved between home producers and the constraints exerted by international capital markets.

At its crudest this view implies that the state is a simple, non-autonomous reflection of the economy with little or no causal influence of its own. However, as Jessop (1982 , p. 10) notes, such a mechanistic interpretation is not advanced explicitly by Marx and Engels. Rather they argue that different forms of state and state intervention are required by different modes of production and that the nature of state power is determined by the changing needs of the economy or the changing balance of class forces. In this approach, different forms of state and state intervention are required at different stages in capital accumulation. For example, a less interventionist state is appropriate at the height of competitive capitalism, which contrasts to the absolutist form required during the transition from feudalism to capitalism, or the more authoritarian state which emerges with the development of monopoly capitalism.

Jessop points out that the view that the state is an instrument of class rule can be assimilated to economic reductionism through the assumption that the economic base determines the balance of class forces in the struggle for state power as well as determining the institutional form of the state. In recent Marxist theory, however, the emphasis is more on class relations than the 'logic' of capital as the primary determinant of state forms. This tends to lead away from simple reductionism because the 'action' component of class relations inevitably involves a less closed and deterministic causality then implied in 'capital logic' approaches. Class analyses also focus more on the potential autonomy of political and ideological forces. This contrasts with the crude economic reductionism of, say, the Second International, and the implication that the spontaneous development of the economic base is the sole cause of social and political evolution. The logical cul-de-sac of this approach effectively rules out a consideration of factors outside the economic base for it follows that its nature and dynamics cannot provide a sufficient explanation for those of society as a whole (Jessop, 1982, p. 12).

Marx and Engels were generally, if not always, alert to the difficulties of simple reductionist or instrumentalist theories of the state, especially in their empirical studies. They offer numerous qualifications which indicate that the correspondence between base and super-structure was not straightforwardly linear, or mechanistic. These qualifications indicate a second approach to the relationship between classes and the state to that found in *The Communist Manifesto* or *The German Ideology*. This approach sees the state as possessing a *measure of independent power* and not as being linked necessarily to the interests of the dominant class, at least in the short term. Nor are state institutions and their workings to be simply 'read off' from existing class arrangements, for they have at least a partial autonomy. For most interpreters, *The Eighteenth Brumaire of Louis Bonaparte* (1852) best exemplifies this second approach to the state by Marx and Engels. Constructed as criticism of Hegel's argument that state bureaucracy efficiently and impartially represents the general social interest over particular interests, *The Eighteenth Brumaire* examines the Bonapartist regime of mid nineteenth-century France as both an exploiting and independent political power. The very size and scope of bureaucratic institutions are seen as giving the state the power not only to steer social arrangements but also to constrain capital. Moreover bureaucratic mechanisms and procedures exert enormous influence on political decisions and outcomes.

It is not clear whether the relative autonomy of political institutions portrayed in Bonapartism is to be regarded as 'exceptional', as the result of the balance or temporary equilibrium of class forces that prevented the political dominance of any one class, or as a more regular feature of capitalist democracies. There is no definitive resolution to this uncertainty in their work for Marx and Engels do not provide a coherent abstract definition of the state of the kind found in their conceptions of the capitalist economy (e.g. commodity, or value). It is clear from their substantive studies, however, that Marx and Engels regard the bourgeoisie as generally lacking the capacity and unity to control the state itself. It only occasionally rules directly. The political governance of the landed aristocracy on behalf of capital in Britain in the nineteenth century is a case where rule is exercised, not directly, but on behalf of the economically ascendant class. A more important issue is to account for the imperatives on state bureaucracies, irrespective of composition, to function on behalf of the bourgeoisie in capitalist society. How is the dominant mode of production successfully reproduced when the economically dominant class does not itself directly inhabit leading state positions? The explanation is that the state in capitalist societies is ultimately dependent on the capitalist economy to provide the means of material existence for that society, and any state executive that seriously threatens the private owners of the means of production runs the likelihood of substantial social unrest as the result of economic decline. Additionally, state institutions rely for their existence on the resources generated by commerce and industry and, in the long run at least, this tends to ensure that state policies are consonant with the interests of capital.

Although the level of autonomy enjoyed by state executives varies according to such factors as location in the world economy, success in inter-state imperial and military rivalry, the internal level of productive forces, and the balance of class forces in a society, state executives have their own distinct interests in preserving the status quo. As Held (1983, p. 28) observes, even when Marx discussed the relative autonomy of states, his focus was essentially on the state as a conservative force. Thus:

> though Bonaparte usurped the political power of the bourgeoisie's representatives, he protected the material power of the bourgeoisie – itself a vital source of loans and revenue. Accordingly Bonaparte could not help but sustain the long term economic interests of the bourgeoisie and lay the foundation for the regeneration of its direct political power in the future, whatever else he chose to do while in office.

Leninism

Many interpreters of the Marxian theory of the state recognise as significant the analysis of the Paris Commune (1870–1) offered by Marx in *The Civil War in France* (1871). This work is regarded as important not only because it complements Marx's substantive account of state power in France under Bonaparte, but also because it provides one of the few accounts of how public affairs could be administered under socialism. Moreover, the study had an important impact on Bolshevik rule in its early stages following the Russian Revolution in 1917 because of its apparent influence on Lenin as expressed in his work *The State and Revolution* (1917).

In *The Civil War in France* Marx suggests that existing state machinery cannot be adapted for the purpose of socialist administration. State institutions are essentially apparatuses that are deployable in the interests of the bourgeoisie and its political allies. The inappropriateness of the capitalist state for furthering and consolidating working-class revolution, a consequence of its irredeemable repressive character, required the 'smashing' and reorganising of the state to meet socially necessary ends. In Marx's view, the Commune is the revolutionary new form of political organisation that secures the freedom of labour and ensures that public decisions follow from direct and extensive participation by the people in the deliberation of social affairs. The Paris 'communists', therefore, were not simply challenging Bonapartism or a particular form of bourgeois state, but the state itself. They sought to capture direct political control for the proletariat on behalf of the people as a means of abolishing classes and class rule.

It is important to recognise, however, in his early writings on the Paris Commune, despite their influence on Lenin's class-reductionistic interpretation of state rule, that Marx offers a humanistic, Hegelian and almost Weberian view of the state as a system of political domination, in which its effectiveness is located in its institutional structure as much as in the classes that control it (Jessop, 1982, p. 27). It implies a particular conception of both socialism and public administration that contrasts with Marx's later writings which are more clearly characterised by a concern with political economy.

A number of valuable observations on the place and importance of Marx's propositions on the Paris Commune have been made by Harding (1984). He suggests that in Marx's writings can be found two different conceptions of socialism which are associated with two contrary models of the state. The 'Commune' model belongs to Marx's earlier phase when his view of socialism was centred on the necessity to overcome alienation through the transformation of the patterns of authority within society. In this view, the state, along with private ownership of productive property, was a major source of man's alienation, comprised as it was of separate bodies of armed men standing outside and above society. Its abolition would involve the elimination of a standing army, the police and the judiciary, whose functions were to be appropriated by the people in arms. Thus all officials were to be elected, subject to recall, and paid workmen's wages. This would avoid the establishment of a separate set of bureaucratic interests and mystique that sustain state exploitation of society. Rather, self-governing communes, in which the people would directly make and implement decisions, would take the place of a national state bureaucracy and would take responsibility not only for legislative and executive decisions, but also for judicial, policing and defensive functions.

However, Harding points out that this model became contrary to the aims of the mature Marx who, in his later writings, regarded the state as having a much more activist role in building socialism. He came to regard the Communard model as too similar to the plans of the anarchists for it to serve as a blueprint for a socialist society. Rather, socialism was increasingly viewed as overcoming material want rather than human alienation. The need for the transformation of property relations to end exploitation and to provide for the economic needs of all required not a weaker but a stronger state. The dislocations and deprivations of unregulated capitalist production could not be transformed without state ownership and control of the means of production. This would secure the twin goals of rational planning and equitable distribution. Moreover, a strong 'dictatorship of the proletariat' would be required to combat the inevitable resistance from the propertied classes.

The advocacy of a powerful, interventionist state was the culmination of Marx's critique of the liberal view that economic life was the non-political preserve of the individual. On the contrary, Marx argued that socially useful production was the sole purpose of politics and the state and did not constitute a distinct sphere. It required a directing and efficiently administered state for the maximisation of production, with the goal of creating a modern industrial, but socialist, society that was characterised less by Communard populism or industrial democracy than by a disciplined workforce accepting managerial and state directives.

This second model of the state in Marxism, concerned more with overcoming relations of property than patterns of authority, is clearly attractive for socialist executives for it legitimises strong state rule in the service of economic production and material consumption. The Paris Commune interpretation of the state, however, sustains oppositional Marxist critiques of bourgeois states because of its 'anti-authority' characteristic. It has also provided a useful legitimating function for state socialist societies seeking greater autonomy from the USSR, while it also gave ideological impetus for the early stages of the Bolshevik revolution. Indeed, the excessive freedom that characterised the immediate post-revolutionary period in the USSR was an important contributory cause of the much firmer period of state centralisation that followed in the 1920s (Harding, 1984, p. 15).

Lenin's *The State and Revolution* (1917) accepted and built upon the image of socialist administration outlined by Marx in his analysis of the Paris Commune. Lenin started from the basic assumption that the bourgeois democratic republic is the best possible political shell for capital and that, once it has gained possession of this shell, 'capital establishes its power so securely that no change of persons, institutions, or parties can shake it' (Jessop, 1982, p. 27). It also followed that as capitalism in its financial monopoly form was defunct, to be replaced by socialism, then so was the bourgeois state, capital's ruling arm and intelligence. Lenin's distinctive contribution to this interpretation, along with that of Bukharin, was to locate the capitalist state within imperialism and to see it as providing the military and administrative framework and support for capitalist penetration abroad. Increasingly the imperialist capitalist state develops its own dynamic, expressed through its pursuit of war and territorial annexation, which feeds off but ultimately debilitates capitalist productive forces.

Consequently, through Lenin's influence, the Commune model became the practical programme of the Bolsheviks in their first years in power, during which factory councils and soviets (communes) provided the form of popular self-administration (Harding, 1984, p. 18). The aim was a radical change in relations of authority and a steady dismantling of the state. It was assumed that the reshaping of economic ownership and distribution would follow naturally from the socialist administration of everyday life. Yet it was a model that was unable to withstand or manage the repeated economic and administrative crises that beset the Soviet Union following the ending of the First World War. Lack of food turned the peasants back into growing for themselves, thus starving the towns and the industrial workforce, while the extensive possession of property and factories by local committees added to managerial dislocation.

The result, by the early 1920s, was a recognition by Soviet leaders that strong central co-ordination was needed to renew the industrial structure, to provide the means of socialist education, and to defend Soviet society from its external enemies. The theory of the 'dictatorship of the proletariat' advanced the view that the working-class was so physically and ideologically undermined by material deprivation and bourgeois resistance that, by itself, it was no longer capable of advancing its class interests. Rather, the party would rule on its behalf, using the state to impose industrial and social order and discipline. The primary purpose, as envisaged in Marx's later model of the socialist state, was to secure the means of material existence for the people as a whole, not to give them direct participation in decision making. Socialism was thus defined as state ownership of production and legitimated as the form of administration that was best able to achieve technical efficiency and economic growth. The consequence was the creation of a new standing army, the development of a national bureaucracy, official support and encouragement for hierarchy, discipline and more autonomous management and control, and the view that industrial democracy was the road to anarchism and economic weakness. As Harding (1984, p. 29) observes, 'Just as the magnates of financial capitalism had to utilise state power against sections of their own bourgeois class, so too the state power of the proletariat would have to be turned inward against sections of the proletariat . . . which had been infiltrated and disoriented.' The theory of the dictatorship of the proletariat charged that 'the proletarian state, not the proletariat itself, was the true vehicle of proletarian interests' (ibid.). The result was that such particularistic bodies as trade unions and workers' councils could only be regarded as potential challengers to state authority, which was exercised by the party on behalf of all workers' interests. In this view, 'mature' scientific Marxism regarded the existence of oppositions, conflicts and the clash of alternative groups and policies as features of an 'adolescent' Marxism and a disintegrating bourgeois democracy. Lenin and his successors therefore excoriated local and direct worker control. Managers and officials were made responsive to the state, not the workforce. As state employment expanded in the 1920s by about eightfold, there appeared in official Soviet thinking the familiar 'bourgeois' refrain that the expenses of state administration had to be reduced in order to protect and increase the efficiency of the productive process (see also Chapter 4).

Weber: bureaucracy and the state

The major response within classical political sociology to Marxism's claims that state institutions were derived directly from class relations came from Max Weber. He was extremely critical of the view that state systems could be cast aside with the end of capitalism and the growth of socialism. Weber regarded modern state institutions as essential for ordering complex societies whatever their political colouring. Moreover, the growth of bureaucratic administration and the development of central state institutions laying claim to the monopoly of legitimate violence within a defined territory, Weber's definition of the modern state, he regarded as both pre-dating capitalism and as subsequently evolving with it in a mutually supportive way in the core western European societies.

But rather than socialism being able to overcome the state, its commitment to equality was much more likely to result in the extension of the universalistic, rational–legal criteria associated with bureaucratisation. The dictatorship of capital would be exchanged for the dictatorship of state bureaucracy. Moreover, bureaucratic organisation with its advance in technical efficiency ensured that it was not only the state that was increasingly characterised by bureaucratic organisation, but also companies and associations in the private sphere. Weber thus anticipated a steady convergence in rule by officialdom in modern industrial societies, not only between capitalist and socialist forms of governance, but also between public and private organisations (Gerth and Mills, 1958).

As Held (1983, p. 35) indicates, Weber believed Lenin to have confused and conflated two separate issues on the state: its class nature, and its necessity for social order and the administration of public life. The crucial choice for Weber was 'between bureaucracy and dilettantism' in the field of administration. As the technical superiority of bureaucratic administration ensures its continued growth in increasingly complex, differentiated societies, it provides officials with the potential for wielding enormous influence through their control of information and knowledge. How was this influence to be constrained? In Weber's view it was crucial that effective leadership in modern nation-states continued to be discharged by politicians, who were sensitive to social and moral values, and not by soulless officials governed by dispassionate technical criteria. A strong parliamentary democracy was vital in enabling potential political leaders to become steeled and tested in public debate and communication and in a position to control officials. Although Weber believed that politicians should always be on guard lest national goals become usurped by large capitalists and landowners who only have their private interests at heart, he was extremely sceptical about both the desirability and possibility of abolishing the private ownership of the means of production. Nationalisation and state ownership of production was likely only to result in a more officious, rule-bound and ineffectual senior management. Moreover, in common with the proponents of liberalism, Weber recognised the desirability of a strong private sector both as a counterweight to possible state authoritarianism and as a vital source of change and new ideas.

Weber emphatically disavowed the Marxist claim that in capitalist societies the question of power was to be conflated to the understanding of class struggle. Although Weber follows Marx in identifying classes as groups with an economic base, Weber's notion of stratification possesses two further important elements: *status*, involving specific 'styles of life', which may bisect class relationships, and *party* which is orientated towards the acquisition and maintenance of political leadership. Status groups, political parties, and nation-states are important agencies in relations of power. It was inescapable to Weber that a key feature of the power of the modern nation-state was the ability to generate strong feelings of national identity which could be mobilised in times of war and external competition. But this could not be constructed as simply the consequence of capitalist imperialism, for Weber recognised that the national-state structuration of modern capitalism had its origins in the pre-capitalist, medieval conflicts between absolutist rulers in northern Europe. Nor was all national rivalry to be deplored. The competition and conflicts between states could be a vibrant characteristic of the modern order, often supplying politicians with the popular support and leverage required to keep the deadening grip of bureaucratisation and officials at bay (Gerth and Mills, 1958).

Despite the importance of Weber's analysis of the state for contemporary political sociology, especially his focus on the external relations between states, it invites a number of important criticisms. For example, Weber tends to overlook the problematic nature of bureaucratic control in modern organisations, especially the ability of subordinates or clients to use their 'everyday knowledge' of on-the-ground operations and practices to circumvent central direction and hinder the implementation of decisions. Moreover, as Held (1983, p. 39) notes, 'in his historical account of the patterns of bureaucratisation in diverse societies he did not isolate the degree to which certain bureaucratic processes may be specific to, or influenced by, capitalist development per se', and the result is a rather incomplete account of the relationship between the development of the state and modern capitalism. At a moral level, too, Weber's nationalistic enthusiasm for the German state and the need for strong political leaders has, in theaftermath of Nazism, cast a shadow over his own political values and interpretations. Nonetheless, Weber's analysis of the modern state's legitimacy based upon correct procedure and legality, and which attaches to claims for greater economic and administrative efficiency, provides important insights for contemporary analyses of legitimation crises in modern democracy, including both Marxist and non-Marxist interpretations.

Recent Marxist theories of the state

Until the 1970s major Marxist theories of the modern state in orthodox communist circles in the USSR and elsewhere were organised around the notion 'state monopoly capitalism', or to use Jessop's abbreviation, 'stamocap' (Jessop, 1982). It refers to a specific stage of capitalism in which ascendant monopoly capital interests ally with leading sections of the bourgeois state, not only against the working class but also against non-monopoly fractions of capital. One of its earlier Soviet theoreticians, Bukharin, argued that 'stamocap' is characterised by the increasingly direct involvement of the state in economic exploitation, the reorganisation of relations between different sectors of capital through state monopolies in trade and production which favour large capital, a decline in parliamentarism and an extension of the secret and repressive apparatuses of the state. A powerful state is able to use social institutions such as education, parties and economic associations as agencies of control, and undertakes international capitalist competition and wars in the name of the nation-state. However, a major difficulty with such an analysis is its underestimation of the potential conflicts of interest between state and capital, of the dysfunctionality of extensive state interventionism for capitalist production, and of the role of class conflict in limiting bourgeois power. The political strategies that derive from 'stamocap' theories for Marxist parties are based on the construction of 'anti-monopoly alliances' between labour, small capital and other intermediary classes. Such alliances may gell in the face of exceptional forms of stamocap such as Nazism, or in localities where a strong local Communist Party is well-entrenched, as in parts of France, but in most circumstances overlooks the distinct market and status conflicts within such a diverse grouping, especially between state-employed labour and small capital (Jessop, 1982, ch. 3).

Stamocap theories also suffer from a major defect of derivationist approaches in largely ignoring the relative autonomy of state institutions and ideological practices in favour of analyses of capital and class struggle. A more satisfactory approach is found in the work of Gramsci and his followers. This seeks to understand how bourgeois states are able to function cohesively despite inherent class division, and focuses on the stabilising tendencies of capitalism and the role played in that by the state, rather than on immediate crises or radical socialist transformations. It is an approach that emphasises the role of ideology and political practices rather than simple economism.

As Jessop (1982, p. 142) points out, whereas the views of Lenin and Bukharin were decisively shaped by the revolutionary process in backward Russia, Gramsci (1971) was concerned primarily with the conditions for a successful revolution in more advanced capitalist societies. Many of Gramsci's ideas were developed in his prison writings of the early 1930s, following his part in the Turin factory council movement. A major theme in his work was that the complex relations among a plurality of social forces, rather than the pure mode of production, determined state power in any particular society. Economic effects were regarded as always mediated by political and ideological factors which were relatively independent of productive forces. Economic crises may politically debilitate states but do not by themselves create revolutions. Their impact depends on the strength of the institutions of civil and political society and the balance of class forces in a society.

A central element in Gramsci's analysis of state power is the means by which the state secures the consent of the dominated in parliamentary democracies. Two basic strategies are identified; force and hegemony. Hegemony is the concept created by Gramsci (1978) to refer to 'the successful mobilisation and reproduction of the "active consent" of dominated groups by the ruling class through their exercise of intellectual, moral and political leadership' (Jessop, 1982, p. 148). This process is not simple indoctrination or the imposition of a 'false consciousness', but involves the bourgeoisie claiming popular, not just class, sentiments for its 'national' goals. It involves an organisation of popular culture and its direction and appropriation for class goals. (A recent British example is the appropriation of popular 'anti-bureaucratic' sentiments by Conservative administrations for the purposes of extending the commodity form and reducing public expenditure, and for associating socialism with the stigma of statism.)

Gramsci suggests that hegemony is operated primarily through the ideological practices of institutions and groups in civil society, such as the schools, media, the churches, or political parties. A problem with Gramsci's analysis is that he tends to assume that the state includes all agencies involved in hegemonic mediation, which blurs the necessary distinction between state institutions and civil society, and defines the state in terms of functional effects rather than structure. However, Gramsci does not argue that bourgeois domination or hegemony is always successful (Jessop, 1982, p. 150). The takeover of state institutions by the Italian fascists, for example, is explained by the ideological and political weaknesses of the Italian bourgeoisie in securing both popular support and a class base free from that of the large landowners. The decisive contribution by Gramsci to Marxist accounts of the state was in locating the importance of hegemonic forms of state power and the formation of 'popular political blocs' rather than regarding state institutions as directly reflecting simple class or 'base' interests.

Miliband and Poulantzas

There has been a remarkable renewal of interest by Marxists in theorising the modern state since the 1960s. In large part, as Held (1983, p. 30) observes, it stems from the ambiguous nature of Marx's own theoretical contribution to the analysis of the state which became highlighted as western Marxists sought to account for the emerging repression of the Soviet state apparatus, became dissatisfied with Leninist–Stalinist 'statist' interpretations of socialism, and sought to understand the extensive growth and increased interventionism of the state in liberal democracies. An influential figure in the revived Marxist theorisation of the state was Nicos Poulantzas. Poulantzas not only built upon Gramscian accounts of state power and the cohesive function of the state in capitalist societies but, in an important debate with Miliband, also helped to extend and renew theoretical work on the state in Britain.

Miliband (1969), in *The State in Capitalist Society*, was concerned primarily with rebutting the dominant liberal democratic interpretation of the state in western societies, seen as either another form of interest group amongst a plurality of such groups, or as a neutral arbiter between contending social interests. Miliband distinguishes carefully between 'government' and 'the state', emphasising that while the government is the most visible form of the state, it is not necessarily the most influential part. The state system also is made up of what Dearlove and Saunders (1984, p. 228) call the 'secret state', the huge bureaucratic systems that include the civil service, the Bank of England, the public corporations, nationalised industries, military, police, judiciary, local and regional authorities, as well as representative assemblies such as the Houses of Parliament. Not only may control of government not ensure control of the state, but it is important to understand how these institutions are interrelated.

Miliband locates the coherence of the state system by critically exposing the formal separation of state power and civil society as largely illusory. Although there is no necessary connection between economic power and state power in capitalist societies, there are a number of basic processes that ensure that the state operates in the long-term collective interests of capital. It does so not by directly responding to capitalist demands, but to some extent autonomously, with a relative independence that allows it both to preserve the general unity of the capitalist class and, if necessary, make short-term concessions to labour. Miliband advances Marx's non-derivationist model, in which the political effectiveness of the state on behalf of the capitalist class is provided by the relative autonomy of the state and its ability to distance itself from particular class fractions. Moreover, in abnormal circumstances, such as war, the state takes on an even greater degree of autonomy from immediate class interests. A major reason why the leading élites constitute a dominant ruling class is their narrow social background and affiliations which produces a similarity of ideological predispositions that are supportive of capitalist interests. The personnel in the highest command positions are either drawn from particular élite families and institutions or else have subscribed to bourgeois values as they have risen to the top. Labour governments, for example, may seek socialist reforms, but the rest of the state system exercises sufficient constraint to force them to retreat. Although Miliband recognises the structural constraints exercised on governments by the necessity for capitalist accumulation upon which state and society depend, the thrust of his critique is to emphasise the inhibitions on non-capitalist strategies arising from the values and outlooks of individual decision makers.

Miliband's interpretation of the state's cohesion and role in capitalist society is emphatically rejected by Poulantzas who, in his earlier work, offered a much more structuralist account of state power than Miliband. In a well-known debate with Miliband, Poulantzas argues that the social characterstics and networks of political and business leaders do not explain why the state functions on behalf of capital. Individuals are less significant than the structural logic of the system, and reflect rather than create systems. Capitalists are forced to act as capitalists, and state bureaucrats are constrained to act on behalf of capital because of the logic of the capitalist system, irrespective of their personal beliefs or affiliations. However, Poulantzas, like Miliband, does not suggest that the economic base simply determines the political and ideological superstructure. Each level has its own particular dynamic, and the state has a relative autonomy from the economic. Indeed the state is only able to function as the unifier of capitalist interests and in a position to impose political solutions on often conflicting business sectors if it is able to operate at a distance from them. However, the extent of the state's autonomy from capital is contingent on levels of class conflict in a society, for the state tends to be a forum or reflection of class conflict as well as having particular effects on class divisions. Thus, when the working class is relatively powerful the state will tend to introduce policies and reforms that benefit the working class, even against some opposition from capital, whereas policies advancing the interests of capital tend to be generated when labour is weak (e.g. in times of high unemployment).

Jessop (1982, p. 154) argues that Poulantzas, despite the structuralist cast of his earlier work, can be located within the post-war European reception of Gramsci. Unlike state monopoly capital theory, which sees capitalist unity as imposed by a dominant capitalist fraction, Poulantzas sees the state as the basic source of ruling class cohesion and, like Gramsci, regards hegemony as much a strategy for unifying the ruling class as a means of mobilising popular support for it. For both Poulantzas and Gramsci the process which ensures that the state operates in the interests of capital is class struggle rather than the logic of capital. However, state institutions have highly important consequences for class relations, for they sustain the notion that members of classes are merely free and independent individuals and that the state is a neutral system serving the national community. Its rational–legal, 'technical' appearance is reinforced if a 'power bloc' is organised that includes representatives of the dominated classes but which rules under the leadership of capital.

Poulantzas is sensitive to the different forms of bourgeois state and their respective constraints on the power bloc. For example, while the liberal state may be the best structure for consolidating the political power of capital in its competitive phase, a more interventionist state is required for the more organised stage of monopoly capitalism. Similarly, 'normal' forms of capitalist state occur when capitalist hegemony is well-established and elicits general acceptance, whereas the 'exceptional' state is characterised by challenges to the dominant ideology and the use of state repression against the dominated classes. The latter involves the subordination of democratic institutions such as assemblies and political parties, a legal arbitrariness, a decline in the separation of powers, and the increased use of coercive agencies such as the military and the police. Two examples of exceptional forms are fascist states and military dictatorships. The former tends to possess a degree of flexibility as the result of a mobilised mass political party which acts as a channel of support and a source of power against traditional state and economic élites. Military dictatorships, however, lack popular legitimacy and political cohesion and tend to degenerate into inflexible and fragmented groupings.

Poulantzas (1978) argues that 'authoritarian statism' best characterises recent forms of normal capitalist state, with a drift from legislative to executive power, a growing indistinctiveness in the separation of legislative, administrative and judicial agencies, and an increase in functional corporatism at the expense of parliamentarism. In large part this is a response to the growing economic role of the state. In the monopoly stage of capitalism, rather than simply securing the general conditions of capital accumulation (e.g. stable monetary system, good communications), the state intervenes directly in both production and the reproduction of labour power. Political institutions take over the major responsibility for the reproduction of capitalist relations from economic agencies, although this carries attendant dangers for the state and capital as the state becomes firmly embedded in periodic capitalist crises. It is forced to take more direct responsibility for securing the interests of capital which may require actions that threaten its 'popular-legitimating' function. Moreover, it is prevented from intervening too directly into the economy for fear of socialising the means of production. The state is thus forced into a series of reactive and often incoherent strategies that reduce its effectiveness and legitimacy.

This increased emphasis on the more problematic success of the state in advanced capitalism in securing the interests of capital is a move or two away from Poulantzas's earlier views on the stabilising tendencies of the state, and more clearly preserves the possibility of a socialist transformation. However, there are a number of problems with his analysis. First, as Jessop (1982, p. 181) notes, if in the long term the policies of the capitalist state only correspond to the political interests of the bourgeoisie, how does 'macroscopic necessity' (bourgeois state) emerge out of 'microscopic diversity' (class struggles)? Given the increased emphasis on class struggle, which is more indeterminate than structural causation, it means that either Poulantzas's theory is void because it cannot move from an infinity of contradictory policies to an unambiguous final resolution, or else it is tautological because he merely postulates the resultant that his theoretical approach demands. As Cawson and Saunders (1983), Clarke (1977) and others have observed, it becomes possible in Poulantzas's analysis to 'explain' any given intervention by the state, for policies which advance labour interests can be accounted for by the autonomy of the state, while those favouring capitalist interests are accounted for by the fact that this autonomy is only relative. The concept relative autonomy 'thus explains everything and nothing' (Cawson and Saunders, 1983, p. 9).

Secondly, Poulantzas falls into confusion over the relationship between the economic and the political as this involves the relationships between class, and political and ideological forces. For example, he ascribes a necessary class belonging to political parties and groupings, although claiming that such groupings cannot be reduced to the class categories of capital and labour. Not only is this logically unclear (Hirst, 1977), but it neglects the role of non-class movements. As Jessop (1982, p. 188) notes, if one accepts his claims about the separateness of civil society and the capitalist state, 'then the influence of non-class forces and non-class ideologies must assume a central place in political analysis'. The important question then becomes how we 'identify those situations in which the functional interests of capital and labour are directly represented in political struggle, and to distinguish these from those cases where political mobilisation takes place on other than a class basis' (Cawson and Saunders, 1983, pp. 10–11).

Crises and contradictions: Offe and Habermas

It is remarkable how many of the theoretical difficulties experienced in orthodox sociological accounts of modern society were replicated in Marxist accounts of the state in the sixties and seventies. In its concern to rebut what it considered bourgeois social science's benign view of liberal democracy and its prioritisation to locating the causes of stability rather than conflict and class inequality Marxism tended to ignore many of the advances in the methodology of the social sciences. Particularly, Marxist accounts of the state became confronted with the problem of functionalism, and in terms similar to those found in the debate over American structural functionalism (see Chapter 1). Yet, as we have noted, there is no logically consistent reason why the capitalist state should inevitably function to preserve a social order compatible with the long-term interests of capital. Moreover, Poulantzas is increasingly regarded as having over-emphasised the stability and crisis-resolving tendencies of modern capitalism and underestimating its persisting dislocations and contradictions, which provide the possibilities of socialist and working-class advance.

Particularly influential within Marxism as theorists offering a more problematic approach to the stabilising capacities of modern capitalism are Offe and Habermas. They emphasise how endemic economic crises and social conflicts generate an increasingly interventionist state with responsibility for their resolution or containment. However, the continued failure of state strategies steadily erodes popular acceptance or legitimation of both the state and capitalist society. Habermas (1976) refers to this as a 'legitimation crisis', in which the requisite amount of normative commitment is lacking. Although Habermas refers to at least three other crisis tendencies in late capitalism – economic, administrative and motivational – legitimation crises are crucial. They stem from the necessity for the capitalist state to meet what are often opposing or conflicting goals: the support of capitalist accumulation, and eliciting popular support for a 'neutral democratic' state. As the state intervenes in more areas of life it is seen as having responsibility for them which, combined with its democratic characteristics, stimulates greater calls on it – for benefits, participation – than it is in a position to grant, at least without threatening capitalist production. The state's appearance of neutrality is gradually stripped away as it is forced to acknowledge openly its support for the dominant class.

Offe (1984), like Habermas, is also concerned with examining the 'crises' of modern capitalism, especially the breakdown of the post-war welfare consensus. He argues that the private capitalist economy is not spontaneously self-correcting, as classical political economy claims, but is inherently subject to crisis. In his view the interventionist welfare state develops both as a means of ordering capitalism, and as a way of legitimating it by being regarded as the source of impartial administration and reform. Consequently the state becomes deeply embedded in the contradictions of capitalism, balancing precariously the needs of accumulation with those of legitimation. It is also faced increasingly with its own contradiction. The state itself is dependent (for revenue) on a successful capitalist economy, but is unable to intervene too directly to sustain the conditions of re-commodification through the provision of market incentives, infrastructural investment, and deploying corporatist forms of decision making (see Chapter 5). None of these strategies works effectively and the continual crisis nature of capitalism throws open, along with the tendency towards de-commodification and the socialisation of the means of production, the possibility of socialist advance.

Both Offe and Habermas display more concern than Poulantzas with the specific institutions of the modern state, their differentiation, and the particular ways in which they sustain an order in which capitalist arrangements are predominant. Importantly, Offe points to the *institutional* self-interest of the state in safeguarding the capitalist economy which, in contrast to Poulantzas and Miliband, 'does not result from the alliance of a particular government with particular classes also interested in accumulation, nor does it result from any political power of the capitalist class which "puts pressure" on the incumbents of state power to pursue its class interest' (Offe and Ronge, 1975, p. 140). However, because of the unlikelihood of capitalist states successfully and continually managing the contradictory pressures on them, states are forced to be 'structurally selective' in favouring those groups, such as organised labour and monopoly capital, whose support is crucial for the maintenance of the existing order. This leads to more secretive, corporatist forms of decision making, away from parliamentary and public scrutiny (see Chapter 5).

In contrast to Weber, Offe argues that bureaucracy is insufficiently superior as an administrative device for solving the problems of the capitalist state, while its rigidity renders it unsuitable as an instrument of production, for it lacks the flexibility required to meet market objectives. Moreover, the two other forms of strategy available to the state – reprivatisation and corporatism – are regarded as no more effective in the longer term. The former challenges the power of organised labour, which Offe feels is too deeply entrenched for the strategy to work, while also overestimating the ability of the commodity form to meet both capitalist and social needs (e.g. for energy, education, health, transport, etc.). Corporatism, on the other hand, in breaking the bourgeois distinction between politics and the economy creates many of the problems of the capitalist state which it seeks to remedy.

The recent experiences of the state in British society suggest that Offe underestimates the capacity of politicians and state administrators to overcome apparent structural deficiencies in policy forms. For example, organised labour has not prevented effectively the 'reprivatisation' policies of Conservative administrations. Moreover, Offe and, especially, Habermas may overestimate the necessity for legitimation and normative commitment to the existing order for it to function effectively. The instruments of surveillance and control available in the apparatuses of the 'secret state', and the dependency of labour and the poor on either the labour market or the state's social service payments for daily comfort and sustenance, provide a compelling framework for individual compliance to state authority, largely irrespective of levels of normative commitment to the existing order (Abercrombie *et al.*, 1980; Held, 1984). Nonetheless, as Held and Krieger suggest (1983, p. 490), 'Offe's emphasis on the way capitalist states are pushed into providing a range of services which directly benefit the best organised sectors of the working class, surmounts some of the limitations of Poulantzas's account of the state as functionally interlocked to the needs of capital.' Rather, the state has an institutional self-interest in defending capitalist class *society*, not simply the interests of one class.

Conclusion: 'post-Marxism'

Offe is recognised as making a decisive contribution to the theory of the state and, in breaking with many traditional Marxist assumptions, as having had a formative influence on recent 'post-Marxist' analyses of the state (Pierson, 1984, p. 565). This approach is generally critical of the 'base-superstructure' model in which the state is simply derived from the logic of capital or from class contradictions. In some accounts, notions of 'relative autonomy' are regarded as failed attempts to make notions of mechanistic economic determination more theoretically respectable (Hindess, 1983, p. 40). Instrumentalist theories of the state, which regard the state as necessarily acting in the interests of capital (or a particular fraction, or only in the long term), are also regarded as unsatisfactory. In contrast the state is viewed in 'post-Marxist' views as possessing the ability to sustain important civil and political liberties within both capitalist and future socialist society. Rather than being 'smashed' and the bourgeois distinction between politics and the economy dissolved, the state has the capacity to guarantee the independence and vitality of civil society, which is no longer conceived only in class terms but as containing a variety of social identities and emancipatory movements, e.g. race and gender (Cohen, 1983; Urry, 1981). Thus the state is conceived as essential to any developed society, but as requiring an extension of democratic rights of representation and liberty to new, non-class, social forces for its power to be both harnessed and constrained.

A feature of 'post-Marxist' accounts of the state is the move away from purely abstract considerations of the state, as if there existed one generic model, and a willingness to consider the biographical variety and historical trajectories of different nation-states. In part this is associated with attempts to turn from simple 'internalist' accounts to examining the international context of relations between states (Jessop, 1982; Urry, 1981). Jessop, for example, argues for discarding general theories of the state on the grounds that a simple theory cannot grasp the variety of causes of states formation without degenerating into a crude reductionism. Capitalist relations of production, in his view, do not ensure that the state form is essentially capitalist nor that it will necessarily serve in turn to reproduce capitalist relations of production, for the state is located within actual societies not simply pure modes of production. Moreover, Jessop sees no valid grounds for assuming that the state is essentially class unified rather than fragmented and with a plurality of institutions whose unity must be constituted, if at all, politically. This is not to overlook that the state's operations have asymmetrical effects for different social forces, not least in the opportunities for access, and is no neutral instrument. Different systems of representation (clientalism corporatism, parliamentarism, pluralism, *raison d'état*) have distinctive consequences for different political forces in accessibility to the state, and a major aim for class struggle is the reorganisation of the state apparatuses in order to redefine accessibility.

A number of affinities exist between post-Marxist theories of the state and those found in Weberian political sociology. These include the emphasis on non-class forms of social differentiation, the necessity for examining specific institutions and configurations in different states, especially in their historical dimension, and the importance of recognising the particular institutional interests of state institutions as a sphere distinct from civil society. Post-Marxist theories of the state, however, are subject to criticism from both the political left and right. For example, orthodox Marxism points to the relative failures and strategic compromises of radical groups that seek to include a variety of non-class interests. Economic liberals may also question why the state should act as a protector of the liberties and pluralism of civil society in the absence of a materially-based countervailing power, i.e. private property. As Pierson (1984, p. 569) remarks, 'the new theorists need to address this issue of private property head on, since its defence as the protector of individual freedom against an overweaning state is a major plank of the neo-liberal defence of inequality'. Nonetheless, recent Marxist and Weberian work on the substantive histories of different nation-states located in an international context and focusing on relations between states, suggest a much firmer empirical basis for theoretical accounts of the state than hitherto.

In summary, therefore, we have in this Chapter distinguished the issue of the relationship of the individual to the state from the related problem of the relationship of state to private power. At the centre of a number of issues on the state–society relationship is the question of whether the state is regarded as the instrument for securing justice and freedom, or as a danger. Socialists generally, but not always (as we have seen), tend to see the state as the means for achieving and sustaining a better and more equitable society, while liberals tend to be suspicious of the state as threatening the liberties generated by private property, the family and a constitutional state. However, we have noted also the ambivalence in Marxism on occasions to the alienating possibilities of state authority and the view that it is an essentially bourgeois and authoritarian form. In recent 'post-Marxist' accounts there is increased recognition that the state may pose a threat to the pluralities and freedoms of civil society. In the next chapter we explore the substantive development of the modern state in this century, noting particularly the increased role for the state in the economies of both East and West.

4

Liberalism, Collectivism and State Socialism

Introduction

Theorists from both left and right of the political spectrum hold that there is an integral connection between economy and polity. Forms of government and the ends they pursue are regarded as primarily dependent upon the nature of the economic system with which they are situated within territorially-defined nation-states. These assertions are particularly pronounced in considerations of the role of the state in capitalist societies. It is claimed that there is both a logical and historical connection between the development of capitalism as an economic system and the growth of liberal constitutionalism as a political arrangement. Specifically, the democratisation of liberal regimes with the extension of political and other rights and the development of electoral politics are clearly linked to the individualism and demands for market freedom of the bourgeoisie. Competitive capitalism, it is argued, provides a necessary if not sufficient condition for competitive politics.

Of course, left and right differ in their interpretations of liberal democracy, particularly on the extent to which its 'freedoms' confer general, cross-class benefits. So-called 'market society' theorists such as Friedman and Hayek, for example, argue that the economic freedoms that constitute competitive capitalism also generate political liberties because the separation of political and economic power allows the existence of distinct and counterbalancing spheres – that of economic interest and political authority. Economic power can be used to prevent the abuse of political power and political power can be employed to offset deficiencies in the market. Power thus becomes dispersed rather than centralised.

We should be careful to recognise, however, that although the 'market society' school of political economists seeks to reduce levels of state intervention in society, it does not advocate total state abstinence. Rather a pure *laissez-faire* economy is regarded as a chimera. State interventionism should be specific, fine-tuned, remedial and authoritative. At the very least governments should seek the maintenance of social order and should provide a minimum safeguard for the economically and socially-dependent, such as the infirm or the unemployed. However, the emphasis wherever possible should be to allow the market to provide the bulk of such social provision through private insurance and other schemes. Thus it is accepted that some guarantee of 'social reproduction' must be provided by the state, and interventionism is required to maintain the conditions in which competitive capitalism can operate, such as an appropriate legal and monetary framework.

Similarly, as we noted in Chapter 3, some Marxists argue that the liberal state is an especially appropriate political arrangement for that stage in the capitalist mode of production that is characterised by competitive or non-monopoly market relations. Particularly the relative autonomy of the liberal state from the economy allows it to function effectively in the long-term interests of capital as a whole. Acting as a 'collective capitalist' it is able to resolve or contain the conflicts between the different 'fractions' of capital, which can have different and competing interests, and sustain capitalist accumulation more generally. This has special utility in periods of economic depression when the state assists the restructuring of capital, not least by allowing the inefficient to go to the wall. However, the legitimacy of the liberal state conferred by periodic electoral success reinforces conceptions of an apparently 'neutral' state arbitrating between various claimants. It is thus argued that the institutional separation and relative autonomy of the liberal state, rather than sustaining individual freedom more generally, primarily aims to secure the subordination of the working class to the interests of capital. Moreover, the liberal state lasts only as long as competitive capitalism, which may not be very long. The 'capital logic' school of Marxism maintains that the historical tendency for the rate of profit to fall in capitalism inevitably produces more authoritarian and interventionist state forms as the result of an increased need to more directly protect and restructure capital (Altvater, 1973). This suggests that the liberal state is not the ideal norm for the capitalist mode of production as a whole, whether or not that state is also democratic, but only at an initial stage of accumulation when the fullest possible freedom is required by individual capitals (Holloway and Picciotto, 1978). However, the advent of monopoly capitalism and the tendency of the rate of profit to fall is associated with increased economic intervention by the state and a growing political influence on the part of the working-class movement (Mandel, 1975).

As Jessop (1978) points out, a problem with these theories is that capitalism, even in its early development, is not universally associated with liberal democracy. We noted in Chapter 2, for example, that Barrington Moore (1968) clearly demonstrates the absence of a unilinear pathway for capitalist development. Although liberal democracy was an important correlate of competitive capitalism in the 'stateless' Anglo–American societies, the process of capitalist 'take-off' in Japan and Germany was largely state-induced. There a weak commercial bourgeoisie allied with the landed upper-class and the imperial military bureaucracy, exchanging the right to rule for the right to make money. Moreover, the timing of capitalist accumulation has been an important factor in the form of capitalist development undertaken by particular nation-states, not least the part played in it by government. In Germany and Japan, for example, as essentially labour-repressive economies ran into difficulties as a consequence of competition from more successful capitalist economies, particularly Britain and the USA, it was an authoritarian state that was forced to rationalise the political order and facilitate capitalist accumulation and industrial construction.

Only in those countries that industrialised early, notably Britain, do we find an extended period of competitive capitalism where the political counterpart was a liberal, generally non-interventionist, state. Furthermore the liberal state need not necessarily be a liberal democratic state, although it was usual for it to become associated with parliamentarism and extended franchises. As McPherson (1966) has pointed out, until well into the nineteenth century the liberal state was generally thought to be endangered by democracy. The separation of political from economic power, where the state established individual rights of appropriation, served to reinforce economic power and class inequality. But this separation is threatened by demands for increased political representation to redress economic exploitation by state intervention. Democracy, in seeking to 're-couple' state and society, was potentially harmful to capitalism.

However, the introduction of democracy on liberal grounds served to avoid these dangers. The market society itself produced a pressure for democracy because liberalism had always justified itself as providing equal individual rights and equality of opportunity. When it did come, democracy was demanded and admitted on liberal grounds, as an extension of rights to individuals (not classes) prepared to accept, in exchange, both the state and the 'responsibilities' associated with citizenship. McPherson (1966, p. 5) remarks that 'Democracy had to accomodate itself to the soil that had already been prepared by the operation of the competitive, individualistic market society, and by the operation of the liberal state, which served that society through a system of freely competing although not democratic parties.' Nonetheless, the advent of democracy, alongside changes in advanced capitalism, established a persisting tension in the liberal state between the needs of capital accumulation and the requirements of electoral support, which served to gradually undermine liberalism in both the economic and political spheres. The signs of this emerging collectivism became apparent in the last decades of the twentieth century.

Liberalism and collectivism

Gamble (1981a, p. 38) notes that following the civil war in Britain in the seventeenth century a relationship between state and economy was established which had considerable reverberations for later industrialisation. The differences between various forms of property were largely dissolved and served to cohere the wealthy into a unified group that was characterised by a shared concern for the pursuit of market reward without legal fetters or personal discrimination. In such circumstances the 'nouveau riche' find fewer obstacles in entering existing ruling strata. It produced an alliance of property owners cemented by a shared commercial outlook, acceptance of an expanding market order, and sustained by a view of the state as primarily engaged in protecting private interests. The economic rewards of unfettered capitalism, bolstered by the markets and raw materials obtained in colonial expansion, were large. Together with the profitability and productivity generated by advances in industry and agriculture, the sphere of civil society attained a potency that, by comparison, appeared to diminish the state. The view that the state was an inferior agency to that of economic interest and social affinity could seem to be well-justified. As a consequence, nineteenth-century Britain witnessed a steady, liberal reform of major state institutions, characterised particularly by the recognition that a reformed Parliament represented not corporate interests but forged its 'will' from the discursive engagement of rational, individual and representative demands.

A marked feature of the liberal design that steadily emerged in the nineteenth century was the process through which some matters came to be accepted as public and others as private. Commercial interests were especially concerned to limit the powers of state activity and wished the state to establish parameters within which business activity could be left relatively untrammelled. An interesting example of this is provided by the changing conception of a 'corporation' (Wolfe, 1977, p. 20). Originally a mercantilist notion, it referred to an exclusive grant by the state to a private company for the purpose of providing something that was in the common interest of the whole society. Clearly it was a means of restraining trade in which corporations received rights to develop essential parts of the economy on behalf of the state. The main impulse was considered to be not private reward, although this was an inextricable and non-reprehensible factor in any such arrangement, but benefit for society generally. Railroads, for example, were incorporated because of their 'public character'. Corporate charters were very difficult to obtain, inevitably, and in England it required a private Act of Parliament. This mercantilist conception of a corporation came under sustained attack from the industrial bourgeoisie in nineteenth-century Britain who gradually succeeded in having it accepted that 'corporations' were private and unexceptional, rather than public and special. It came to refer to any group of people who obtained limited liability from the state in pursuit of their private advantage. This greatly facilitated the growth of joint-stock companies. Yet the important point is to recognise that it was political action that brought about the change. To place limitations on state prerogatives required state interventionism. The liberal state is not a *laissez-faire* state, but one in which interventionism may be required to create or maintain the conditions for private accumulation. It demands at least some level of involvement in the public sphere by the bourgeoisie. As Wolfe (1977, p. 22) observes, 'One had to have power in the state in order to make it impotent. Few clearer examples exist of how the struggle over legal parameters cannot be accepted as a given but becomes part of the activity of the state itself.'

The extension of capitalism tended to reduce earlier mercantilist notions of state economic activity and the political control of trade. Instead public action on economic matters consisted largely of the construction and management of legal, fiscal, monetary and financial frameworks for the autonomous self-regulating operations of the allocative mechanisms constituted by the markets for land, capital and labour (Poggi, 1978, p. 115). Thus, the state still played an important if not particularly visible role in capitalist production, not least through the provision of infrastructure (e.g. land) or finance for large industrial schemes, and through military and diplomatic support for colonial expansion.

Clearly, therefore, the nineteenth-century liberal state, the first in which industrialists played a significant role, was not a *laissez-faire* state. It displayed active and often aggressive tendencies to intervene both in the economy and in social life. Wolfe (1977) suggests that 'the accumulative state's' role during this period of expansion was to: define the broadest parameters of economic activity, preserve discipline in order to increase production, adjust macro-economic conditions, provide direct subsidies to private industrialists, and to fight wars. Moreover, the new bourgeoisie in Britain were quick to turn to Parliament to reform and unify the existing localised forms of social control which did not fit well with the requirements of an emerging capitalist society. Before the 1830s, the largest towns such as Birmingham and Manchester had no police because they had no political representation in general, while the police system, under the amateurish control of the aristocratic Lord Lieutenants, concentrated its strength in the rural parish, rather than in the new industrial towns where it was needed. Not only were the bourgeoisie increasingly successful in ensuring that the magistrates for the industrial towns were chosen from themselves and not the gentry, but the strengthening of the metropolitan police and the reforming and centralising of the administrative structure of the English prison system helped meet industrialists' demands for increased professionalisation. As it developed, police control expressed the movement of a more interventionist state. As Wolfe (1977, p. 26) notes, 'early Victorian social legislation – such as the factory acts, the municipal acts, the public health acts, and the railway acts – were pushed by those who urged police reform and resisted by those who opposed it'. Both were influenced by the same philosophy, and both became governed by similar administrative structures. As a result, the need to keep order helped also to facilitate a more active state and indicates the relationship between social control and the economic role that the state played. The instillation of work discipline and the securing of social stability were inextricably tied to the emergence of labour.

The development of local chambers of commerce and other forms of business association in the second part of the century was part of attempts by capitalists to overcome the inadequacies of communication and legal institutions and to bring some form of order to the local economic system. In the increasingly impersonal world of continental markets and trans-oceanic contracts the loopholes for dishonesty or sharp practice were becoming far greater. Consequently local business associations successfully sought such reforms as codification of mercantile law, the provision of a district registration of partnerships, heavier penalties against the fraudulent use of trade marks, and longer sentences for jailed debtors. It was a reflection of the impatience of the commercial entrepreneur with the practices and institutions of the landed gentry and the desire for more 'businesslike' laws and procedures. Many local officials, particularly in the law courts, often held appointment for life, having purchased the office and with the work being done by underlings paid a small fraction of the salary. Bankruptcy Commissioners, for example, sat irregularly and were inefficient and expensive. Businessmen wanted Tribunals of Commerce composed of businessmen and commercially-minded lawyers to provide cheaper and business-informed practices (King, 1983).

The success of business in its claims on a supposedly *laissez-faire* state challenged the notion that the state did not intervene to help business. Transportation and communications policy, particularly when it concerned the railways, was based on the use of public money. Business took a pragmatic attitude; it was concerned less with principled objections to public subsidy than practical consequences for trade. The concern with the railways was more over the monopolisation of ownership of the railway companies and fear that the result would be higher rates and a more inefficient service. At least the state could help to provide a standardised infrastructure that would enable private capital to expand. Moreover, the state's support for a uniform communications system ensured 'fair' competition; it helped prevent certain localities or overseas competitors from gaining a competitive edge as a result of patchy provision. This seemed to be a more important consideration than ideological commitment to an inactive state. While continental Europe, particularly Germany towards the end of the nineteenth century, was more likely to see direct state participation in strictly manufacturing as opposed to transportation industries, this was primarily the result of the need for such countries to catch up with the manufacturing capacity of Britain as quickly as possible.

Although the liberal state was supportive of capital, the extension of the state's activity also contained attendant potential dangers for capital. Notions of equality and civic rights, despite the individualistic twist given them by liberalism, paved the way for increased demands and participation of the disadvantaged and the disenfranchised. A developing capitalism implied a growing working class and new, more intensive forms of social fissure. Social and political demands from an increasingly large group of the population inevitably confronted business with a potential threat in a political system where governmental power was gained by voting (i.e. numerical) strength. It posed two conflicting and potentially contradictory constraints on the state – the need to maintain the conditions of capital accumulation, especially in the face of international competition, and the requirement to attract or maintain popular support. With an expanding economy, the two aims could both be secured. But the polarity increased with recession and declining resources. Moreover, if an active conception of the state was admitted, there was no logical reason why the working class should not also benefit from government. Clearly it cannot be assumed that liberal democracy is somehow functional for capitalism for the indeterminancies and changes created by electoral politics can generate serious impediments to a successful capitalist economy (Miliband 1982).

Throughout the nineteenth century the extension of formal

liberal rights in conjunction with often deepening social disparities ensured that the question of equality was necessarily broadened. As Bendix (1964) suggests, where legislative means are used both to protect the individual's freedom of contract and to deny the lower classes the rights needed to avail themselves of the same freedom (by denying the right of association and prohibiting trade unions, for example), then equality is no longer sought through freedom of contract alone, but through the establishment of social and political rights as well. Moreover, the abstract principle of equality underlying the legal and ideological recognition of the independent individual was often the direct cause of greatly accentuated inequalities; for example, in England, when *laissez-faire* proponents suggested that adult males do not need protection and were thus denied the right to combine. In France, too, the plebiscitarian tradition of direct state–citizen relations, enshrined in the famous revolutionary Loi le Chapelier (1791), was further strengthened under Napoleon and reinforced the tendency to restrain associations.

In several European countries, however, the extension of rights of association and the development of trade unionism were used to assert claims to elements of social justice, such as reasonable working conditions and basic levels of health and education. The extension of citizenship to the lower classes was given the special meaning that as citizens the members of these classes were 'entitled' to a certain standard of well-being in return for which they were only obliged to discharge the ordinary duties of citizenship (Bendix, 1964). Such developments marked a move away from the radical individualism of the liberal state. Nor was this confined to changes in the status of labour. The extension and changing conception of 'incorporation' referred to above and the attribution of legal personality to business firms is of doubtful legitimacy in the face of strict liberal ideology. The very concession of corporate status to the joint economic endeavours of individuals – going public – has strong pre-liberal as well as anti-liberal antecedents (Poggi, 1978, p. 127).

We have noted in previous chapters that the distinction between the public and private spheres found in liberal states can be characterised as that between relations of interest and affinity, on the one hand, and authority on the other. The liberal emphasis on the competitive market, as a sphere in which relations between individuals are based on self-interest rather than power, appears to reserve for the state a special status as the agency within societies holding a monopoly claim to authority. Yet by the turn of the twentieth century the emergency of large firms cast doubt on the competitive aspects of market relations. Relations between such firms, their control over markets, seemed to become increasingly power-based and characterised by cartelisation, monopolisation and concertation. Moreover, the emergence of employers' associations as well as trade unions added dimensions of negotiation and bargaining into the essentially market relations held to exist between capital and labour. Poggi (1978, p. 124) points out that the impact of this development on the state–society line can be seen in the fact that the rules on such matters as collective bargaining and much welfare legislation came to form a body of law (e.g. 'labour law') that straddled the divide between private and public law. Moreover, as we shall see, the increasing involvement of these new economic organisations in a developing arena of 'pressure group' politics, often to be found 'behind the back' of Parliament and operating within governmental bureaucracies, turned apparently private interests into quasi-governmental agencies. At the same time, the growth of state organisations produced new sets of bureaucratic interests that competed for a share of the social product with the private sector. The division of powers between the different organs of state rule, which aimed at their mutual 'check and balance' in the liberal design was largely overridden as bureaucracies competed to increase their powers, not at the expense of each other, but of society (Michels, 1915; Poggi, 1978).

The development of the modern, increasingly powerful state during the latter part of the nineteenth century induced conflicting responses from businessmen over the extent to which the state should actively secure the basis of successful capital accumulation through increased economic interventionism in the market. Alongside was the question of attitude to be adopted to the working class – should it be recognised and incorporated, or should the class basis of politics be resisted? As Gamble (1981b, p. 198) asserts, all capitalist states eventually have had to face these issues, but they surfaced early and more insistently in Britain, for nowhere else was the working class so quickly a majority. No class of peasants, no smallholders or other potential 'pools of reaction' could be drawn upon, as they could in most of continental Europe, to provide the social basis for a democratic organisation against the interests of the working class. The dilemma was whether to aim for a thorough-going market society, based upon individual desire to accumulate, as in the USA, with its denial of special class interests, or to seek the gradual incorporation of the working class as a privileged interest into the corporate body as a means of securing social stability and a 'moderate' labour movement. Yet the nationalist impetus to capitalist development which in Germany encouraged close co-operation between the state and the major economic actors, was largely lacking in Britain. The result was an erratic, and some would argue basically inefficient, path that oscillated between liberalism and collectivism.

The emergence and development of collectivism

A model of largely autonomous development by relatively isolated nation-states looked increasingly untenable in the face of an expanding international economy in the second part of the nineteenth century. Intensified trading pressure from the first industrial nations, Britain, and then the USA, forced other nations into actions to restructure their own economies. In Germany, Japan and Russia, for example, many ideas, technical innovations and some political institutions were either taken over from abroad or developed in conscious reference to changes that took place abroad. Such borrowing and adaptation was part of a concerted political effort to increase the economic and military viability of these countries (Bendix, 1964). The objective of resisting external domination or containment in a network of modernising societies constrained those in control of the state to seek to increase the resource-producing capacity of the society, often by increasing the extent to which the application of these resources is under the direction of the state. Where such an objective seriously conflicted with the interests of a powerful social class, then either that interest was submerged or the state experienced serious reverses internationally, risking defeat and conquest.

Germany provided a good illustration of just such a dilemma confronting some societies. Before its unification in 1870 Germany was fragmented into very unequal units and lacked a central authority, although one of the units, Prussia, was clearly ascendant over all others by virtue of military strength and efficient administration.

Consequently, following the Franco–Prussian war, political unity was accomplished under the hegemony of Prussia, its army and tradition of monarchical and bureaucratic rule. The success and example provided by Prussia considerably helped the support that Bismarck's conception of an activist, militaristic state received, even from liberals (Bendix, 1964). The state, primarily the officials of an absolutist regime, played a leading role in initiating industrial development, although its reforms met with considerable opposition. Especially in the East, local landowners (Junkers) used their existing local dominance to exact economic concessions from the government and resist efforts at constitutional reform. Their anti-urban bias and distrust of merchants reinforced both economic conflicts of interest between an agrarian east and industrial west and exacerbated fundamental differences between defenders of tradition and advocates of reform. However, the importance of political initiative in promoting economic change paved the way for a later corporatist integration of labour and state-aided and protected industry (Crouch, 1979). It indicates that the development of capitalism was not necessarily associated with a liberal democratic state. Rather, democracy had difficulty in emerging where the bourgeoisie was not politically and ideologically dominant, particularly in societies where radical political action and socio-economic reform was required to secure the conditions for industrial development in the face of intensified competition from more advanced economies. In such circumstances a 'strong' or 'exceptional' state may be supported by a bourgeoisie prepared, to reiterate Barrington Moore's expression, to exchange the right to rule for the right to make money.

Yet it is also important not to underestimate the role that the state played in the development of capitalism in liberal democracies. As Gamble (1981a) notes, liberalism requires a strong, if limited, state, to preserve property and accumulation through the provision of legal frameworks and institutions of social control, not least to counteract liberalism's own subversive tendency to question the legitimacy of all social authority. Moreover, models of society based upon the self-interested behaviour of individuals, as found in liberal political economy, for example, lack a normative account or moral justification for overarching social order. Rather, notions of nationalism and the 'nation-state' came to underpin authority and claims to political legitimacy. Following the French Revolution in particular, all forms of political opinion came to recognise 'the nation' as a prime focus of political loyalty (Gamble, 1981a, p. 132). A strong nation-state could be advocated on either liberal or conservative grounds, as either consolidating political independence and sovereignty, or as justifying opposition to individualism and sustaining patriotism. Conservatives tended to use the traditional and often rural symbols of national biography to argue against free trade and rampant economic individualism, and for protection and state intervention, while recognising the need for nations to industrialise if they were to avoid diminished status. Nonetheless, both liberalism and conservatism, through their embrace of 'nationalism', could ideologically support notions of a strong central authority, even if they differed over the extent to which some authority should be applied to the economy.

At the beginning of the twentieth century, even in Britain, where the strongest advocacy of free trade was to be found, the economy was looking less and less like the liberal model. Firms were larger, production more concentrated, liability more limited, with the functions of corporate ownership and management becoming more distinctive. The need to influence the state grew, particularly as increased foreign competition stimulated demands for protection for home markets. Although free trade was to persist as official governmental policy until well into the twentieth century in Britain, many of the traditional manufacturing industries supported Chamberlain's campaign for tariff reform and imperial preference, linked to a programme of social welfare. The struggle over tariff reform within the Conservative party in the pre-1914 period, and the continued pre-eminence of free trade in party policy, reflected both a more distinctive class-based electoral politics and a heightened conflict over alternative conceptions of the state. During the Edwardian period the Conservative Party became increasingly the party of business, in its social composition and support, whilst the Liberals became the advocates of social welfare, gradually in competition with the emerging Labour Party. In effect the party roles were reversed. Liberals had tended to argue earlier that state welfare provisions circumscribed the freedom of the individual while Disraeli, for example, had stressed in his programme the necessity for the state to extend welfare facilities. Yet, in the pre-war period Conservatism was dominated by 'the individual', and the state, formerly seen as the guarantor of property and order, now seemed to have become a threat to them.

Modern British Conservatism, in its view of the state, became marked by a series of related dichotomies: freedom and order, competitive and functional or co-operative industrial organisation, individualism and collectivism, conflict and harmony (Harris, 1972). The first terms in the pairs express the key elments of liberalism and its notion of a freely competitive market, while the contrary polarities reflect recognition of the state as directing the orderly arrangement of society and economy. Moreover, there was a long-standing cultural tradition in Conservatism that was favourable to notions of corporate representation and which facilitated the ideological acceptance of functional group politics as economic and other circumstances changed in the twentieth century. What Beer (1965, p. 3) refers to as 'Old Tory' thought had an ideal of social reality that was organic and hierarchic and emphasised the central notions of 'degree' and 'order'. It rejected the radical liberal commitment to 'parliamentarism', which ruled out associations formed outside Parliament for the purpose of determining what it should do, for Parliament was held to consist of representatives who deliberated as individuals on the great matters of the day. In contrast, liberals saw parliamentary members as representives of territorial rather than functional constituencies or interests, in which coalitions and alliances were often temporary, comprised of individuals who at any one time shared similar opinions. However, economic and social changes and the extension of state power in the Edwardian period, and powerfully reinforced by the experiences of the First World War, infused older traditions of strong government, paternalism and the organic society. 'Collectivist' politics developed from both left and right as both Socialism and Tory Democracy accepted the emergence of organised capital and labour and attributed to them an important role in government and administration, alongside an acceptance of party government.

The war offered a model of capitalism that differed considerably from the liberal design, for by 1918 the state in Britain had succeeded in co-ordinating for the first time the most important sectors of the economy in order to maximise war production. By the end of the war the state combined and controlled the railways, guaranteed profit margins and had assumed a major role for insurance. It was also the largest employer and produced the major part of national output. Moreover, there was recognition that the state needed to associate representatives of interest groups with government administration, sometimes in statutory form, as with the Education Act. This would provide not only a source of economic expertise and knowledge but also add an extra dimension of legitimacy to state action. It would also extend the potential influence of civil servants.

Almost without precedent the impact of the First World War required the British government to mobilise massive national public support for its war needs, especially for armaments and conscripts. Mobilisation of support increasingly involved government attempts to more actively 'create' public opinion through the use of propaganda. These, as Middlemas notes, were 'transmitted into an increasingly formal network of information-gathering and use essential to the functioning of an interventionist state authority' (Middlemas, 1979, p. 20). In the pre-war period, however, although the state apparatus was expanding, it lacked the centralising bureaucracy and organisation found in the more 'statist' continental countries. Although the Treasury tended to exercise increasing control over the state apparatus, the collective influence of civil servants may even have counted for less than that of the political constellation of outsiders.

The war also created a need for new organisations for the representation of industrial interests. Business organisation had remained predominantly localistic and highly fragmented in Britain, although the rapid growth of trade unions in the second half of the nineteenth century led to the creation of a large number of employers' federations. The growth of large-scale corporations with wide overseas markets also encouraged collaboration between firms to control prices and output, particularly in the iron and steel industries, and this was reinforced by fears of growing foreign competition. Yet the failure of the tariff reform movement and the confirmation of a free trade policy also limited industry's political involvements, whereas in other countries tariff policy provided high rewards for industrial ventures into politics (Blank, 1973). The free trade issue also created divisions between employers and limited support for organisations claiming to speak for industry as a whole. There were no systematic attempts by government to encourage the formation of representative industrial organisation, and most industrialists acted through their trade associations or approached government themselves. Although a system of conciliation had become well-established at the Board of Trade before 1914, neither employers nor unions were prepared to concede long-held de facto rights, and certainly not in favour of a system of legally-constituted institutions, bound down to agreements made under the competence of the state bureaucracy.

The war effort in all countries required an unprecedented degree of organisation and was based to a considerable extent on centralised control and planning. The state relied heavily on the co-operation of businessmen. At local level employers virtually ran the war effort in Britain and, often with government assistance, trade and other employers' associations were formed to help run the war machine. The state's control agencies were staffed with businessmen and, as in Germany, the business community reached to the heart of government. The formation of three new 'peak' employers' associations, including the Federation of British Industry (FBI), highlighted the increasingly close relationship established with government. However, in all the major countries engaged in the conflict, France, Germany, Italy and Britain, the first stage of the war down to 1916 brought almost unmitigated conflict between government, employers and trade unions. In Germany, as Middlemas (1979) has noted, the absence of a parliamentary tradition combined with rapid industrialisation had resulted in only very weak links between the trade unions and the political parties, while the Reichstag had acquired only limited power of control over the bureaucracy and the Chancellor. Moreover, the political isolation of the working class led the Chancellor and government to seek what had been rejected in England – industrial collaboration between state, employers and the trade unions, in which the latter, unlike their British counterparts, sought status as legal corporations, capable of making binding collective agreements.

In Britain, government was at pains to preserve normal economic incentives and disturb the structure of business as little as possible. Yet mutual suspicion characterised relations between both sides. The government acknowledged the contribution made by the trade associations towards the war effort but was concerned about their monopolistic aspects, while industrialists were concerned about intervention from state bureaucrats (Grant and Marsh, 1977). Many of the trade associations were valued not because they facilitated closer relations with government but often because they limited these connections, protecting the autonomy of their members (Blank, 1973). One consequence was that the FBI was never very effective as a representative influence on government as the great majority of members of the organisation did not feel the need for a stronger, more authoritative body. On the labour side, too, the TUC was unable to become an institutional representative of the whole trade union movement and faced considerable opposition from the national growth of the shop steward's movement. Nonetheless, it would be a mistake to underestimate the levels of successful co-operation that did occur between state, industry and the labour movement in comparison with what occurred before the war. After 1916 the TUC became the government's only lasting safeguard against the shop steward's movement and the prospects of mounting industrial and political unrest. However, only in England did co-operation tend to occur outside as well as inside Parliament.

In the 1920s the FBI was much less involved with government than it had been during the war, and it established itself primarily as a service and defence organisation for its members. However, there were halting steps taken towards institutional co-operation between capital, labour and the state in the 1920s, primarily around questions of structural change in industry, despite the intense conflicts engendered over wage-bargaining. These developments were similar to patterns of industrial organisation in France and Germany, although in Britain they were linked to the re-emergence of the class-based, two-party system, in which Labour took the place of the Liberals. However, increasing TUC disillusionment with Labour Cabinets exemplified the dissonance existing between the party's need for electoral appeal, on the one hand, and trade union obligations to defend members' interests on the other. The TUC deliberately dismantled the joint committees that had been established with Labour and developed its own research and policy-making organisations. Middlemas (1979) suggests that during the 1930s organised labour settled down to live with organised management. An expanded secretariat and new buildings emphasised a new professionalism and flowering of administrative capacity within the TUC under a new generation of leaders. However, although the TUC could only become an authority by accommodating to individual unions and could not take real policing power, it assumed the role of rule-maker and arbitrator for the movement.

On the employers' side, the effective end of free trade and introduction of extensive protection in 1931 following Britain's departure from the gold standard, necessarily increased government intervention in the economy. The government's first efforts were devoted to establish tariffs acceptable to the most important sectors of business opinion, and beginning the development of agriculture in order to reduce imports. Making protection work meant using the state to force industrial concentration and co-ordination through the use of state grants and conditional offers of tariffs. The result, not without appreciable resistance, followed a more complete rejection of liberalism than hitherto. As Harris (1972, p. 77), notes, many 'liberal' Conservatives however accepted with equanimity the decline of competitive capitalism and the creation of monopolies, provided they retained unimpeded control of business. Liberal conservatism faded imperceptibly into pluralist corporatism, where the corporations were business firms rather than estates.

Although the powers of the state expanded greatly in the inter-war years, it was less the growth of an all-powerful central authority that characterised the period than the development of shared powers between the public and private sectors. The so-called 'franchise state' (Wolfe, 1977) had the advantage of encouraging co-operation among businessmen who would have resisted having it forced on them through the state. State power (and responsibility) could be parcelled out to 'semi-governmental' private agencies, such as trade associations, as a means of accommodating public and private authority. A 'deep strategy of crisis avoidance' (Middlemas, 1979, p. 18) was an essential part of the triangular co-operation between institutions as the trade unions and employers associations gradually became 'governing institutions' rather than interest groups. They came to display some of the characteristics of the state, which, for its part, welcomed moves that helped avoid and control a myriad of individual demands.

Middlemas (1979) suggests that the emergence of a 'corporate bias' or collectivism in British politics cannot be ascribed solely to the needs of capital accumulation. Rather, the state increasingly had its own, distinct concern in the maintenance of social order and avoidance of conflict in an increasingly conflictful world. In a less religious and deferential age, British public administrators were perhaps the first in the newly-industrialised countries to value the arts of good public management, 'not by invoking authority . . . but by the alternate gratification and cancelling out of the desires of large, well-organised, collective groups' (p. 18). Certainly if the needs of capital accumulation had been uppermost, one might have expected either a strategy that pushed Britain towards a radical bourgeois model on the lines of the USA, or one which used the state in a more direct manner to effect a more thoroughgoing reconstruction of the economy and to suppress the working class. Either may have helped avoid the long decline of the British economy (Gamble, 198lb, p. 80). However, 'the state' is no monolithic entity, with an overall 'intelligence' or 'steering capacity', and government departments differed in the strategies they pursued and the groups they encouraged. Moreover, there is a strong argument that suggests that a particular fraction of British capital – the financial sector – was able to dominate state policy and hamper internal, manufacturing investment, to the possible detriment of the long-term interests of capital as a whole (Longstreth, 1979).

Fascism

Nor should the 'corporate bias' in Britain in the 1930s referred to by Middlemas be confused with the corporate state of inter-war fascism found in Germany and Italy, which were much more 'statist' in their subordination of the economy to government. Fascism sought to concentrate power in the state, crushing groups such as trade unions, political parties and the churches. Its doctrine of national self-sufficiency, or autarchy, was part of the attempt to insulate the nation from the depressions and slumps that characterised the world economy in the inter-war years. In effect, the doctrine implies not so much an isolationism as unlimited expansion and imperialism. To become 'self-supporting' required access to prime raw material sources and the development of a colonial empire (Bracher, 1973). The increasing competitiveness of the world economy heightened nationalism within the advanced societies, and resulted in a race for colonial annexation, tariffs and general protectionism. The fascist state in Germany, at least, helped accomplish the reorganisation of German industry into cartels and monopolies that enabled it to compete more competitively abroad, while its military excursions and conquests sought to remedy Germany's exclusion from the vital raw material resources available to its major industrial competitors (Neumann, 1944). Poulantzas (1974) even more explicitly links the emergence of the fascist state to monopoly capitalism and imperialism. He argues that fascism is an 'exceptional' form of state that belongs to the imperialist stage of capitalism in quite specific circumstances. Following Lenin, the 'imperialist chain' of countries is characterised by the unequal development of its links, the strength of some depending on the weakness of others and vice-versa. It is argued that although a socialist revolution was made in the weakest link in the chain – Russia – fascism arose in the next two weakest links. This weakness is not simply economic backwardness but refers to an accumulation of political and ideological contradictions as a consequence of capitalist development carried out under the hegemony of the Prussian Junkers and not the bourgeoisie. The result was a dissonance between the increasing economic dominance of monopoly capital and its comparative political weakness. The immobilism of the Weimar republic, its inability to intervene and support large-scale capital, was a major factor in the fascist assumption of power and the eventual restructuring of capital in the interests of its monopoly sector.

The inter-war period is characterised by the decline in the liberal state and the emergence of collectivist politics based on the major classes. Whilst in Britain this took the form of institutional co-operation, outside as well as inside the political arena, and was characterised by the indentation of the public and private sectors, elsewhere more state-directed developments were found. The German fascist state exemplifies the increasing power of central authority in one of its extreme forms. However, the post-1917 revolutionary development of socialism in the USSR provides the classic case of twentieth-century state power in its non-capitalist form.

State socialism

In Chapter 3 we referred to two different conceptions of socialism in

Marx's writings, with which are associated two contrary models of the state. A 'commune' model is centred on the need to overcome alienation through the transformation and dissolution of state authority through the creation of self-governing communities in which people would directly participate in decision making and its implementation. An alternative model conceived a strong state as necessary for the transformation of property relations, for the overcoming of material want and inequality, and for defending the socialist revolution from its enemies. The early Bolshevik conception of the state, outlined by Lenin, took its lead from Marx's commune model. In the immediate aftermath of the 1917 revolutionary seizure of power the new regime encouraged the development of factory councils and soviets as a means of popular self-administration. However, as Lane (1985, p. 60) observes, 'the activities of the soviets and workers' control were always regarded by Lenin as taking place within the context of the leading role of the party', which effectively ruled out more extreme versions of local self-administration, such as syndicalism and workers' control. Yet the Bolsheviks' early distrust of the state as being primarily a capitalist construction exacerbated the social disorder and rapid decline in output that characterised the first years of the new regime and fuelled demands for greater political freedom by left socialist groups.

The chaos and disruption that followed from civil war and foreign intervention in the period of 'war communism' (1918–21) effectively prevented the intended centralised planning and control of the economy. The seizure of land by the peasants and its distribution into smaller holdings not only contributed to the diminished efficiency of good production, adding to the dislocation in the supply of food to the towns and the military, but also provided an obstacle to the creation of large-scale, party-controlled, collective farming. As a consequence, the period of the New Economic Policy that followed aimed at restoring production and output through the introduction of market mechanisms. Alongside the nationalised financial and large-scale industry sectors was developed a privately-owned sector in which smaller industry and virtually all agriculture were located. Here, prices were determined by supply and demand, while professional 'specialists' received differential wages in order to provide them with incentives to effectively discharge complex industrial tasks and to develop a general motivation for education and training. Efficiency was encouraged by the adoption of profit yardsticks and the requirement for enterprises and state institutions to adopt commercial practices. By the late 1920s industrial production returned to, and then comfortably surpassed, pre-war levels.

Although these economic advances reinforced the legitimacy of the Bolshevik regime, the political aim of the New Economic Policy was to consolidate the post-revolutionary economy until the hoped-for revolutionary uprisings in other countries allowed a more thorough-going socialist transformation of the countryside and the economy. In the meantime, however, the extension of private ownership and commercialism risked the development of bourgeois attitudes and groups inimical to socialism. The failure of other socialist revolutions to occur in the West, and the military and political threats to the Bolshevik regime posed by encroaching capitalist powers, effectively brought the New Economic Policy to an end, to be replaced by the doctrine of 'socialism in one country'. It marked the full official recognition that massive industrialisation was required for Soviet military protection and for the consolidation of internal Communist Party power through the enlargement of the working class. A further feature was the ideological adoption of Marx's later model of the socialist state, as a strong, centralised agency that scientifically and rationally secures the means of material existence for the whole people. Under Stalin, the 'socialism in one country policy' provides the impetus for industrialisation, the collectivisation of agriculture and strong central party control. From 1928 the Soviet economic structure changed dramatically as high rates of growth, especially in capital goods, were aimed for and achieved. As Lane (1985, p. 69) remarks,

> The essence of Stalin's policy was to strengthen the country politically and economically by the creation of an industrial base and the formation of an urban working class. It was not the prime objective of the government to promote the short-term interest of the Russian workers in terms of general standards of living.

The often forcible collectivisation of agriculture into larger units not only increased the supply of food and labour to the towns and factories, but ensured political control of the countryside. It involved the expropriation of the rich peasants (*kulaks*), regarded as class enemies by the regime, and took away the ordinary peasants' ownership of his produce and his control over his working environment, and made it subject to the will of the collective unit, which was led by Communist Party members or sympathisers. The other vital part of Stalin's objective was a firmer central grip on the party apparatus and, in turn, stronger party control of political processes. Under Stalin the party became more hierarchically directed by the general secretary, and provided the base for the massive purges of the party and extreme political coercion that took place in the 1930s and 1950s as Stalin sought to root out any potential opposition that allegedly debilitated the resolve of the regime in its policy of socialism in one country.

By the end of the Second World War the Soviet Union had an industrial base that was comparable with other advanced industrial societies. Its political system rests on the assumption that the Communist Party expresses the political interests of the working class, and, as revolutionary state ownership and control of production effectively eliminates class conflict, no other parties are required. The liberal–democratic role of political institutions in western societies, in which different interests and demands are articulated and harmonised through the activities of relatively autonomous pressure groups, is absent in state socialism and regarded as debilitating the collective leadership of the working class by the Communist Party. The party has become 'the authoritative source of values and now has a monopoly of political organisation' (Lane, 1985, p. 146). The highest political body of the Communist Party is the Politbureau, with a membership of between 12–20, below which is the Central Committee, to which the Politbureau is formally accountable, and the Congress of the party, consisting of various territorial delegates. As such, the party is the dominant political body which seeks to control other administrative institutions by laying down general policy for all levels. The principle entailed is democratic centralism, which involves elections from the lower tiers to the top but the compliance of the lower levels to the highest ones.

The government in the USSR is formally and organisationally distinct from the party, and possesses the legal power to enforce policies, if necessary through the application of physical force and other sanctions. It is made up of ministries whose heads form a

Council of Ministers, and comprises the executive arm of government. Constitutionally the government is responsible to the Supreme Soviet, the apex of a system of territorially-organised elected assemblies and the chief legislative body. Effectively, however, the ministries are subject to little influence from the Soviets. In recent years there is evidence that although the party remains the source of normative power the ministerial bureaucracies have achieved greater organisational power, not least because the sheer volume and technical nature of work in a modern state, together with the relative lack of professional training amongst party officials in comparison with state bureaucrats, inevitably leaves government bodies with considerable power (Lane, 1985, p. 227).

As the Soviet Union has emerged as one of the major advanced industrial societies, various theories have suggested that its political and economic processes are little different to those found in western societies. Some 'convergence theories', for example, suggest that there is an evolutionary tendency for societies to converge in a single type of industrial society (Clark Kerr *et al.*, 1973; Galbraith, 1967; Parsons, 1966). As western societies become more planned and managed by bureaucratic élites, so the USSR, with the rise of technology, the growth of bureaucracy and the ideology of technical rationality becomes more like the West. There is, therefore, a double convergence which is characterised by a high level of structural differentiation and 'adaptive capacity' (Parsons, 1966). In this view, modern technology and science' leaves no freedom of choice for the social patterns of the division of labour and co-operation, but directly defines the appropriate labour process and, through this, defines the wider social relations as well' (Rakovski, 1983, p. 395).

Convergence theories have been adopted by both the political left and the political right in the West. For the latter, it justifies claims that modern capitalism is no longer controlled by uncaring, rapacious entrepreneurs but is managed in a socially responsible, benign and class–neutral way be professional élites. For the political left, convergence theory is recalled to provide support for claims that the USSR is a capitalist society (albeit 'state capitalist'), like those in the West. The difficulty with this interpretation, however, is that quite wide variations in systems of social stratification exist between industrial societies and patterns of distribution can be altered quite radically by political regimes (Goldthorpe, 1968; Parkin, 1969). There are also other crucial differences, particularly in property relations, that distinguish state socialist societies from capitalist societies. In the USSR there is no legal freedom for enterprises that limit the Soviet state's direct influence on economic behaviour, whereas the predominance of private property in capitalism prevents non-market relations becoming uppermost. More generally, the distinction between the public and the private found in the West is hardly drawn in state socialism, where the state more clearly and directly controls communications, education, and group associations as well as the economy. The Soviet state is not determined by the economic base to the degree found in capitalist societies, but exercises a more directive and influential control of property relations.

Nonetheless, patterns of occupational recruitment, educational achievement and social mobility in the USSR do reveal the almost universal tendency for those in privileged positions to ensure at least a head-start for their children (Lane, 1971). An important element, despite the 'positive discrimination' in favour of the working class in the allocation of higher education and other places exercised by the Soviet state, is the 'cultural' as opposed to private capital possessed by the educated middle class, which is handed down to offspring in the form of encouragement and preparation for education. In the view of some Marxist critics, the socialisation of the means of production in the USSR has generated a new ruling class, despite official ideology. 'State capitalist' theories, associated with the work of Tony Cliff (1974) and the Socialist Workers Party in Britain, regard the state bureaucracy in the USSR as a ruling class like the western bourgeoisie because of its collective control of the means of production which is used to exploit the workers through the extraction of surplus value. In Cliff's view, the level of capitalist production at the time of the revolution was too low for there to be a fully socialist revolution without the occurrence of simultaneous revolutions abroad. The state was thus forced to develop industrialisation and undertake the necessary stage of capitalist development, which inevitably leads to a division between ruling and exploited classes. Thus, capitalism was restored under Stalin, not only in the form of private capital but as a form of state-controlled capital, in which industrialisation was achieved by extracting surplus from the peasantry (Westoby, 1983, p. 221).

The difficulty with state capitalist theory is that it underestimates the absence of the main mechanism of capitalist accumulation in the USSR and the predominance of state and non-market forces in comparison with the situation in capitalist societies. Another Marxist criticism of the USSR derives from Trotsky's denunciation of Soviet Russia under Stalin in which he takes issue with the state–capitalist interpretation by disagreeing that the Soviet bureaucracy is best described as a ruling class. He argued that because the private ownership of the means of production had been abolished, Soviet society was essentially a proletarian state, but one that had become perverted or 'degenerated'. In this 'degenerated workers state', bureaucrats become a privileged ruling stratum, maintaining a system of unequal distribution and drawing on surplus values for its own use. This bureaucratic stratum is based on the state control of the economy, but also the necessity to quickly develop the industrial sector in the face of international capitalist hostility. As Westoby (1983, p. 223) notes, both state capitalist and degenerated workers' state interpretations associate the privileges and oppressive approach of the state bureaucracy with economic backwardness, for 'the state, directly or as a surrogate for the market, must coerce the surpluses for industrialisation'. A problem with 'degenerated workers state' theory, however, is the continuance and stability of this (apparently) perverted state form, particularly once industrialisation is achieved and the worst shortages are eliminated. Recent advocates of this view (Mandel, 1979) argue that Soviet Russia is a transitional society between capitalism and socialism, in which its parasitic ruling bureaucracy will finally be purged by an upsurge of class consciousness and political revolution by the working class. Yet there are few signs of transition or instability in the Soviet regime to support such an interpretation.

Conclusion: post-1945

A feature of western capitalist societies in the three decades following the ending of the Second World War is the increase in state involvement in the economy. Not only has the state's share of employment increased considerably but its proportion of overall expenditure has steadily expanded, partly as a consequence of the state's role in 'transfer payments', such as social insurance, where resources are redirected rather than appropriated. Thompson (1984, p. 83) notes that nationalisation has been a significant characteristic in Britain and other capitalist economies, where major sections of industry have been taken into public ownership, especially heavy manufacture, energy and communications, areas which are vital in supporting capitalist accumulation generally. He identifies five major motives for nationalisation in Britain:

(a) a number of nationalised industries, such as gas and electricity supply, were already in local government ownership as 'natural monopolies' and requiring a high standard of public service, before being centrally reorganised in the interests of national planning and efficiency;
(b) the strategic importance of some industries, such as air and communications, to Britain's defence;
(c) the inability of private owners to raise the capital required to reconstruct badly-declining industries, such as coal or rail;
(d) the argument that national planning of the economy, especially the use of Keynsian macro-economic techniques, required state ownership of major industries; and
(e) socialist arguments that nationalisation would provide a means for the redistribution of wealth and power.

It is doubtful that nationalisation and other forms of state intervention in modern capitalist economies characterise a major change in the nature of the state. As in the 1939–45 war years, 'The state's involvement in the economy, although expensive, was largely confined to the regulation of exchange, and production itself remained in the hands of private capital . . . the private ownership of capital meant that the economic basis of the class structure was unchanged' (Harris, 1983, pp. 74–5). Moreover, the relative unconcern by socialists with either the specific organisational structure and operational running of the nationalised industries has helped their integration 'back into the "market mechanism" despite their changed status in terms of property rights' (Thompson, 1984, p. 88). Nationalised industries are expected to operate as commercial concerns, although few governments have been able to resist intervening in the setting of price levels in the pursuit of specific fiscal or political objectives. Under conservative and 'market liberal' administrations in recent years, however, particularly Britain under the leadership of Margaret Thatcher, determined and largely successful efforts have been made to 'return' a number of the nationalised industries to private ownership.

In some views, the post-1945 decades have been characterised by the development of corporatism, in which state direction, if not ownership, of the 'mixed economy' led to the increasing involvement of organised business and labour in national economic policy making which, under administrations of both left and right, was marked by a 'consensus' that governments adjusted levels of demand in the economy to meet the prime 'Keynsian' objectives of low levels of unemployment and inflation, economic growth, and a trade surplus (Pahl and Winkler, 1974). It is an interpretation in line with that offered by Middlemas (1979), in which the emergence of corporatism is traced to the social and political turmoil of the early years of the twentieth century, although Middlemas places heavier emphasis on political factors, such as the need for political and social order, than do recent, more 'economistic' analyses. However, it is doubtful that corporatism is properly used as a description of a type of economy, while the resurgence of liberal or social market remedies for modern economies indicates the precariousness of any theory that assumes an inevitable convergence of advanced societies in an increasingly state-directed form. (These are issues we take up in the next chapter.)

In this chapter we have provided a more empirically-detailed account of the development of the modern state since the last decades of the nineteenth century. We have examined particularly the emergence of more collectivist forms of state–economy organisation which, in the West, have become characterised by concertation between organised labour, business association and the state. The influence of war in the move away from the earlier liberal design of a largely non-interventionist state is noted, as are the consequences and further threats of war in the development of state socialism in the East. Although significant differences in economic and political arrangements characterise East and West, there is increased resemblance in the existence of both market incentive and state economic involvement. Finally, we examined a crucial state strategy used by governments in the post 1945 decades in the West to ensure sufficient demand and full employment in economies – Keynesianism – and its assumption of incorporated labour. The chapter, therefore, indicates three major forms of state strategy for managing increasingly complex modern societies – liberalism, bureaucratisation and corporatism – and we turn to their more explicit consideration in the next chapter.

5

Corporatism

Pluralism and liberal democracy

As we noted in Chapter 1, a key feature of western liberal democracy is held to be the role of regular elections and the necessity for political leaders to struggle competitively to attract the people's vote. This is a major distinguishing factor from one-party or 'totalitarian' regimes which lack clashes between parties and leaders with opposing philosophies and alternative policies. In recent years, however, this rather élitist interpretation of democracy, in which leadership circulation and periodic appeals to the electorate loomed larger than classical democratic concerns with more direct forms of citizen participation, has been supplemented by the rediscovery of interest groups. As we indicated in Chapter 1, interest, or pressure, groups which develop alongside or within formal institutions have been seen to play an increasingly crucial representative role in democratic systems. It was pointed out that in the structural functionalist approach to comparative politics that dominated Anglo-American political sociology in the immediate post Second World War decades interest groups undertook specialised functions in advanced societies that complemented those of political parties. In this view, to quote Berger (1981, p. 8),

> The defining characteristic of interest groups is that they articulate the claims and needs of society and transmit them into the political process. In the most developed political system the division of labour between interest groups, parties, and government is one in which interest groups transmit 'pragmatic specific' demands to parties; parties aggregate these demands, integrate them into a general programme, and mobilise support for them; and parliaments and bureaucracies enact them as policies and laws and implement them.

This legitimation of the function of groups in the democratic process was sustained by a pluralist interpretation of society. As we described in Chapter 1, pluralism's major exponents, such as Dahl and Polsby, extended the analogy of the competitive market which was already being used to charactise the electoral system to the pressure group world. Here, too, the world was open, fluid and voluntary. No particular group is necessarily dominant and no group is without at least potential political influence. Power is widely distributed between groups and any group of individuals can organise and ensure that its preferences are taken into account by decision makers if it is so determined. The number of interests and potential interest groups is in principle unlimited with no single set of interests (e.g. capital, or the state) necessarily victorious. This is because 'the overlapping memberships of groups, social mobility – all work to maintain a fluidity in the relations among various organised interests and to undermine the bases on which a situation of permanent domination could be constructed' (Berger, 1981, p. 5). Thus power is distributed non-cumulatively and public decisions reflect demands from the political market. Not that there are too many of these, as most people are either generally satisfied with their governance, or apathetic, or seeking economic or domestic goals and are uninterested in politics. Relatively low levels of participation are not the mark of a polity's 'ill-health' for pluralists. For the system to remain stable there should be a fairly high level of apathy. Otherwise, as Dahl argues, too many demands are imposed on government for them to be met, at least with equity and in an orderly manner, and new interests will find little space to organise.

In this view the state is construed as either a neutral and rather passive switchboard for contending interests, or its agencies as simply one set of interest groups among all the others. Weber's idea of the state as a monopoliser of legitimate violence and authoritative domination recedes rapidly from view. Indeed the classical bourgeois distinction between state and society fades in pluralism as the former dissolves in the latter. As Offe (1984, p. 162) notes with reference to social contract theory, 'the state is based upon *nothing but* the associated individuals who decide to enter into a contract with each other; that is, public authority is [based] . . . on the [hypothetical] will of its subjects'. Insofar as the state has a distinctive purpose at all it is to promote and define the 'individuality' of subjects with legal rights and physical protection.

Political rights are granted only to the extent that their exercise does not interfere with the political rights of others.

The pluralist view of the pressure group world and its benign and open influence on democratic processes, a central component of the sociology of democracy in the 1950s and 1960s, has undergone serious criticism and revision since the early 1970s. In large degree this stems from the rise in social conflict and economic recession in advanced capitalist societies that mark the recent period and which cast doubt on pluralist interpretations of the political system. Berger (1981), for example, suggests that pluralism was compatible with the conditions of economic prosperity and political stability of the 1960s because it created fluidity in the relations between organised interests. The interest group system consisted of an unspecified number of organisations and was competitive, 'state-free' and self-determined, and not hierarchically-ordered into varying layers of superordination. However, the end of rapid growth in the world economy, mounting inflation and levels of unemployment, provided conditions which led to the view that pluralism created an unstable system of interest representation with destabilising effects on governance and economy. Pluralism is seen as a source of the increased 'ungovernability' of advanced western societies as 'rising expectations', conceived increasingly as rights or 'entitlements' rather than simply preferences, and generated by competing interest groups and parties, disseminated by the media and encouraged by legitimation of a more socially responsive and interventionist state, results in 'overload' of the state bureaucracies. Under the impact of fiscal constraints – the mutually-feeding relationship of rising 'social expenses' and reduced growth – the state is unable to meet these expectations, and the concomitant decline in governmental authority provides no effective basis for resisting such demands. For writers such as Schmitter (1984) new forms of interest group intermediation with the state provide a better basis than pluralism for securing increased social and economic co-ordination to add to the system's regulative capacities. Corporatism is better able to manage demands for goods of a kind (e.g. collective consumption, welfare) which pluralist systems of interest representation with their narrow, self-interested and exclusive definitions of group goals have never provided. It is less the problem of 'overload' that corporatism is designed to meet than the problems of identifying and *ranking* problems, and securing a view of the state as operating for the public good rather than private or class advantage.

It is doubtful if we can plausibly ascribe to pluralism all of the ills attributed to it, not least by conservative-inclined theorists of 'ungovernability'. As Offe (1984, p. 165) observes, ' "rising expectations" may often turn out to be a misnomer for increased insecurity and structurally induced need'. It could be argued, for example, that the modern welfare state actually encourages a dependency and helplessness from many of its recipients as a direct form of control and surveillance. Very little of life in highly urbanised and socially insecure conditions lies untouched by the state. Some Marxist interpretations extend the analysis further by arguing that large-scale state suppression and authoritarianism, designed to combat rising class conflict and preserve the profitability of capital accumulation, will actually promote more class and popular demands of the state. However, both Conservatives and Marxists share a belief in the increased 'ungovernability' of liberal democratic regimes, although Marxists see this as less the consequence of pressure group activity than as a structural imperative derived from the private possession of the means of production and the increased weight that the veto power of capital achieves under conditions of low economic growth (Poulantzas, 1973; Miliband, 1977). Finally, we should note too that élitist analyses of power have questioned the pluralist claim of the non-cumulativeness of power resources. Some empirical studies of local community power structures, for example, have indicated major economic interests as pervasively dominant in political decision making (Hunter, 1953; Bachrach and Baratz, 1970). (See Chapter 6.)

The emergence of corporatism

The notion of corporatism has a long historical background in the view of some authors stretching as far back as feudal society with its emphasis (at least ideally) on organic harmony. Newman (1981) traces the corporatist idea to the Standestaat (see Chapter 2), and sees both as essentially tripartite, with the partnership of monarch, aristocracy and burghers in the former period matched by that of state, employers and trade unions in the latter. Like others, however, Newman sees the development of competitive capitalism and liberal democracy as erasing corporatism until the onset of crises in both in the early twentieth century. Order, hierarchical authority and national consensus as means of overcoming internal division and securing external and imperialistic victories were notions that drew upon and replenished corporatist thinking (Harris, 1972). Crouch (1979) suggests that the First World War helped found a new co-operation between government, business and the trade unions as all combined for the clear purpose of winning the war. Certainly, as indicated in Chapter 4, both the two great wars of this century have legitimised a more active and interventionist state, while the consequent economic and social dislocations of the inter-war period again sustained corporatist notions of a rational and organic unity. Both left and right derived corporatist solutions from medieval notions of separate industrial or economic corporations, with the former inclining towards syndicalist or guild socialist notions of more local forms of self-governance, and the latter finding extreme expression in fascist notions of a strong, hierarchically-ordered, state-disciplined society in which large scale corporations would be formly wedded to national goals.

Like Crouch, we noted earlier that Middlemas (1979) also regards the First World War as a critical watershed in the emergence of corporatism in Britain. Certain key economic interest groups, such as the British Employers Confederation and the Trade Union Congress became part of the state apparatus in the exercise of the war effort. In Middlemas's description, they became 'governing institutions', which are defined as 'a body which assumes functions devolved on it by government' and which shares governmental interpretations of the national interest and even comes in its administrative trappings to resemble government departments (p. 20). As we noted earlier in Chapter 4, Middlemas suggests that such a system contains a 'corporate bias' rather than being a full-blown form of corporatism, and it emerges as a response to a problem of political order or statecraft as governments seek crisis avoidance by utilising the disciplinary potential of the major interest groups.

Middlemas reinforces the view that corporatism is a response to crisis. During the First World War it was characterised first by increased state intervention in the economy and areas of social policy, and then by a change in the nature of key economic interest groups from primarily private associations to ones with regular and mutually supportive relationships with government. These developments have come to be seen as deriving from the inability of the market and liberal democratic institutions to provide both the conditions of capital accumulation and conflict-resolution in modern complex and class-divided societies. Corporatist analysis therefore underlines the importance of relationships between the state and those groups corresponding to the social organisation of economic production and distribution. These relationships are characterised by exchange: the leaders of these groups help construct and even implement state policy, and in return are expected to successfully secure agreement from members for state policy and if necessary overcome internal dissent. Corporatism therefore seeks to generate class collaboration and the view that national goals and a united effort to secure them are more beneficial to all interests than narrow, sectional and class-divisive campaigns.

Interpretations of corporatism

An important explanation for the emergence of corporatist forms of interest representation is provided by Cawson (1982) who links the decay of pluralist policies to the decline of a competitive market economy, suggesting a transformation in the way interests are represented in politics similar to the development of the corporate economy. In the same way that modern capitalist economies become stratified between a large and concentrated business sector on the one hand, able to dominate markets, and a competitive small and medium-sized sector on the other, where company failures and mobility are more clearly marked, so does the political market reflect the unequal influence of some interest groups as opposed to others. This is not simply analogous. Large corporations come to exert economic power in the market and also political power that enables public policy to discriminate in their favour. Cawson (p. 10) notes that at the same time as a corporate sector grew in the economy as both a cause and consequence of state intervention, 'the democratic political market was beginning to be eclipsed by the power of interest groups, especially those of the economic producers, both capital and labour'.

In the same way that the processes of corporatisation in the economy develop unevenly, and as a consequence of the uneven expansion of the role of the state, some interests become corporatised while others remain pluralistic. In the corporatist sector are to be found more permanent, bureaucratically-organised associations comprised of individuals having a common location in the socio-economic structure. The functional power of capital and labour, for example, is determined less by the association's resources, membership and publicity than by their obstructional capacity for production. The state negotiates or bargains with these groups on a particular basis – not openly, but secretly and silently – in the pursuit of orderly governance and capital accumulation. In the pluralist sector, however, are to be found more transitory and poorly-organised groups formed voluntarily by individuals with shared beliefs or interests, which, generally lacking close relations with government, rely on highly-publicised, campaigning activity to advance their cause. Their interests may be of little concern to government and there is little inclination or facility for controlling members in the interests of state-defined national goals.

Cawson is careful to note that even in the corporatist sector groups have a degree of independent power and autonomy that prevents simple 'incorporation' or 'co-optation', i.e. a total subordination of the group or only token participation. His characterisation of a corporate society (rather than corporate state) rests upon the notion of a fragmentary or decentralising state parcelling out or sharing its power with those centres of influence that have developed outside the formal democratic processes of the state. The state thus engages in genuine bargaining and accommodation with these associations. This model of corporatism and the state has elements more in common with pluralism than, for example, Marxist accounts of a powerful and authoritarian state ruling on behalf of monopoly capital. Some forms of corporatism share with pluralism views about the importance and influence of formal interest groups. However, in corporatism, while power is relatively dispersed it is not pluralistically or competitively distributed as in the market model, but to corporate groups essential to society. The formation and development of these groups is not 'state-free' as in pluralism but symbiotically linked to the state in a manner that blurs conventional liberal distinctions between the public and private spheres.

Until recently the role of the state in corporatist analyses has been variable and often unclear, and the notion of a fragmentary state differs from an earlier and influential treatment of corporatism by Pahl and Winkler (1974). Rather than seeing corporatism as a system of interest group relationships with the state, Pahl and Winkler see it as a new economic system, distinctive from both capitalism and socialism in its combination of private ownership and state control. In response to fundamental changes in the economy, such as increased international competition, monopolisation and cartelisation, lower rates of return on investments, and more sophisticated technology, the state moves from a facilitative to a more directive role. Its attempts to give positive direction to private economic activity necessitates more governmental controls over company decision making and trade union strategies. This mode of allocating resources, however, is legitimised and operated according to four principles: unity, order, nationalism and success, which secure the co-operation of the different classes and their assent to curbs on autonomy through the emphasis on national goals achieved through collaboration and restraint.

There are a number of well-observed difficulties with the Pahl and Winkler model. One, elaborated by Westergaard (1977), is that the state interventionism associated with corporatism does not run counter to capitalist criteria, but rather seeks new methods for providing the conditions of successful private accumulation. Patterns of resource allocation and wealth distribution change little, if at all, under corporatism, not least because of the external competitive pressures on state policies from the world capitalist economy. Moreover, the problematic interpretation and status of notions such as 'national interest', 'consensus' and 'success' in class societies suggest very real boundaries to stable and persisting corporatist arrangements. As Offe (1984) has noted, too, there are also strong pressures on the state in capitalist societies to limit its interventionism. The modern 'welfare' state is a self-limiting state, required to perform two incompatible functions *vis-à-vis* the economic subsystem: commodification and decommodification. The state is impelled both to intervene in the economy and create through non-market or decommodified means the pre-conditions for accumulation, as these are not provided 'spontaneously' by market forces, and is also obliged not to encrouch on the private power of capital upon whose successful operation the state and its revenues continue to depend.

Although Pahl and Winkler designate a more directive state than does Cawson, both conceptions recognise the characteristic mode of state intervention in corporatism to be a delegated enforcement of policies which discriminate between categories on a corporate rather than individual basis. State administrators turn to the key interest groups for support in alleviating fiscal and planning problems, and the co-operation of labour leaders is regarded as particularly important in excluding 'excessive' wage and other demands from their members. Archetypal examples of corporatism, in the view of most corporatist theorists, are nationally-agreed tripartite policies on prices and incomes forged by capital, labour and the state.

Market, bureaucratic and corporatist forms of decision making

Claus Offe (1975), and Cawson and Saunders (1983), have sought to distinguish corporatist modes of state decision making from market or bureaucratic modes. For Offe this takes the form of analysing the strategies available to the modern capitalist state in aiding production. There are three such strategies, none of which is adequate. First, new bureaucratic machinery is incapable of generating innovative solutions to problems of generating support for business. Second, pluralist decision making may solve the problem of consent, but poses severe risks for capital accumulation by allowing more influence to non-capitalist interests. Finally, corporatism involves the major social groupings in decision making but is unstable because it is class-biased in favour of capital and thus generates working-class opposition, while as a mode of decision making it lacks legitimacy.

Cawson and Saunders extend Offe's analysis and combine it with a model of state spending formulated by O'Connor (1973). O'Connor distinguishes between three main categories of spending: *social expenses*, which consists of projects and services necessary for social order and legitimation, such as the welfare system, but which are not directly productive; *social investment*, which consist of services that increase productivity and profitability, such as land clearance or transport systems; and *social consumption*, such as social insurance, which socialises and lowers the reproductive and other costs of labour. This model of state expenditures is incorporated by Cawson and Saunders into a theory of different modes of state action that generates an ideal-typical framework for analysing resource allocation.

a. The market mode

This rests on the assumption of invisible and spontaneous mechanisms in the market that allow resources to be allocated independently of the exercise of political authority. The state's role is minimal and facilitative, guaranteeing only basic requirements for accumulation such as private property and the legal enforcement of contracts. 'There is no attempt to plan the allocation of investment or other economic resources; capital flows to where the rate of return can be maximised' (Cawson and Saunders, 1983, p. 15).

b. The bureaucratic mode

In this mode resources are allocated authoritatively by state institutions. Associated with state socialism, the allocation process is governed by explicit rules and commands. The inefficiency, inflexibility and inability to take account of unforeseen consequences make it an inappropriate method for resource allocation in capitalist production.

c. The corporatist mode

In contrast corporatist decisions are neither imposed by objective laws nor by a determinate political authority, but reflect the outcome of a bargaining process between corporate interests and the state. The assumption is that each party is able independently to exercise some form of sanction. 'Power is thus neither pluralistically dispersed, nor concentrated, but polycentric within an overall hierarchy' (ibid. p. 16). This form of state interventionism is institutionalised by ad hoc or quasi-autonomous agencies on which the major interests are directly represented and which implements policies discriminately rather than as in the bureaucratic mode through a universally applicable code of rules. Privilege is accorded to firms or sectors with high accumulation potential, for example through specifically negotiated planning agreements. In this mode the state is neither directive nor coupled to an autonomous private sphere, but is intermeshed with it in a complex way which undermines the traditional distinction between public and private.

Cawson and Saunders suggest that ideal-typically the different forms of interventionism and resource allocation are linked to the different types of state spending. For example, social investment can be operated bureaucratically as the state does not require the active co-operation of external groups while the fiscal importance of such spending necessitates that it be firmly controlled. The distribution of taxation revenue such as social security benefits can be organised reasonably efficiently and bureaucratically on the basis of universal criteria, such as citizenship, embodying notions of individual need. Social investment on production, however, tends to be operated in a corporatist manner, with an emphasis on planning and closed negotiations with functional associations to mask its discriminatory nature. On the other hand, social consumption, as expenditure on the reproduction of labour power rather than production directly, can be left subject to the uncertainties of pluralist decision making. Because social consumption expenditure is often located at local government level, threats to production as a consequence of local control or influence from non-capitalist interests can be circumscribed by centrally imposed controls.

Corporatism may develop out of the failure or instabilities of the market or bureaucratic modes. Offe (1984), for example, argues that there is little basis for the liberal belief that market mechanisms are self-corrective or that labour power and capital expelled from the commodity form will be reintegrated spontaneously and automatically into exchange relationships. Rather, 'the key problem of capitalist societies is the fact that the dynamics of capitalist development seem to exhibit a constant tendency to paralyse the commodity form of value' (p. 122). On the other hand bureaucratic solutions for the failure of exchange principles threaten capitalist accumulation because of 'over-regulation'. Corporatism, however, recognises the need for non-commodified forms of support for capital by the state but without challenging the private ownership of production by limiting, and if necessary retreating from, its interventions. Nonetheless, corporatism also has its attendant dangers for capitalist accumulation and orderly governance. It dissolves the institutional separateness of the state from society and undermines it as a coherent and strictly circumscribed apparatus of power. Rather, policy-making powers are 'contracted out' to consortia of semi-private representatives, and the shift to functional forms of representation breaks down the bourgeois definition of politics as the struggle for institutionalised state power.

Offe may underestimate the importance of the state recognised in market strategies. Those governments adopting such strategies in recent years, such as those of the New Right in the USA and Britain, in seeking to withdraw the state from a range of activities do so as a means of *strengthening* its authority, as a strategy that protects the fiscal position and governance of the state from 'overload' and the rising expectations encouraged by the welfare state. Nonetheless, to suggest that corporatism seeks to obscure the distinction between the public and the private presupposes that there is some real tension or distinction between the two respective organising principles of market society and political democracy that must be mediated. As Offe observes, this is by no means an undisputed assumption. Marxist–Leninists, for example, see bourgeois democracy as serving only capitalists' interests and as means for persuading the masses that it does not. There is no incompatibility between the two spheres. Alternatively, pluralist democratic theorists claim that there is no tension between the two realms because democratic arrangements control capitalism in the social interest. However, there is a well-established tradition of thought, spanning both left and right, and which is a vital source of reinvigorated corporatist theory in the 1970s and 1980s, that regards mass democracy as constituting at least a potential threat for capital. Consequently the compatibility of capitalism and democracy depends on institutions that serve to contain popular or working-class demands. Historically the gradual development of mass party systems and the welfare state are seen as serving this purpose. Michels (1915), Weber (1958) and Offe and Wiesenthal (1980), are among those that have referred to the very dynamic of the organisational form of the large-scale working-class party, allied with the imperatives of electoral competition, as debilitating class politics and radicalisation. In this view at least three consequences of the organisational form of the competitive labour party – ideological deradicalisation, deactivation of the membership, and erosion of collective identity – contribute to the compatibility of capitalism and democracy.

For Offe, the decline in party systems in both articulating and resolving conflict leads to the development of alternative institutions. Corporatism is one such alternative (social movements and authoritarian repression are others). It seeks to 'depoliticise' public policy and defines issues as 'technical' or 'scientific', thus reducing the scope of legitimate participants and public accountability. In comparison to both parliamentary and bureaucratic forms of policy making, its functional superiority derives from its informal and non-public procedures. However, as we shall see in considering corporatism as a form of interest intermediation more closely, corporatism also has its limitations and dysfunctions.

Corporatism as interest intermediation

The literature on corporatism has expanded rapidly since the 1970s and increasingly includes a range of empirical work. However, the topic has come to be marked by ambiguity and misunderstanding. As Panitch (1980, p. 159) points out, 'considerable confusion must attend a field in which the central concept is variously understood to connote a distinct economic system or mode of production . . . , a state form . . . and a system of interest intermediation'. To which we could add that corporatism is also used to distinguish a particular ideology, often associated with social democratic parties, that of 'social harmony' or 'class collaboration'. Yet there are definite signs of agreement amongst corporatist scholars that corporatism designates a distinct pattern of interest intermediation. Following Schmitter (1979), one of its leading theorists, we see corporatism as different from pluralism in the amount of decisional authority a group acquires from the state and the role of interest groups as co-responsible 'partners' in governance and societal guidance. Thus corporatism involves not just bargaining between the state and functional groups but also the implementation of public policy through the groups themselves. The term 'intermediation' rather than representation is used to distinguish it from pluralism and to connote the 'Janus-faced' character of corporatist interest organisations. Not only do such interest groups represent or advance their members' interests but they are also prepared to enforce on their members compliance with agreements reached with the state and perhaps other groups in the 'national interest'.

Apart from interest intermediation and policy implementation as distinguishing traits of corporatism, 'there is a strain towards representational monopoly in corporatism which contrasts with the opposite stress on heterogeneity and diversity of all pluralist theories' (Crouch, 1983, p. 455). Membership discipline of the corporatist kind cannot easily be maintained if members can easily form or join a multiplicity of competing organisations. Nor is disciplined and detailed co-operation really possible if a variety of groups have to agree. The state has an interest in minimising the number of groups it has to deal with and in legitimising the more 'responsible' and representative groups. As Streeck (1982) has noted in a study of West German business associations an important way in which the state can lend such groups organisational support is by setting rules of access to political influence that are favourable to them. By, for example, not seeing individual firms but only 'peak' associations. Although some theorists, such as Lehmbruch (1979), place less emphasis on tendencies to representational monopoly in corporatism, preferring instead to stress concertation and bargaining between the groups themselves, most follow Schmitter (1979, p. 13) in his ideal-typical representation of corporatist organisations as 'recognised or licensed (if not created) by the state and granted a deliberate representational monopoly within their respective categories in exchange for observing certain controls on the selection of leaders and articulation of demands and supports'.

Clearly the role of the state is less passive than found in pluralist accounts. However, the extent and type of interventionism varies according to which of two sub-types of corporatism is being referred: societal or state corporatism. Schmitter denotes state corporatism as imposed 'from above' as public policy in which territorial or functional groups are closely subordinated to central bureaucracies. Representation is entirely replaced by the disciplinary role and the state uses 'corporations' for its own purposes and derives its legitimacy from elsewhere. In societal corporatism the system of interest intermediation is more 'bottom up' in that the legitimacy of the state is substantially dependent on the activities of autonomous interests which perform the dual function of representation and discipline. This type of corporatism is more likely to be found in multi-layered, patchworked political systems and cultures with competing ideologies and parties. It is clearly much closer to pluralism than is state corporatism and 'seems a concomitant, if not ineluctable companion of the post-liberal, advanced capitalist, organised democratic welfare state; state corporatism seems to be the defining element of, if not structural necessity for, the anti-liberal, delayed capitalist, authoritarian, neo-mercantilist state' (Schmitter, 1979, p. 22).

A criticism of some corporatist analyses is the variable way in which the role of the state is conceived. In some accounts the state has a marked directive role, whereas in others (e.g. Nedelman and Meier, 1979) a corporatist state typically leaves matters to the interest groups. In similar fashion, while some Marxist interpretations of corporatism see it as a means of excluding popular demands by concentrating power in the higher executive reaches of the state, others regard corporatism as indicative of a 'franchise' or 'fragmentary' state in which power is parcelled out to functional groups (Cawson, 1982; Wolff, 1977). One response is to suggest that this interpretative variety simply reflects empirical reality. For example, the state generally has played an active part alongside unions and employers' associations in establishing incomes policy in the Netherlands and Austria, while in Sweden and West Germany the emphasis is on bipartite arrangements relatively free from government interference (Crouch, 1983, p. 455).

Certainly in comparison with pluralism, and whatever the type of corporatism or its circumstances, there is an assumption in corporatism that the state more actively forms and sustains the system of interest intermediation and is deeply interested in its outcomes. It is not the essentially passive recipient of the demands of organised interests. Corporatist models also tend to incorporate variables other than socio-economic ones in accounting for interest group formation, particularly the impact of national historical experience, the weight of intra-organisational factors in defining interests, and the role of the state in structuring relations among interests (Berger, 1981). In response to new public policies groups may have to organise to defend themselves against the state, or because other groups in similar issue areas have organised in response to state policy.

Offe (1981) suggests that the state shapes interests through the incentives that particular regime types provide for particular patterns of organisation and through the authoritative attribution of public status to interest groups. This way provides a group with legal rights to participation in law-making and implementation and to public funds. Inevitably corporatism raises questions of representation and accountability within groups that tend not to be regarded as significant issues in pluralism. Rather, in pluralism the existence of groups was explained by the rational calculations that a self-interested individual would make about the utility of associating with others to pursue objectives. As we noted in Chapter 1, Olson (1965), for example, developed a theory that only where individual self-interest and collective good coincided would groups be formed at all. As even non-members benefited from collective goods sought by organisations, the provision to members only of goods or 'selective incentives' was required to generate membership. In corporatism, however, the leaders of organisations may have to strike a balance between membership demands and the requirements of public policy. There may be inherent organisational needs in interest associations that lead away from pluralism and towards corporatism, such as the offers of additional resources by the state on a more reliable basis. Consequently, organisations have to balance a concern with the 'logic of membership', the structure and kind of membership interests within an organisation, and the 'logic of influence', which ultimately is concerned with the conditions and processes of political influence (Streeck, 1982).

It is difficult to say where the state ends and private interests begin in corporatism as part of its development is that interests take on semi-public characteristics. In Britain particularly it has long been difficult to precisely locate the boundary between the public and private sectors within the economy. The development of shared powers between the public and private sectors has had the advantage of encouraging co-operation between government and businessmen who would have resisted having it forced on them through the state. Although corporatist developments have occurred in Britain, it is generally regarded as little-formed because of the strength of a liberal culture, a decentralised but strong trade union movement, the disorganisation of the business sector, and powerful financial interests. Grant and Marsh (1977), in a study of the Confederation of British Industry (CBI), came to the view that tripartism, as a sub-type of liberal corporatism, could not be said to genuinely exist. Neither the CBI nor the Trades Union Congress (TUC) is fully representative of the interests they are supposed to represent, and neither can control their membership. We can, however, point to the relatively recent development of quasi-governmental agencies ('quangos') as displaying corporatist characteristics. Quasi-governmental agencies help to combat decision difficulties by 'factorising' administration so that different decision functions are allocated to different agencies. The picture is one of 'non-executant' central departments in which a generalist civil service controlled by elected politicians controls only overall funding while detailed policy implementation and operational administration rests with the professionals (Dunleavy, 1983, p. 279). These corporatist characteristics reflect the organisational fragmentation of policy-making in the modern state and are a response to the difficulties in managing advanced complex societies.

The dimensions of corporatism

Although most attention generally has been paid to the national level in the corporatist literature, and whether a particular country can be properly described as 'corporatist' or not, it is now recognised that corporatist arrangements can be found in particular sectors or issue areas even if it is generally lacking elsewhere in a country. 'Micro-corporatist' arrangements may influence the organisation of a society more than highly publicised tripartite bargaining which may not endure. A recent study of the micro-electronics industry leads to a similar conclusion. Here, as in other policy sectors in the British system 'are to be found tripartite structures and a tendency to concentrate on smaller manageable problems rather than try for agreement on radical change' (Richardson, 1982, p. 346). Grant (1985) notes that corporatism can be associated with a retreat of the state. In Britain the dissolution of most of the statutory training boards under the 1979 Conservative government led to their substitution by arrangements generally constructed by the relevant employers' association and monitored by the tripartite Manpower Services Commission. It also expanded the number of 'public–private' organisations, including local enterprise agencies and bodies such as the Financial Institutional Groups (FIG) as part of a policy to induce private investment into inner-city areas. FIG is comprised mainly of seconded senior financial managers from the private sector working under government direction and devising schemes for facilitating local authority–private company ventures to develop industrial projects in blighted urban areas. The state may also encourage or recognise corporatism as an alternative to bureaucratic control. Moran (1983), for example, describes the 'anticipatory corporatism' of the financial organisations that comprise the City in London and its development of self-regulatory mechanisms as a means of avoiding more direct controls. Similarly, the British government's refusal to grant chambers of commerce the public law status and compulsory membership of their continental counterparts has contributed to more liberal corporatist forms of public support for chambers (King, 1983). Although economic and other associations may genuinely regret corporatist arrangements, in contrast to bureaucratic and legal modes of resource allocation and regulation, members are more likely to accept them and to feel less rigidly controlled and able to avoid their more irksome consequences.

Following Offe (1981), therefore, it is useful to regard corporatism as an 'axis' of development, rather than a situation, and to have as the criterion the extent to which public status is attributed to organised interest groups. Thus corporatism depends on the number of dimensions in which groups are affected, and increases with:

a. *resource status*
The extent to which the resources of an interest organisation are supplied by the state, e.g. direct subsidies, tax exemptions, forced membership, etc.

b. *representation status*
The extent to which the range of representation is defined through political decision, e.g. a public definition of the range of substantive areas in which an interest organisation may operate and/or of the political membership.

c. *organisation status*
The extent to which internal relations between rank-and-file members of the organisation are regulated.
d. *procedural status*
The extent to which interest organisations are licensed, recognised and invited to assume, together with a specified set of other participants, a role in legislation, the judicial system, policy planning and implementation, or even granted the right of self-administration.

The delineation of specific dimensions of corporatism allows us to recognise that positive readings on one scale could be accompanied by negative showings on others. Moreover, as Streeck (1982) observes in a study of West German business associations, corporatist arrangements tend not to be the result of a grand corporatist design but tend to emerge almost unnoticed by, and sometimes even against the will of, participants who still hold strong pluralist convictions. The devolution of public authority to associations is resorted to pragmatically, or opportunistically, by both sides as an expedient solution to individual problems.

Moreover, the routinisation and demands of large complex political institutions tend to draw many economic interest groups especially into a web of public contacts and decision making once they cross the 'state parameter'. As Streeck (1982, p. 271) observes,

> The pluralist ideal of independently-defined interests that are independently pursued by self-sufficient actors presupposes a degree of strategic autonomy that business associations enjoy no more than anyone else . . . given the unpredictable pressure and needs of day-to-day political decision-making . . . interests may be best advanced by investing in 'interwoven' structures of continuing contact and communications with state agencies that provide for guaranteed presence in the decision-making process and that permit associations to react pragmatically to whatever issues the system may produce.

The result tends to be an ambivalence in attitudes to the state, with interest group leaders often retaining pluralist self-definitions of their role, especially in dealings with the membership. As ideology pluralism has greater legitimacy than corporatism, which may suffer from its earliest fascist connotations, not least among state officials whose professed belief tends to be that all interest groups are voluntary organisations free from state determination.

Who benefits?

An issue that features large in the corporatist literature concerns the outcome of corporatist processes, namely the question 'who benefits?' The 'class-theoretical' approach to corporatism, exemplified by Panitch (1980), argues that corporatism, primarily defined as tripartite agreements between state, business and unions, is a device for drawing the workers into the capitalist system. Once integrated they are forced to accept policies inimicable to their interests, such as prices and incomes restraint which lowers wages and standards of living. Thus corporatism is a political structure designed to protect capital in periods of crisis and declining profitability. As such, Panitch regards corporatism as inherently unstable, for the working class, particularly the trade union rank-and-file members, resist incorporation into the state.

This class-theoretical approach challenges the tripartite, group interpretation of corporatism by arguing that despite the formal equality of partnership in negotiations, the outcome of corporatist agreements are class-biased and asymmetrical. This is a persuasive approach as governments have sought to protect capital accumulation and restrain wages in this way. Moreover, the organisational form for capital is rather different from that for labour. Capitalist associations generally lack the intermediary capacity of trade unions and do not control their members in the same way. While trade unions are vital for workers in creating the bargaining power and collective will to overcome the market weakness of individual workers, business organisations tend to represent existing power, that which is defined at the level of individual capitals or members firms. Offe and Wiesenthal (1980) argue that capital has at its command three different forms of collective action to define and defend its interests: the firm itself, informal co-operation, and the business association. Workers are dependent on formal association alone. Capitalist associations defend in the political arena those individual interests (tariffs, tax, etc.) that are shared, and they have little substantial control over the actions that their members choose to pursue. Indeed, as King (1985) observes in a study of a major British chamber of commerce, the problem that business organisations tend to face is less one of controlling demanding members than of resurrecting any interest at all from the bulk of the membership in their representational activities. Corporatism, therefore, unlike the situation for labour, involves little political control of capital.

However, it would be mistaken to assume that corporatism imposes no costs on capitalists. Jessop (1979), writing from a Marxist perspective, points out that business does not fully support corporatism and that the contradictory needs of capital (such as that between finance and manufacturing capital) creates difficulties in establishing stable corporatist arrangements. Certainly capitalists are often very reluctant to become involved in corporatism and it is doubtful that we can simply attribute this to an inability to perceive their own true interests. Corporatism has the tendency to spread over time, imposing irksome constraints on entrepreneurial sovereignty and endangering property rights, which 'is a rather heavy potential price to pay for predictable labour costs and social peace' (Schmitter, 1982, p. 277). Cawson (1985) makes the point that where labour organisation is sufficiently strong and social democratic parties entrenched the outcome may be redistributive corporatism, as found in Scandinavia. At local level, too, in Britain can be found a form of 'left-wing corporatism' as some authorities adopt 'restructuring for labour' policies in which public investment is extended to firms willing to agree to change industrial relations practices to increase the level of employee and union participation.

Governments are also aware of the potential costs of corporatism at the national level. New Right administrations have seen the post-war welfare state as interfering with the ability of the capitalist economy to reorganise production following the oil price rises and other crises of the 1970s. The 'supply side' of the economy, particularly labour, becomes more rigid and 'sticky' and unable to respond to changing market forces. Offe (1984) suggests that corporatism may favour and facilitate a non-statist socialist strategy by threatening the coherence and relative autonomy of the state and opening up new areas of social contestation. Consequently corporatism may only develop when capital and labour recognise that both stand to gain, perhaps as a means of securing new investment and combating unemployment. In some cases the cost of mutually-recognised interests between capital and labour may be passed on to the consumer, which is the party to lose from class-collaboration.

Corporatism tends to be attractive to business only under special circumstances. Business is inevitably favoured politically by the dependence of government on the privately-owned means of capital accumulation in market societies, in which a large category of major decisions is turned over to businessmen who become a kind of public official (Lindblom, 1977). Given at least the potential costs of corporatism the often lukewarm attitude of capitalists to it is understandable. It is a less preferred source of influence for capital than the market and may occur only when its economic power is sufficiently weakened to threaten its influence in the political process, perhaps as a result of increased political power for trade unions and socialist parties.

However, corporatism should not be judged simply in terms of its contribution to economic performance but also as a distinctive mode of governance (Grant, 1985). Despite its lack of legitimacy in comparison with pluralism, corporatism may provide new opportunities for political participation and contribute to political order and stability. Schmitter (1981, p. 313), for example, detects 'a strong positive relationship between a societal corporatist mode of interest intermediation and relative governability' in advanced capitalist societies. Such a view suggests that in at least some circumstances corporatism is the best or at least a stable political shell for capitalism and perhaps the predominant form for the future. If so, there may be signs of its development at local level, too.

Local corporatism

The relevancy of corporatist analysis for local political processes is still being established. Cawson and Saunders (1983), for example, extend their typology of state expenditures and different modes of decision making to the allocation of functions between central, regional and local government. This allocation to different levels of government plays a vital role in resolving the contradictory pressures on government in market societies. Cawson and Saunders's 'dual-state' model locates social investment expenditures within central and regional government structures that are insulated from popular control. At this level are more likely to be found corporatist arrangements reflecting the state's primary interest in securing the needs of capital accumulation. Politics is class-based and expressed in the hierarchy of capital and labour associations. On the other hand, social consumption expenditure is largely in the hands of local government, and here are found non-class, consumption–reproduction struggles (over education, housing, health-care provision etc.), and policy making is characterised by an imperfect pluralism in which other than capitalist interests are likely to prevail. However, because of the financial and institutional dependency of local government on the centre, local consumption demands and decision making can be severely bounded.

We should be clear, however, that the Cawson and Saunders model consists of a set of 'ideal types', and the thesis predicts only tendencies towards functional specialisation across institutional levels. In reality most expenditure could be classified in two or more categories, with education, for example, being seen as either investment, expenses or consumption. Furthermore, it may be that expenditures take on particular functional characteristics as a consequence of the level of government which undertakes it, rather than governments simply responding to a predetermined set of functional requirements on the state apparatus (Dunleavy, 1984, p. 72). For example, in circumstances where education is nationally administered it may take on more of an investment function, whereas when it is locally administered it may assume more of an expenses or consumption function. That is, the level of government determines the type of expenditure, rather than the reverse.

The model advanced by Cawson and Saunders allows for local corporatist developments, particularly if the local state becomes more involved in production issues, and they discern 'corporatist elements' in certain strategic planning functions undertaken by English county councils. More recently, Cawson (1985) has pointed to corporatist developments as a consequence of increased local state intervention in the economy, particularly by a number of the metropolitan counties. Simmie (1981) and Flynn (1983) have also pointed to corporatist characteristics emerging in the planning process in Britain at local level, and the formation of ad hoc bodies allowing more direct involvement by larger firms in the policy process. Economic decline can also generate corporatist alliances between local politicians, capital and labour in defence of local economies (Urry, 1983), although generally local tripartism as opposed to capital–state bilaterism may emerge less frequently as trade unions traditionally have been disinclined to become involved in local as opposed to national public policy. Chambers of commerce in the United Kingdom have also become more formally involved in local public policy making and implementation, particularly in the administration of the urban aid programme (King, 1983).

Corporatism and welfare

A persisting question in the literature is whether corporatism is a phenomenon confined to the economy and economic associations. A number of writers have sought to extend corporatist analyses for an understanding of the welfare state. Cawson (1982), for example, argues that corporatism as a specific combination of representation and intervention is not a phenomenon confined to the economy. 'To dismiss the significance of corporatism because of the instability of one of its forms – tripartism – is to overlook the much more firmly embedded structures of corporate representation in a far wider area of social policy making' (p. 41). He suggests that the National Health Service is particularly characterised by corporatist policy making, and that the most significant groups are the professions (e.g. medical practitioners) and the public sector trade unions. These groups cannot be reduced to the division between capital and labour. Rather, reinterpreting the growth of the welfare state in corporatist terms suggests that it results from the bargaining process between the state and providers, rather than a responsiveness to the needs of consumers or clients. Similarly, if the welfare state is successfully defended from a strategy of welfare expenditure cutting it will be because it directly challenges the power of corporate groups.

It is worth noting that in Cawson's interpretation corporatism remains in the sphere of 'production' even in the field of social policy. He is not suggesting, of course, that all social policy decision making is corporatist – the administration of social services benefits is bureaucratic and legal–rational – but that in some areas, education, for example, the collaboration of professional producer groups in the determination of goals has been regarded as important by the state. Moreover, corporatist institutions, especially at regional level, are emerging in the health service outside the direct control of local authorities, and the integration of health policy-making in largely appointed regional and area health authorities seeks to insulate it from popular pressures.

A more explicitly consumption-based corporatism than Cawson's emphasis on production is offered by Harrison (1984). However, he also notes difficulties with a class-orientated approach to welfare corporatism in that welfare institutions are seen too much as integrated and largely dependent mechanisms subordinated to the process of a wider emergent corporate industrial state. Harrison's solution is to think in terms of a state-organised consumption structure which involves access by some interests and the exclusion of others. Full recognition of needs is far more readily accorded to higher-status groups, while other groups are often seen in terms of a 'public burden' concept, rather than an incorporation of recognised and deserving consumer interests. In this latter group are to be found many of the unemployed, the severely disabled, the low paid, ethnic minorities, and many disadvantaged females. As we have noted earlier, however, it may be that corporatist analyses, especially of the welfare state, underestimate the distinctive professionalisation of policy making and too readily seek to subsume it within corporatist, pluralist and bureaucratic categories. Dunleavy (1984), for example, argues that Offe's typology of pluralist, bureaucratic and corporatist decision modes 'seems restrictive in leaving no readily identifiable location for policy systems dominated by the professions' (p. 76). Although the professions form important interest groups it is their 'ideological' influence – the communication of new fashions and ideas – that helps constitute a distinctive technocratic mode of professional decision making.

Conclusion

Corporatist models have been criticised by those who argue that there is little that is distinctive about corporatism that cannot be understood as effectively within a pluralist paradigm (Martin,

1983). In this chapter we have sought to delineate the major characteristics of corporatism, its 'private–public' characteristic and most notably intermediation and policy-implementation by functional interest groups, which do mark it off conceptually from pluralism. This is not to suggest that corporatism, particularly the liberal form, does not share features with pluralism, such as a certain distribution of power, the importance of interest groups, and the relative absence of a dominating and increasingly all-powerful centralised state as found in some accounts. Encouragingly, there is evidence of increased empirical investigation within the corporatist model, particularly in the long-neglected area of business association. Corporatism is also providing an impetus to empirical analysis of local or 'micro' groups as a suitable corrective and complement to the well-established emphasis on national tripartism. In Chapter 7 we look more closely at some of these developments within the field of local politics. First, however, we examine the notion of power and critiques of its behavioural conceptualism in the sociology of democracy as opposed to a more structuralist interpretation, for many of these are substantially located in the study of urban processes.

6

Power

Introduction

We examine here differing concepts of power presented by sociologists and political scientists in recent accounts of political processes. Consequently we shall be less concerned with terminological definitions of power and associated concepts, such as authority, influence, force, coercion, etc., than with exploring the different philosophies or values – ways of seeing the world – that underpin various approaches for understanding political decision making. As we shall see, this is no easy task for social scientists are considerably at odds as to how to go about assessing power. Many share Steven Lukes's view (1974) that the concept of power itself is an 'essentially contested concept' which rules out a universally accepted agreement because different conceptions of power are tied to quite fundamental differences of values. Nonetheless it is possible to identify a number of major approaches for studying power which elucidate the primary methodological issues involved.

Sociological approaches to power raise a central concern: whether behaviouralism provides the best, or only, approach for the analysis of policy processes. Associated with this issue is the problem of 'decisionalism' – to what extent, if at all, it is useful to consider policy outcomes as the consequences of choice(s) made by autonomous individual(s), perhaps in conflict or co-operation with others? How should we explain those situations of inequity or injustice, for example, which are not the consequence of any obvious 'decision', or which provoke no objection? This, of course, raises even trickier problems, that of specifying 'interests'. Specifically, what are we to understand by an individual's or group's 'interests'? Is the individual to be regarded as the sole judge of his or her interests, and in what circumstances?

The sociological discussion of power cuts to the heart of these methodological dilemmas because in recent years the previously well-established behavioural or individualistic orthodoxy in conceptualising power has been severely and persistently challenged. For many years the study of power seemed a relatively unproblematical exercise and was largely based on the work of Weber. The central assumption was that power is a characteristic of conflictful, observable relationships between two or more individuals in which one set of wills prevailed over another. The advantage of such an apparently commonsensical and simple approach was that it was perfectly congruent with the established methodological canons of social science. Power is assessed by requiring observation, empirical testability, and data on individual action. Moreover, while some theorists, such as Talcott Parsons (1967), doubted the emphasis on conflict as the revelatory mechanism by which power relations were exhibited and argued that power was a collective resource usable on everyone's behalf, few theorists challenged the notion that the exercise of power usually involved a conflict of wills and preferences between knowledgeable individuals. Individuals were aware of their interests which became reflected in preferences or demands articulated more or less strongly, depending on how intensely a person felt about a matter, in social and political arenas. The absence of preference articulation, i.e. inaction, indicated satisfaction that interests were either being advanced or not endangered, while power was a reflection of success in the relatively public clash of policy preferences.

In recent years, however, a more 'radical' approach to power has challenged a number of these assumptions. It rests largely on the claim that the positivistic, behavioural and conflictful conceptions of power ignored the role of ideology in human affairs. Ideas, beliefs and values are not necessarily the fully voluntary or reflexive constructs of autonomous individuals, but can be used as symbolic or cultural resources in securing or maintaining dominance by one group over another. The result of such an exercise of power is not necessarily conflict but its absence, not action but inaction. Perhaps most contentiously of all, the successful imposition by the powerful of its 'definition of the situation' over the powerless leads to the view that, in some circumstances at least, individuals may not be aware of what is in their best interests and therefore may not be the best judge of them.

Some of these objections to established conceptions of power are not new. Marxists, for example, have long argued that individual consciousness was a social class product and not simply ideational reflection by free individuals. There is also a tradition in non-Marxist sociology, perhaps best exemplified by the work of Emile Durkheim and Talcott Parsons, that emphasises the normative and value constraints on individual action and which questions the assumption that individual preferences are freely constructed. However, this view regards values as a collective, social resource, not as in Marxist accounts, the manipulative means for obtaining compliance from individuals in the interests of particular groups or classes. Nonetheless, recent critiques of behaviouralist approaches to power now more clearly recognise the need for empirical substantiation of claims about power relations when these involve reference to inaction and the causal influence of ideology. That is, claims about power must have empirical application and be able to generate hypotheses that can be framed in terms of it that are in principle verifiable. Mere assertions of 'false consciousness', for example, are regarded as generally insufficient without an identification of those contrary conditions that open such assertions to tests of falsifiability. Moreover, recent critiques of orthodox conceptions of power differ in the extent to which they depart from methodological individualism and to the degree to which relevant tests of power are to be hypothetically constructed or empirically located. To understand this we need to explore in greater detail the different conceptions in sociological approaches to power in decision making.

Three conceptions of power

A useful framework for discussing the analysis of power is provided by Steven Lukes (1974). He distinguishes three 'conceptual maps' that underlie three major models of power. First, there is the one-dimensional view, associated with the work of Max Weber but which predominated among political scientists in the USA in the post Second World War years, particularly in the work of the pluralists (see Chapter 1). Secondly, the two-dimensional view offers a critique of Weberian or pluralist behaviouralism through the use of the notion 'non-decision', although it is clear that this provides only a partial critique. Consequently, a three-dimensional view has emerged which offers a more thoroughgoing challenge to the methodological and theoretical assumptions of 'decisionalism' and which it is claimed gives a deeper and more satisfactory analysis of power relations than the first two models.

Decisional or pluralist accounts of power

Although several British and other European writers have contributed to contemporary theoretical debates on power, most of the empirical work that has underpinned these discussions is derived from analyses of power relations in American local communities. Very few community power studies have been carried out in Britain, partly because of the view that community power analysis is based on the relative weakness of local political institutions compared with private community organisations and groups. In contrast to the United States, British local government is held to be both the formal and real source of power in local communities, and is relatively immune from control by external groups or individuals (Newton, 1976).

Whatever the accuracy of this view, the corpus of substantive power research is undoubtedly American, behaviouralist and primarily local or urban. The seminal study of American community power is Hunter's (1953) study of Atlanta, Georgia, in which Hunter adopted a much more individualistic methodology than those of earlier studies. As Dunleavy (1980) points out, Hunter argued that power could be understood as the property of particular individuals, and this could be measured by the use of a reputational methodology. This involved the observer asking a number of expert 'judges' or 'inside dopesters' in the city (e.g. newspaper editors, leading businessmen and politicians), to nominate a small number of community influentials from lists drawn up by local organisations. Interviews were then carried out to discover the extent of personal interaction between 'influentials' and also which individuals were the chief members in any élites or cliques that were unearthed.

The problem with this technique was that it tended to look for those individuals with the *reputation* for possessing power rather than for those who actually *exercised* it. Yet it is possible for individuals to be falsely attributed with having power and while it may be argued that even false reputations provide the basis for power of a sort, this is not the intention of the methodology. An adequate conception of power should distinguish between dispositional (reputation or potential for power) and episodic (exercise of power) usages, and Hunter's approach did not. Moreover, it was a technique that tended inevitably to produce a picture of élitist, privately-dominated community power structures when replicated elsewhere because it involved a step-by-step winnowing and narrowing of community leaders from ever-shortening lists of potential community influentials.

Consequently, an alternative methodology associated with pluralism developed that challenged both Hunter's reputationalist approach and also its élitist conclusions. A number of theorists, such as Dahl (1961), Polsby (1963) and Wolfinger (1971), argued that to study power researchers should look at actual decisions involving cases of overt political conflict and reject reputationalism. The most influential work was Robert Dahl's study of New Haven, *Who Governs?* Dahl argued that any group with a serious grievance or goal could make it known in New Haven's relatively open political system. He suggested that the researcher could see whether a group was powerful or not by seeing how successful it was in the policy process. Dahl concluded that in New Haven power was widely diffused, and no group was significant across all issues, although some were in particular decisions.

While the pluralist study of power structures aimed to demonstrate that power within the American political system was distributed less cumulatively than Hunter claimed, observers have generally failed to note the essentially similar conception of power employed by both Hunter and the pluralists. Hunter was criticised for ignoring *actual* behaviour or the exercise of power in observable, concrete decision making, but not for his view that power was to be conceived individualistically. For both, power was interpreted as the capacity of one actor to do something affecting another actor which changes the probable pattern of specific future events (Polsby, 1983). We should be clear, therefore, that the notation pluralism refers to a type of power structure, to be distinguished from élitism, rather than a description of a methodology for studying power. The one-dimensional view is probably best characterised as the issue–outcome or the decisional approach, and while it is often associated with pluralist *findings*, this does not follow inevitably.

Dahl describes his 'intuitive idea of power' as the successful attempt by *A* to get *B* to do something he would not otherwise do. This reference to a successful attempt is central, for it indicates that Dahl is referring to the exercise of power in a social relationship. Power is conceived episodically and is to be distinguished from dispositional conceptions of power as an individual's property or capacity in which the individual has a potential for power which may or may not be exercised. The operationalisation of Dahl's concept of power, as found in *Who Governs?*, involves identifying a number of key decisions in the local community and then determining for each decision which participants had put forward proposals that were eventually accepted, which had successfully opposed proposals from others, and which had suggested proposals that were not adopted. Overall, the participants with the greatest proportion of successes out of the total number of successes were then considered to be the most influential.

The emphasis in this approach is seeing who wins or loses in actual decision making by studying concrete, observable behaviour. This behaviour may be observed directly by the researcher, or may be reconstructed from documentation, newspapers, interviews and other sources. Whichever, the approach rests on producing empirical data as evidence for propositions about the exercise of power that have been operationalised for particular settings in a way that enables these propositions to be verified or falsified. Moreover, this data is action-based and exhibited by public policy preferences in decision making. A further central assumption, however, is that decision making involves actual and observable conflict. As Lukes (1974) notes, the pluralists speak of the decisions being about issues in selected (key) issue-areas – the assumption being that such issues are controversial and involve actual conflict. For example, Dahl (1961) argues that one can only strictly test the hypothesis of a ruling class if there are cases including key political decisions in which the preferences of the hypothetical ruling élite run counter to those of any other likely group that might be suggested, and in such cases, the preferences of the élite regularly prevail. However, as Lukes (1974) remarks, this focus on behaviour in the making of decisions over key or important issues as involving actual or observable conflict is not required in Dahl's definition of power, which merely refers to *A* successfully affecting what *B* does, and which presumably could occur in the absence of observable conflicts. As we shall see, critics of the decisional or issue–outcome view make use particularly of the possibility of non-conflict or inaction as part of a successful exercise of power in their critique of its behaviouralist assumptions.

In summary, therefore, conflict over freely-made and articulated preferences by individuals, which is accessible to the observer, provides the empirical test of power in the decisional or one-dimensional approach. This raises the concept of interests employed in the analysis. Interests are defined as articulated policy preferences. To infer that an individual's interests may be unknown to the individual or mistakenly perceived is rejected as unscientific for it then becomes impossible to disprove any empirical proposition on power relations. The presumption by the observer of a set of 'real' interests not recognised or articulated by an individual only involves a substitution by the observer of his own prejudices. But it is around these particular issues that alternative conceptions of power to that found in decisionalism have been constructed.

Non-decisionalism or the two faces of power

An important group of critics of Dahl's approach are known as 'non-decisionalists', as described because of their stress on the importance of issues not discussed within the political arena. A problem with the decisional approach is that the issues selected for study are those already recognised by the political system as issues. Moreover, the behavioural definition of interests as articulated preferences suggests that issues involve conflict of policy preferences which are regarded as conflicts of interest.

Yet conflicts of interests may not be indicated by conflicts of articulated policy preferences for the possibilities for effective political action are not evenly distributed. Not only do individuals and groups differ in the resources that they possess (e.g. wealth, time, literacy, etc.), but they differ also in the way they are regarded by society. Those groups with low public or social esteem may have great difficulty in having their claims taken seriously. Some groups may find that a consideration of their wishes or interests never takes place in the political arena, and any analysis of the distribution of power based solely on the analysis of decisions would not detect this. The most powerless would not be those who did least well in having their preferences accepted, but those whose wishes or interests were never considered at all.

The assumption of the decisionalists is that when people do not advance policy preferences then this is because they either do not particularly care about, or are generally satisfied with, existing or proposed arrangements. If they did feel intensely about a matter then the political system is sufficiently open for people to be motivated to express their views. However, this raises the question of the process whereby the will to engage in political action becomes manifest. Moreover, as Saunders (1979) notes, if the objective possibility for such action is present (i.e. through access to the necessary resources), yet inactivity results, then we need to explain why the will to act has apparently failed to develop.

This clearly suggests that analysts of power may be as concerned with inaction as they are with action. Instead of assuming, with the decisionalists, that inaction indicates satisfaction or agreement with existing arrangements, inaction may reveal an inability to advance a set of interests which, over a period, may induce a fatalism or resignation about even trying. On the other hand, too, inactivity may not be a reflection of weakness or suppression, but the reverse. The very powerful may rarely need to act to advance or maintain their interests because they are already taken into account by decision makers. The supreme exercise of power may be the capacity not to have to act at all.

One of the earliest attempts to challenge the one-dimensional or issue–outcome view that political inaction indicated unconcern or satisfaction is found in Bachrach and Baratz (1962; 1970). Referring to the 'two faces of power', they suggest that while power may be reflected in concrete, observable decisions ('the first face'), it is also exercised when powerful individuals use social values and institutional practices to limit political discussion to only those issues that are relatively harmless to them ('the second face'). Not only may those in powerful positions simply ignore claims by the less powerful, but the less powerful may not advance its claims because it anticipates that it will not succeed or, if it fails, invite retaliation.

Bachrach and Baratz develop the notion of 'non-decision-making' to criticise the decisional approach for ignoring those areas of policy making where certain interests have been prevented from having a public airing. One reason for this may be a 'mobilisation of bias', which refers to a set of predominant values, beliefs, rituals and institutional procedures (rules of the game) that operate systematically and consistently to the benefit of certain persons and groups. For example, it is often argued that in capitalist societies business and business groups have little difficulty in having their views or proposals accepted as legitimate matters for serious public discussions, whereas labour or the poor encounter much greater suspicion for their aims or objectives. Bachrach and Baratz therefore employ the notion 'non-decision-making' to criticise the behaviouralist assumptions in the one-dimensional or issue-outcome approach to power for unduly emphasising the importance of initiating, deciding and vetoing, i.e. for stressing political *action*. Yet Bachrach and Baratz's position is a difficult one to maintain, particularly when it comes to operationalisation, for it has been pointed out that when it comes to considering non-decision-making there is a multiplicity of events that have not happened from which the researcher may choose. It is in response to such criticisms that Bachrach and Baratz moderate their anti-behaviouralism, for they assert that non-decisions which limit the area of decision making are themselves observable decisions. However, these non-decisions are more covert and less accessible to the investigator than decisions because opposition is thwarted before it reaches the formal stages of authoritative decision making. But signs of this opposition and its thwarting may still be empirically detectable if the analyst digs deep enough.

Yet, as Parry and Morris (1974) argue, if non-decisions are actually observable practices (albeit harder to observe than decisions) the conceptual distinction between decisions and non-decisions tends to collapse. In many cases non-decisions are decisions, although not necessarily the sorts of key decisions studied by Dahl and the decisionalists. What happens, they suggest, is a series of lesser decisions or choices each of which forecloses other courses of action. Therefore, either non-decisions are observable, in which case they may be regarded as a type of decision, or else they are not observable and therefore not open to empirical enquiry. Parry and Morris (1974) suggest that non-responses by élites or the mobilisation of bias against the powerless usually involve some form of visible behaviour sufficient for the vigilant researcher to be alerted to enquiry why claims were not followed through. However, these are properly recognised as decisions, for to do otherwise will be to collapse distinctions between very different political techniques. For example, the term non-decision includes both action and inaction, but some non-decisions involve conscious choices while others may be the outcome of the unconscious acceptance of community values. Therefore, to understand the power and penetrability of any community it is better to replace blanket terms like non-decision with a more precise analysis of the many different patterns decision making can take.

The problem with Parry and Morriss's formulation (and also Bachrach and Baratz's) is that there are cases of non-decision-making where the powerless take no action because, for example, they are aware of the futility of pressing a claim. Indeed, the utility of a notion such as non-decision-making is that it points to the everyday or routinised nature of many power relationships, and it recognises those situations where dominant interests exercise such a degree of influence over the beliefs of the less powerful that it effectively determines not only whether certain demands come to be articulated or taken into account, but also whether people even conceive of such demands. It is not clear from Bachrach and Baratz's analysis whether their acceptance of a behaviouralist interpretation of non-decision-making is based solely on methodological or moral grounds. That is, it could be argued that whilst it may be difficult to empirically test 'false consciousness' propositions it does not follow that situations of 'false consciousness' never occur, only that it is difficult to verify such propositions in a way that allows for their falsifiability (Lukes, 1974). Thus, as with pluralism, observable conflict or action provides the test for power relations and the assumption is that conflicts occur over interests that are consciously articulated as policy preferences, even if it is recognised that some preferences may never reach the formal 'agenda' of public decision making. In the end, therefore, Bachrach and Baratz's notion of non-decision-making reasserts positivism and the decisional paradigm, and rests on the assumption that decisions are choices consciously made by individuals.

However, in criticising Bachrach and Baratz's methodological individualism, Lukes (1974) argues that the bias of a system can be mobilised, recreated and reinforced in ways that are neither consciously chosen nor the intended result of particular individual's choices, but by the socially structured and culturally patterned behaviour of groups and practices of institutions as a function of collective forces and social arrangements. Consequently, it has been argued that the two-dimensional view underestimates the significance of ideology, the imposition of beliefs and the manipulation of values in securing stability and the absence of conflict. While an individual may exercise power over another individual by getting him to do what he would otherwise not do, he also exercises power over him by influencing, shaping and determining his very wants. This takes us on to a consideration of the 'radical' view of power.

Radical approaches to power

Radical approaches to power offer a critique of the behaviouralist assumptions of both the decisionalists and the non-decision-makers. They tend to rest on the claim that rather than actual conflict being necessary to power, the very absence of conflict may reveal the most thoroughgoing use of power in which potential grievances are prevented through the shaping of individual perceptions and wants. Social and political arrangements can be legitimated and accepted by the powerless despite a contradiction between the interests of the powerful, which are advanced or maintained by such arrangements, and the real interests of the powerless, which are not. The necessary methodological corollary is that the observer is able to distinguish between the subjective interests of the participants and their 'real' or 'objective' interests as these are theorised by the observer.

Clearly, such an assertion provokes scientific and moral indignation by those that regard notions of 'false consciousness' or associated concepts as a shorthand way of saying that people do not know what is good for them. As we have seen, too, if it is difficult enough to verify the claims made in Bachrach and Baratz's essentially behaviouralist interpretation of non-decision-making, how much harder it is to meet criteria of adequacy for propositions about the manipulation of cognitions and preferences. However, because such a task is methodologically difficult does not mean that claims for 'false consciousness' should be theoretically ignored, or that, in the absence of conflict, we would assume the existence of consensus. Nonetheless, the identification of real or objective interests, as Lukes (1974) asserts, must rest on empirically supportive and refutable hypotheses.

It is interesting to note, as does Saunders (1979), the seminal role played by Parsons's work on power in the formulation of an empirically verifiable, non-behavioural conception of power. An essential feature of power for Parsons (1967) is that it is less an individual capacity than a facility or system property for achieving collective goals. In liberal democracies the inevitable asymmetry of power possession is justified if power is used for the benefit of society as a whole. That is, the legitimacy for wielding power is dependent on more than the subjective agreement of societal members but also on demonstrating that the objective interests of the powerless have also been met by the powerful. As Saunders (1979) notes, the approach necessarily rests on the central premise that it is possible to identify the real interests of a given individual or group independently of the way in which such interests may be subjectively conceived by those concerned.

But how are these real interests to be identified? First, by rejecting on philosophical grounds the behaviouralist assertion that interests and wants are necessarily the same and that a concept of objective interests which is not consistent with people's own wants or perceptions of their interests is unacceptable. Not only is it possible for someone to want something that he recognises is against his interest (e.g. a cigarette), but it is also possible for someone to mistake his interests. Individuals are often not aware of their motives for acting in a particular way. Scientists have long recognised the existence of unconscious wants. Similarly, theorists of the so-called Frankfurt School, such as Habermas (1976) and Marcuse (1964), have suggested that ideological distortion in advanced capitalism prevents individuals from necessarily wanting their true needs, although they accept that in the final analysis, in the appropriate circumstances, individual wants and needs should be synonymous. But these appropriate circumstances are where social and political mechanisms allow truly autonomous individuals to be the judge of their own interests, freed from the influence of dominant ideologies. These conditions do not presently obtain in the real or empirical world, for they require (for Habermas, 1971, at least) undistorted, rational communication within a context of ideological neutrality and political equality. To understand empirically unobservable but real individual interests requires the analyst to mentally reconstruct or hypothesise the conditions of open discourse that allow autonomous will-formation and the authentic individual identification of interests. (The method is similar to Weber's 'verstehen'.) However, such constructs or hypothecations are obviously difficult to verify or falsify empirically.

One step towards a methodology allowing empirical test of 'false consciousness' claims may be to look for those situations in the empirical world where ideological constraints have been loosened and then seeing whether the hypothesised forms of action actually occur. These situations may be exceptional, but if individuals or groups do act in ways consonant with their 'real' interests, i.e. if subjective and objective interests converge, then it is possible to argue that the appropriate 'counterfactual' has been adduced. Certainly this notion of relative autonomy is more likely to be empirically available than the hypothesised situations of full individual autonomy or open, discursive will-formation of the kind advanced by Habermas. Lukes (1974) for example, suggests that in the absence of observable conflict, situations where ideological or coercive power is weak or has been relaxed provide grounds (albeit indirect) for asserting that if *A* had not acted (or failed to act) in a certain way, then *B* would have thought and acted differently from the way he does actually think and act.

A number of writers, including Lukes, have used Matthew Crenson's (1971) study of the politics of air-pollution control in two American cities as one of the more successful analyses of the indirect exercise of power and as indicating that 'radical' approaches to power are in principle open to empirical verification and falsifiability. The study seeks to explain inaction as well as action, i.e. to explain why certain actions did not occur. Specifically, why was the issue of air pollution not raised as early or as effectively in some American cities as it was in others? Crenson starts with the apparently reasonable axiom that individuals prefer clean air and good health to bad, and explains the slower speed with which one of two similar towns adopts air pollution controls to its dominance by one company. In Gary, Indiana, which was a company town founded by US Steel, the major employer in the town, the issue of air pollution surfaced slowly and spasmodically on the political agenda. In East Chicago, which was not dominated by one employer, the question of air pollution had a much higher political visibility. Legislation to restrict air pollution in the town was introduced after a relatively open, pluralist decision making process.

The advantage of Crenson's study is that he showed that where the steel industry enjoyed a reputation for power it could effectively prevent the issue of air pollution being raised through its power reputation operating on anticipated reactions. It did not have to enter into open, public discussion or overt policy processes. Moreover, as Lukes (1974) has noted, Crenson does not interpret non-decision-making behaviourally, because he emphasises the importance of inaction, whilst he also considers institutional as well as individual power. Crenson is able to demonstrate, therefore, that local political institutions and political leaders may exercise considerable control over what people choose to care about and how forcefully they articulate their cares. Furthermore, Crenson's study provides both the relevant counterfactual and the identification of a power mechanism. That is, it is apparently reasonable to suppose that people do not want to be poisoned, even if they do not articulate such a preference, and Crenson provides data indicating how institutions prevented people's interests not being acted upon. (However, one substantive difficulty with Crenson's approach is that we are not sure that people may have *preferred* to risk their health rather than risk unemployment.)

This shows that we must recognise that in many situations it is likely to be very difficult to justify the relevant counterfactual. Individual's interests are even harder to adduce than in the case of air pollution and it is even harder to be sure that people would have acted differently but for the exercise of power. Charges that the observer is simply positing his values over those of the subject are difficult to rebut. Yet we have to recognise that exceptional or abnormal instances of relative autonomy do occur, and perhaps occur more readily than we realise. For example, as Lukes (1974) notes, the intermittent periods of 'liberalism' or relaxation of controls over individual freedom that have occurred in Eastern Europe indicate how differently people can behave when presented with an opportunity to do so. Even in normal times it may be possible for the observer to detect occasions when people escape from subordinate positions, from direct surveillance at work, for example, and to use such data to test propositions that people would act differently, in line with their real interests, if provided with the ideological autonomy and freedom to do so. For another example, Lukes (1974) has suggested that there is a significant difference between the caste system as it exists in the popular conception and as it actually operates. Although caste position is held to be ascriptive and unchangeable, lower castes do seek to rise within the system. When the opportunity arises there is a marked change in behaviour. Moreover, instances may also be available to the observer to detect the specifiable consequences of inaction when acting in a certain way was a reasonable, hypothesised expectation which would have had determinate effects.

However, in seeking empirical applications of notions of relative autonomy, we may forfeit some of its theoretical power. Bradshaw (1976), for example, argues that it is extremely difficult to determine at what stage we arrive at relative autonomy such that the level of influence being exercised by *A* over *B* is sufficiently reduced for *B* to act sufficiently autonomously so that his real interests are advanced or maintained. Moreover, *B*'s hypothesised independence of *A*'s power fails to rule out the likelihood of *B*'s continued subjection to other sources of power which, even though opposed to *A*, may still be inimical to *B*. Further difficulties with 'autonomy' solutions to problems of identifying power and interests follow from attempts to retain the individual as the final arbiter of his own interests in circumstances of (relative) freedom and equality. Saunders (1979) notes that not only do such solutions tend to lead to hypothetical analysis which is difficult to assess empirically, but compel us to accept that a course of action is in an individual's interests, no matter how bad it is, provided that the individual made the choice in a situation of relative autonomy. Thus, he argues, we would be obliged to accept that if the inhabitants of the steel towns studied by Crenson actually opted for their air to be polluted, then provided they made this choice in a situation of relative autonomy, and with full access to all the relevant information, then poisoned air would be in their interests.

An alternative approach which rejects any individualistic conception of power and interests is found in certain theories in Marxist structuralism in which power is the capacity of a social class to realise its specific objective interests. Poulantzas (1973), for example, argues that the interests of a class are determined in the field of class practices by what it can achieve as a social force in conflict with other classes. Moreover, the members of a given class will not always be aware of the extent of their class interests, but this does not hinder class interests, since interests are limited only by what can be achieved. However, such a position, rooted in Marxian historical materialism, is difficult to empirically verify, for it rules out of court by definition the possibilities of a genuine consensus and shared interests between the two principal classes within capitalism. Similarly, Lukes (1974) argues that within a system characterised by total structural determinism, there would be no place for power, because to speak of power in social relations is inevitably to speak of agents, individual or institutional, who, although operating within structurally determined limits, have an autonomy and an ability to act other than in the way that they did. That is, in the case of a collective exercise of power, on the part of a group or institution, this is to imply that the members of the group or institution could have combined or organised to act differently.

While accepting Lukes's strictures on structural deterministic accounts of power, it may not be necessary to go so far as he does in abandoning objective criteria for assessing whether or not interests have been met in any given situation. Lukes (1974) wishes to keep a subjective referent to the identification of interests for he believes that an attribution of power is at the same time an attribution of (partial or total) responsibility for certain consequences.

However, this raises questions as to whether power is being exercised when the consequences of an action on others is unintended. Moreover, following Saunders (1979), it may be possible to go further than Lukes by accepting a definition of interests which rests on the assumption that real interests refer to the achievement of benefits and the avoidance of costs in any particular situation, and that the assessment of benefits and costs is to be determined independently of the desires and preferences of the individuals concerned. That is, benefits and costs are determined by the observer with reference to the context in which they are distributed. For example, Saunders points out that we can demonstrate which groups benefit from local authority density provisions and zoning policies, from welfare cut-backs, etc., and we can identify which groups have lost out as a result, irrespective of whether they recognise or accept the fact.

A major objection levelled at the notion of 'objective interests' and the claim that power is exhibited by the consequential costs and benefits of policies imposed on agents irrespective of their view of the matter, is that the definition of costs and benefits, like that of objective interests, is value-determined. That is, it is argued that there are usually different views of what counts as a cost or benefit and no objective criteria for discriminating between these views. One response, offered by Saunders (1979), is to suggest that it is possible to assess costs and benefits in any empirical context once the nature of that context is identified. The context of lead poisoning, for example, is health. It is clear that the greater the level of poisoning, the greater the cost to those affected. Therefore, we can take certain 'life-chances', such as wealth or health, as providing objective indices of interests. One is able to say that a person's interests are advanced (benefits) or diminished (costs) to the extent that his position in respect of such indices also advances or declines. In political decision making, empirical analysis of the allocation of scarce resources indicates who gains and who loses (for example, who pays most, perhaps in the form of increased taxation, and who receives most, perhaps in the form of increased services). It may also be possible to determine the extent to which such gains or losses are cumulative or patterned.

Individuals, as Saunders notes, may act deliberately against their own interests. For example, a rich capitalist may vote for socialist legislation to introduce a wealth tax because he believes in greater equality. That course of action is perfectly rational and compatible with his beliefs. It is, nonetheless, contrary to his objective interests as a wealthy person. Altruistic behaviour, whilst rational and in accord with a person's values, is literally behaviour against one's interests. Thus, costs and benefits do exist objectively and within specified contexts may be analysed empirically.

The case of business power

In this piece we have emphasised some of the dangers in analysing power behaviourally. That is, we have argued that action or participation (voice) in decision making, in which competing agents seek to resolve conflicts of interest exhibited as policy preferences, does not provide necessarily the best test of power. Instead, it is suggested that inaction or the absence of participation may indicate a supreme power accomplishment – the ability to have one's interests catered for without having to take action at all. To borrow a description employed by Friedland (1982, p. 2), 'political power may be silent, voiceless'.

An obvious but still useful example of 'voiceless power' is provided by the influence of major business interests. Not only do such interests find that their material or economic power may be sufficient to guarantee that their requirements are met by political decision makers without the necessity of participation, but when participation does occur it is to *communicate* existing dominance rather than to create it through the mobilisation of political resources. Until recently, social scientists assumed that the key to discovering business political influence lay in studying the political participation of individual businessmen. As we noted when examining élitist and pluralist approaches, whatever the different conclusions about the distribution of power, the empirical focus for both was on individual involvement by business people. However, the implicit assumption that the political power of business derives from the aggregated individual acts of participation has been criticised. Rather, as Friedland (1982) has noted, interpretation has rested recently on regarding both the participation and the power of individual businessmen as being determined by the organisational structures from which they are drawn. Thus, an individual businessman's source of power derives from his position in an organisation and in the structure of organisational relations. Nonetheless, even with this approach, the emphasis is still on organisational *participation* as being necessary to the exercise of power.

A further view, in keeping with some of the radical or three-dimensional conceptions of power, is to suggest that the absence of political participation by business may not indicate a low level of business influence, but rather the reverse. It may signify a taken-for-granted assumption by governmental decision makers that keeping business sweet is axiomatic for effective policy making. Local governments, for example, invite businessmen to become involved in policy processes as a means of legitimating their own decisions and to give standing to claims to external agencies for local investment. It is control over economic production that may allow business to influence the determination and scope of publicly-acknowledged 'issues'. As Friedland (1982) suggests, from this perspective the political power of businesses, particularly of dominant economic units, derives more from their locational flexibility and control of the material base of the city, than from their present or potential political participation. Capital, particularly in its more liquid forms, may be able to move quickly in response to locational variation in profitability, and it is this control over the investment process that is the source of its power. In comparison, labour is much more spatially 'locked in' or tied to particular localities, and unions are less able to control the local economy or to adapt easily to local conditions through the mobility of their members. Moreover, because labour unions are not locally dominant economic organisations in the way businesses are, to generate power they are required to mobilise their members and participate in the political process.

There is, therefore, less imperative for business to organise politically than for labour. The latter seeks to 'voice' its interests, while capital's power frequently may be silent. Furthermore, as Offe and Wiesenthal (1980) point out, while 'labour' consists of individual men and women, 'capital' consists of units of money. Units of capital can be added together, merged with each other, to provide single 'lumps' of capital, but workers, even when united, remain individual human beings with separate needs and wants. Capital is in that sense always a collectivity and automatically has the advantage of organisation, while for workers organisation presents particular difficulties. Workers require organisation to construct a collective identity out of separate individual identities.

This is not to suggest that business's political power is always 'voiceless'. In Britain, for example, as we noted in Chapter 4, the development of trade unionism helped to trigger business association as firms, in addition to their continued merging of capital, recognised political participation as a necessary means of promoting their collective interests against the challenge offered by labour organisation and political representation in an era of mass democracy. However, business's preferred and most efficient form of action is to respond individually to the constraints and opportunities offered by the market. This is a less hazardous method of control than offered by the political frame of action in which agents perform, however nominally in actuality, on equal terms. If it is accepted that organised political representation is a less preferred source of influence for capital than individual action in the market, this suggests that participation occurs when economic power is weakened and is no longer sufficient for controlling the political process.

Nonetheless, business appears uniquely privileged by political institutions in capitalist societies, and this influence is explained by the structural dependence of the state on a capitalist accumulation. This is not a view confined to Marxists. The distinguished American political scientist Charles Lindblom (1977), best-known for his 'liberal–conservative' positions, has suggested that government regards business not simply as another special interest, but as performing an indispensable function that grants them an exceptionally privileged status. He argues that decisions on incomes, production and distribution are of momentous consequence for the welfare of any society, and in a private-enterprise market system they are in large part decided not by government officials but by businessmen. Delegation of these decisions to the businessman does not diminish their importance or their public aspect. In Lindblom's view, therefore, businessmen become a kind of public official exercising public functions. Employment, production and prosperity in a society rests in their hands and a major requirement for government is to encourage businessmen to perform their tasks, for it is beyond the power of government to organise or control the process of accumulation. Moreover, in liberal democracies, this must be done by inducement rather than command.

Yet Lindblom's observations on the structural rather than the behavioural locus of business power should be qualified. If business is inevitably privileged in the political systems of advanced capitalist societies, why does it need business interest associations? Nor should government institutions be regarded as always or inevitably following capitalist interests. Some sociologists, for example, regard the growth of public administration in modern society as providing state bureaucrats with the capacity to pursue their own interests in the determination of policy. Not only are such interests independent of capitalist interests, but they may be detrimental to them. The expansion of bureaucratic power can constitute a fiscal drag on accumulation, as well as posing potential dangers for entrepreneurial sovereignty. Moreover, the political effectiveness and activity of business vary considerably over time. Vogel (1983), for example, argues that the decade from the mid-1960s to the mid-1970s witnessed a significant decline in the political influence of business in the United States, as a coalition of consumer, environmental, feminist and civil rights organisations were able to influence the outcomes of government policy in a direction antithetical to the interests of business. The consequence was a mushrooming in formal association and representation by business in the late 1970s to counteract lack of influence.

Conclusion

Any analysis of power must recognise the limitations of a solely behaviouralist framework. Our study of the special case of business indicates that power may follow from structural position rather than from political action. Yet we have also noted that totally 'voiceless' or silent power is rarely achieved, even for business, and that more overt behaviour or influence is also detectable, and that this may vary from period to period. The nature of political action must still be analysed in any account of power. However, the structural bases of action (and inaction) must form part of this analysis. Does action, for example, constitute the *source* of power, or does it, as with business associations, simply *register* or *communicate* that which already exists (e.g. as a consequence of economic position, although other statuses, such as religious, could conceivable operate in a similar fashion)? Consequently, any adequate approach to power in decision making must take account of both structure and action. In the next chapter we consider further both more structuralist approaches to power and also local political processes.

7

Urban Politics

Introduction

In all western industrial nations the central state administration is not the only form of public sector agency. Decentralised and specific forms of service provision, revenue collection and legally-allocated authority are well-established features of modern politics, especially in the governance of localities, although the extent and type of decentralisation varies between societies. Friedland, Piven and Alford (1977, p. 450) suggest that all western nations have institutional arrangements that manage two primary and sometimes contradictory functions, economic growth and political integration. Although concerned mainly with the United States, they argue that there is a more widespread but varying tendency for these functions to be structurally segregated between different agencies and programmes. More speculatively they suggest that these variations in the extent and type of governmental decentralisation 'may help to account for differences among nations and cities in the capacity to cope with periodic eruptions of political conflict'.

In Britain there are to be found two fundamental forms of public organisation apart from the central state. One are quasi-governmental agencies, such as housing corporations or the Arts Council, which tend to be single-issue agencies with control over only one policy area. Organised at either national, regional or local level, quasi-governmental agencies are non-elected bodies, appointed by ministers, and with executive responsibilities. Dunleavy and Rhodes (1983, pp. 110–11) suggest two main reasons for their creation. One is simply organisational decentralisation to allow more operational autonomy and efficiency, or perhaps to avoid too direct an implication for government in sensitive areas or potentially unpopular decisions (e.g. the use of the University Grants Committee in cutting higher-education spending). The other is where the administrative function is so large that it must be broken down for its exercise to become manageable. It is difficult to come to general conclusions about the role of quasi-governmental agencies because of the diversity, distinctiveness and rapid change in their organisational forms and influence with government.

The other form of non-central public agency is the local authority, which is an elected body and covers a wide range of local public services. It also has powers to generate income through local taxation and charges for some services. The doctrine of *ultra vires* reinforces the formal control of the centre in Britain by requiring local authorities to obtain specific statutory authority to undertake a function. It derives from the legislative creation of local government by the centre through Parliament in the nineteenth century and was confirmed in the major reorganisation of the 1970s. This is not to deny, however, the many forms of local government in Britain and elsewhere that existed well before its modern creations. As Elcock (1982, pp. 4–5) observes, 'Parliament was not creating a new system of government where none existed before; its role was rather analogous to that of a colonial power attempting to bring order to a series of chaotic tribal states.' We can trace an extensive mixture of local governing bodies, which were generally controlled by local propertied interests, back to at least medieval times and local communities were also responsible for keeping law and the peace through the office of constable. The task of relieving poverty fell on local parishes and vestries as early as the seventeenth century, while the nineteenth century development of towns and cities led to the promulgation of single purpose authorities with responsibilities for water supply and sanitation. Gradually some towns were granted borough status which allowed them to be run by locally-elected members. The political legitimacy that election conferred on the boroughs, heralding also the potential conflict between elected tiers of local and central government, was steadily confirmed by the replacement of the patchwork of local public bodies by the now familiar systems of local authorities including the extension of the local electoral franchise. By the end of the nineteenth century localities had either a single all-purpose authority, namely the county borough council in the large towns and cities, or, elsewhere, were governed through two or three tiers, each with specific functions. However, all were financed by a mixture of local property taxes and central government grants.

A variety of problems which gradually became more acute in Britain after the end of the Second World War, and which were also found in other industrial societies, led to major reorganisations of local government in the 1970s. Prior to the creation of much larger authorities, especially in the metropolitan areas, changing population patterns had resulted in local authorities with similar powers but massive divergences in population, resources, and demand for services. Moreover, many urban authorities lacked land to meet new housing needs and experienced difficulty in securing it from their neighbouring rural counterparts, and there was generally an increased interdependency of town and country in services and communications which cut across many rural–urban authority boundaries. The local authorities also became more financially dependent upon central government in the 1960s and early 1970s and attracted an unenviable reputation for inefficiency, bureaucratisation and, in some quarters, even corruption. Creating larger authorities was regarded as helping to redress these problems, including improving the 'calibre' of local councillors, although some have seen reorganisation as a strategy for linking local government more directly to the needs of capital (Cockburn, 1978; Dearlove, 1979).

Central and local functions and relations

Explanations for the development of modern forms of local government are hampered by the lack of explicitly comparative data on the functions of different tiers of government in different countries. This appears to have presented less of a problem to those who have focused on structured causes of the role of the state in capitalist societies generally rather than particular practices or types of government. In recent approaches associated with the work of Castells (1978) local or urban politics has a specificity in capitalist societies that derives from its function in the provision of collective consumption, namely services such as education, housing and social services. Patterns of public expenditure in such societies do reveal a movement out of the central state in the post-war period which, as Dunleavy (1984, p. 51) observes, 'probably reflects the increasing importance of socialised consumption in advanced industrialised societies, and the key role of local or regional governments as an implementation tier within western "welfare states" '. However, this process largely has been halted or reversed since the late 1970s as the result of fiscal crisis, while it is often overlooked that the growth had been mainly in just two areas, education and housing, and the number of areas where local authorities were engaged in providing services had reduced dramatically. Central government has allowed or encouraged a post-war trend for local government to lose functions to public corporations or other single-function quasi-governmental agencies while increasingly hedging in the control of policy in those areas which remain formally within the local government orbit.

Dunleavy (1984) identifies four existing explanations of the functional allocation of policy responsibilities between different levels of government. First, a conventional public administration approach, which tends to regard some policy functions as generically 'local' and some as fundamentally 'national'. This position derives from a straight-forwardly descriptive and historical analysis of a range of societies and the general tendency in them to allocate particular services to a specific tier of government. Size and scale often appear to be major determining factors so that, for example, defence and economic management tend to be central responsibilities while primary education and small-scale environmental services are generally locally-administered. However, there is sufficient divergence from these tendencies between countries and enough functions that cannot be clearly designated to one category or other to make the approach very problematical. The second explanation of functional allocation is provided by an inter-governmental relations approach which looks less at particular types of policy allocation, because it regards patterns of service responsibility as having functional equivalence, than at overall organisational relations, such as the tendency in large-scale complex societies for policy making to become more diffuse and decentralised and more dependent upon the expertise of relatively autonomous professional groupings. The problem with the model, however, is the difficulty in recognising the substantive conflicts of interest that underlie organisational relations in particular policy areas as opposed to overarching organisational imperatives. Thirdly, a public choice model assumes that local authorities are rational actors seeking to maximise their tax base. It suggests that redistributive services, such as taxing the wealthy to help the poor, are increasingly funded by central government because otherwise differential capacities and competition between individual authorities would result if it was left to local government, with redistributive spending being highest in local authorities with large fiscal capacities and low social needs, but lower in poorer localities where the need for such services is greater. Alternatively allocation services which improve facilities for the community generally are still funded primarily from local sources because competition in this area between local governments is useful in maintaining efficiency of service provision. In some service areas the allocation of policy responsibility between central and local government depends on whether the benefits are confined to a particular locality or not. If not, such as economic development support for companies drawing on a wide travel-to-work area, then local authorities may lack the incentive to provide such services which may then become a central responsibility, (e.g. regional development aid). The difficulty with the model, however, is that it depicts policy processes 'in terms of a depoliticised logic of welfare maximisation, where social conflicts are hidden beneath pervasive assumptions of rationality' (Dunleavy, 1984, p. 63).

Finally, local state theory, although not developing an explicit theory of functional allocations between different state levels, sees the local government system as a means for spatially and ideologically fragmenting working-class movements into localistic or 'community' interests (Dear and Scott, 1984). It also provides local political powers to capitalist interests through increasingly restrictive, secretive and centralised forms of policy making (Cockburn, 1977). The force of this theory, however, is somewhat debilitated by the existence of an alternative interpretation of the local state which regards it as a potential source of working-class or popular insurrection against capital and sees corporate management and other centralising tendencies in local government, and the loss of local powers to national government, as indicating the necessity for the central state to protect monopoly capital from popular local struggles. This latter interpretation has become more attractive in the 1980s, especially to the left, as central efforts by governments of the right to control local public expenditure and influence has stimulated widespread opposition from socialist councils. A return to central power by the left, however, which may have to face recalcitrant non-socialist authorities opposed to its policies may result in this version of the local state again giving way to the former interpretation.

These differences in theorising the local state exemplify the generally ambivalent stance towards local government adopted by many on the left. In Britain particularly, the decentralist view of its functions has largely been obscured by the emphasis given in the Labour Party to the necessity for a strong central state able to implement reforms in overcoming social and spatial inequality. The trade unions, the pre-eminent source of influence in the party, have been concerned more with the need for an orderly system of national wage bargaining than with local government, while the Fabians and Keynesians wanted an efficient system of central macro-economic planning and saw local government at best as training or experimental grounds for this wider aim (Sharpe, 1982, p. 154). Bassett (1984, p. 90) suggests too, that central–local relations were transformed as part of the construction of the welfare state in the 'post-war settlement' between capital and labour. 'Although local government lost some functions and gained others, the overall effect was increased centralisation and the sacrifice of local autonomy to the administrative needs of particular national services.' Moreover, in the early Labour administrations of the 1960s, the notion of a rational, efficient central state was a major part of the aim for a scientific, technological revolution. Bassett argues that the ideology of the party was sustained by the structural characteristics of the British state, in which the power of Parliament over the local authorities was a feature of governance, and which lacked strong regional and intermediate levels of government and local government executive structures as a basis of local power. These features were visible as far back as the nineteenth century, pre-dating the growth of the Labour Party, and were an essential part of the development of the British state in which local government became primarily a means of delivering central policies rather than articulating local demands (Ashford, 1981).

It is not only on the left that can be detected an ambivalence towards local government. The right has criticised it both for its fiscal drain on the private sector and for its bureaucratisation and interventionism. These criticisms intensified as local authority expenditure on consumption increased in the 1960s and early 1970s and were associated with claims of 'taxation without representation' as a result of business disenfranchisement and withdrawal from local politics. It was argued that this left the non-domestic ratepayer with little restraining influence over local politicians in comparison with the 'consumption lobby', resulting in higher council expenditure and bigger rates' bills for companies. These views struck a popular chord in the late 1970s and chimed with wider suspicion of local public officialdoms and the alienating characteristics of town-hall decision making. However, the right also has regarded local government as a vital check on an 'elective dictatorship' from the centre, especially when central governments of the left are in power. Sections of both the left and right, especially in Britain and the United States, draw upon a cultural tradition that regards substantially autonomous local government as an important source of protection of individual liberties against excessive central power. An important feature of western liberalism ascribes to local authorities a vital source of countervailing influence and check on authoritarianism.

Each of these perspectives raises questions of control and influence: the degree of control exercised by local authorities in their dealings with the central state, and the level of influence exercised over local policy processes by particular social interests. The former necessarily involves reference to the growing literature on central–local relationships, including the dual-state thesis, and the latter which we consider first, to questions of 'community power', especially the relationship between government and business.

Urban power

In Chapter 6 it was suggested that much of the empirical work that has underpinned contemporary theoretical debates on power was derived from analysis of power relations in American local communities. Both the reputationalist and decisionalist approaches to community power adopted a view of power as the property of particular individuals, although they differed over how this was measured. Reputationalists sought 'inside' information on who were thought to run a particular community, while decisionalists examined who got their way in actual decision making. The former method tended to unearth small cohesive élites in which business leaders were prominent, but the latter method generally produced a picture of a relatively open local power structure with no particular élite dominant across a range of decision areas. A number of specific difficulties with each approach was identified, but they received two criticisms in common. First, that the individualistic methodologies employed either misrepresented or overlooked the structural determinants of local power, especially that exercised by business. Second, that such approaches and findings were not really relevant to many non-American societies, such as Britain, where local government institutions are both the formal and real source of power in local communities and were relatively immune from control by external groups or individuals. Certainly few 'community power' studies have been carried out in Britain, in part because of the view that community power analysis is based on the relative weakness of local political institutions compared with private organisations and groups.

To take the first point, Friedland (1982) criticises the view that the power of business derives either from the aggregated individual acts of participation by business executives, or even necessarily from the structure of organisational participation represented by individuals. Rather, the origins of its local influence lie in organised control over private investment and the resources upon which local governance depends. The political power of business, particularly of dominant economic units, springs more from locational flexibility and control of the material bases of the city than from present or potential participation (see Chapter 6). Friedland emphasies the importance of national flows of capital for local economies and dispels the view that national corporate élites are no longer powerful political forces in cities. Thus corporations and unions do not simply shape policy, they shape policy making by affecting which local conditions affect local policy and which do not. Friedland found that cities with powerful corporations were more responsive in their policy making to local economic conditions likely to constrain urban growth. Federal urban renewal after the Second World War, for example, was adopted in cities where downtown economies were not only alive but growing, and where the downtown corporate office and retail economies were strong, not weak. Because they controlled investment the corporations controlled the economic conditions necessary to the success of urban renewal.

There are a number of difficulties with Friedland's analysis, however. For example, there is little empirical research as yet to indicate the extent or effect of the locational fluidity of capital, and how sensitive companies are to local policies, as opposed to how sensitive they say they are, is still a matter of conjecture (King, 1985b). It is often forgotten that capital is also dependent on a variety of infrastructural and accumulated ancillary services in localities, many provided by local government. As Friedland points out, urban land is not allocated by the market alone but also by government. Firms are required to use the powers of government to facilitate land-use changes and to provide the public infrastructure that makes their investments profitable.

This takes us to a second point, the proposition that in Britain local government institutions are the source of both formal and substantive power rather than it being the possession of external, private interests, which thus reduces the explanatory potency of community power approaches. This is to posit a false dichotomy and to fail to recognise the reciprocal relationship between public authority and private interests, especially the structural importance of business, in capitalist societies. The key point for analysis is the nature and extent of public–private relationships, for which community power approaches may be successfully employed. A good example is Saunders's (1979) account of urban politics in Croydon, which examines the relative influence on council policy of three major groups – middle class owner-occupiers, working-class tenants, and business – and analyses which groups gained or lost from council decisions.

An important aspect of the study is to indicate that a simple capital versus labour class model did not explain a number of the political alliances that emerged in Croydon in the 1970s. For example, middle-class housing residents successfully resisted plans by builders for high density housing schemes which also meant that working-class residents lost chances for lower-priced private housing or new council homes. The middle-class owner-occupiers were generally very successful in using a wide range of personal contacts in having their interests for low rates and few housing developments protected by the council. Yet the efforts of tenants' associations were generally unsuccessful and hampered by lack of resources, the 'rules of the game' which required 'respectability' from those advancing claims and a limitation on demands, and the unlikelihood of the Labour Party achieving power locally. The commercial business sector gained most from local authority policy in the post-war years, benefiting from the exploding demand for office accommodation and the support of the council in providing infrastructure (e.g. land clearance, roads). The biggest losers were those groups in most need of welfare services, which had been reduced as expenditure was directed towards commercial schemes, and local businessmen who were often badly affected by the competition from the larger incoming companies.

The evidence that Saunders adduces for the ability of the larger firms from outside to profit enormously from the central business area development in Croydon raises several issues about the nature of political participation by business. First, the over-representation of particular types of property on the council did not necessarily lead to these interests being favoured by council policy. In Croydon, the town-centre re-development scheme, which harmed local businessmen and benefited the larger newcomers, was undertaken by a council composed predominantly of the former. Secondly, the relationship between overt or formal political participation and interests appeared highly tenuous. Saunders notes that the influence of large business in Croydon was rarely in evidence in questions of policy formulation, for the consistent support of town-centre enterprises by the local authority took place with little formal prompting from interests outside the town hall. Nevertheless, there were considerable social and civic contacts between leading councillors and senior managers of the companies. Political influence was exerted through membership of a network of local bodies, such as the chamber of commerce, the rotary club, the magistrate's bench and local school governorships. Saunders stresses the importance of shared political values in these relationships which enabled Croydon's political leaders to identify Croydon's interests as being the same as the interests of Croydon business. A similar 'political communion' existed between the authority and the middle-class residents, who had a greater degree of access and influence than other groups and whose demands were regarded, as with business, as 'non-political' and non-contentious.

Saunders's account supports the view that 'conflict in local government is essentially between those who are in most need of its services and who bear only a relatively small proportion of the burden of local taxation, and those who bear a higher taxation burden and have less need of public services' (Elcock, 1983, p. 84).

Specifically, cleavages between housing classes are important bases of local political action including voter alignment, particularly in countries such as Britain where local property taxes are a major source of local authority income, and where council policies have large distributive consequences (see Chapter 1).

A major aim of the Croydon study was to understand 'why some dogs do not bark in the night', and to argue that some groups may fail to pursue their interests because of an anticipated 'mobilisation of bias' against them, or conversely, because they have little need to act as their interests are adequately taken into account by decision makers who share similar values. Studies of local interest groups tend to distinguish between those that enjoy close or 'inside' relationships with officials and councillors and those that do not (Dearlove, 1973; King and Nugent, 1979; Newton, 1976). Dearlove notes in his study of Kensington and Chelsea that groups gaining access and influence with the council have to be seen to be abiding by the 'rules of the game', and 'helpful' associations are those with moderate demands, who campaign quietly, provide a service, and are drawn from 'respectable' social groups. Newton's major study of the interest-group system in Birmingham showed that most 'well-established' groups tended to use their links with officials rather than contacting political parties or councillors, and that quieter methods were regarded as more effective than publicity demonstrations.

A feature of the work of both Saunders and Friedland, apart from their shared view that the essential theoretical and empirical task in analysing urban power is to examine the constraints on voluntarism and the relationship between structure and action, is recognition of the importance of 'non-local' factors in local policy processes. Friedland, for example, shows that after the Second World War major corporations in the United States became fully integrated into a national network of urban policy formation and diffusion. This national network not only shaped federal renewal legislation but speeded its adoption and directed its use in the major cities. Particularly, the National Chamber of Commerce acted as a transmission belt for urban policies generated by other national corporate organisations. Especially in their headquarter cities, national corporations provided essential political support for urban renewal through the original stimulation and financing of central business district studies, the provision of seed money for project proposals, and the loaning of corporate executives to redevelopment agencies.

A similar concern with the national and structural determinants of local policy making, but in a British context, is provided by Dunleavy (1981) in *The Politics of Mass Housing In Britain, 1945–75*. This is a comprehensive discussion of the broad context of high-rise housing decisions which, in Dunleavy's view, undermines the explanatory utility of behavioural models of power, for the ability of local decision makers to ignore the unorganised expressions of tenant resistance to high-rise made pluralist analysis largely irrelevant to the issue. Nor was there much support for élite theory approaches as decision making on high-rise in the three localities analysed was concentrated within recognised channels in the local authority. The primary determinants of high-rise were national and structural and could not be characterised in terms of community élites or interest groups. Such determinants included the cost controls by which the Ministry of Housing and Local Government (MHLG) architects were able to exert considerable influence on local authority architects' departments, the professional influence of architectural ideology in which high-rise was a central image of the 'modern movement', the 'urban containment' orientation of the planning system, and the links between high-rise and industrial concentration in the construction industry. The most important influences on the development of high-rise policy were the pressures from the construction industry directed at both the MHLG and at the local authorities and the influence of the MHLG on the local authorities. Moreover, communication through the national local government system strongly influenced the boundaries within which local authorities operated and provided an important source of values for individual authorities.

The merit of Dunleavy's account is that it provides empirical application of structuralist theory in a policy area where simple behavioural accounts would be inadequate. A problem, however, is that Dunleavy conflates what he admits is the closely-related distinction between actor influences and structural determination on the one hand, and local and non-local political influences on the other. Thus the major structural influences were central government intervention and movements of capital. Central government intervention was crucial to local housing policies as the result of subsidy changes and the pressure directed towards the adoption of industrialised building. Movements of capital exerted extensive influence on local authority policies because of the direct effects on the attainment of outputs and the implications of this for future MHLG allocations. Because construction firms in the 1950s and 1960s could involve their resources in a variety of markets and in a large number of authorities in a period of high demand their willingness to tender for contracts was crucial for a council's housing performance. However, it is not clearly conclusive why, or at least to what extent, national influence on housing policy should be considered to be structural rather than behavioural. It could be argued that most of the structural influences that are given most attention, such as the construction interests, the architects and the MHLG, could be regarded as groups whose influence could well be handled within pluralist or élite theory. Nevertheless, Dunleavy offers a valuable account of the 'nationalisation' of local politics, the close and reciprocal relationship between the public and private sectors, and the incorporation of professional and technocratic influences within public policy apparatuses (King, 1985b).

Urban managers

Although American community power approaches were little used in analysis of British urban politics in the 1960s and 1970s, an influential model at this time was the 'urban managerial thesis' associated with the work of Pahl. As in Dunleavy's study that followed, particular emphasis was placed on examining the relationship between local public authority and market interests, focusing on the mediating agencies between the two sectors and between central and local government. Initially, and in line with community power approaches, Pahl laid greater stress on the values and goals of individual urban managers, such as local authority officials, than on wider structural influences. Although Pahl gradually shifted his approach to allow for wider structural considerations, his analysis has been criticised for ignoring 'logics of structures' by those employing urban political economy and collective consumption methodologies.

Pahl's account of the importance of urban managers in analysing local power rests on three basic elements in Weberian sociology:

> a conceptualisation of the state as an apparatus controlled by individuals with definite aims and motivations; a view of the state's mode of operation in which officials and technical experts are deemed to prevail against elected political leaders; and a commitment to a theory of politics as a realm autonomous of economic class relations. (Saunders, 1981, pp. 122–3)

Thus state policies do not always or necessarily reflect the interests of capital but are rather the outcome of managerial bargaining between agents representing different organisations. In this view public policy makers are regarded as an important influence in the distribution of life chances and the determination of inequalities and class struggles outside the occupational sphere, particularly the allocation of the 'social wage' such as education, health-care and social service. The city, especially, is seen as containing processes that generate specific inequalities, largely as the result of decisions made by individuals occupying strategic allocative locations in the urban system. These 'gatekeepers', who Pahl comes to see primarily as local authority officials with some degree of independence, determine the eligibility of clients for the receipt of scarce public goods. An important set of questions, therefore, centred on the extent to which these officials shared common values and discriminated persistently against certain social groups. A number of studies indicated that officials such as housing managers and planners did maintain consistent forms of bias against the poor and council tenants (Dennis, 1972).

The urban managerial approach encounters difficulties in meeting two particular criticisms. First, how should these managers be identified theoretically? For example, at what levels in the organisation are they located? Are they found in both the public and private sectors? Secondly, what are the level and nature of constraints on managers from, for example, central government and corporations? The response to the first problem has been to confine a definition of urban manager to the public sector, and to regard them as performing a crucial mediating role between the public and private sector, and between central and local government. As Saunders (1981, p. 121) notes, Pahl's analysis becomes:

> situated in a broader theoretical framework in which the key

> variables are the state and the capitalist economy . . . urban managers are significant as allocators of resources, but it is recognised that the initial availability of such resources depends upon decisions made by central government and by those who control investment in the private sector.

The extent of the constraints on managers remains untheorised, however. Pahl suggests that it varies empirically, but this is not especially helpful without a theoretical specification of those types of circumstance when officials either have, or do not have, some freedom of action. A consequence of the theoretical difficulties encountered by the urban managerial thesis was attempts to theoretically provide a 'new urban sociology', which many associated most successfully with Castells and his emphasis on the specificity of collective consumption.

Collective consumption and urban politics

The collective consumption theory of urban politics starts from a critique of theories, such as community power or urban managerialism, which are based on the actions of individual subjects. Rather, the actions of individuals can be explained only through a theory of structure and social totality that constitutes them as subjects. Drawing on the work of Althusser, Castells (1977, 1978) delineates social totality into three analytical levels – the economic, political and ideological – while the economic is further broken down into elements of production, consumption and exchange. In Castells's initial, strongly functionalist formulations each element performs a particular function for the whole system, with consumption, for example, reproducing labour power. Although the urban system may be theorised in the same way as the total social system, with the same units, it has a particular specificity and functionality for the system. While capitalist production is organised nationally and regionally through individual firms, consumption and reproduction are specific to the urban. Moreover, consumption is increasingly provided through the state, which collectivises and politicises it, as a result of the inability of individual companies to provide education, social services, etc., through the commodity mode. This state structuring of the urban system is accounted for by Castells as meeting requirements for the reproduction of labour power and social cohesion, and to overcome a potential contradiction between the profitable production of exchange values and the necessity for the consumption of use values. Yet, as Saunders (1981, p. 189) has noted, there is an ambiguity in Castells's theory of the state that becomes more pronounced in his later work as the explanation becomes based less on the functional requirements of the system than the efficacy of class struggles. Why the latter (practices) should necessarily produce the former (meeting functional needs) is never fully explained.

However, Castells's functionalism does not maintain a constantly self-regulating system in equilibrium, for the increasingly collective nature of consumption generates a fiscal crisis as the consequence of a widening gap between its expenditure and revenues, exhibited particularly in the cities. Yet attempts at cutting housing, education and other forms of collective consumption, given its greater politicisation, provide the basis for popular urban social movements that crosscut traditional class divisions between manual workers, professionals and the petty bourgeoisie. However, Castells argues that without socialist political organisation the various urban struggles will remain fragmentary, secondary and ultimately reformist. Urban political sociology, therefore, comprises two major sub-fields, the study of urban planning (broadly defined as a range of state interventions in the urban system), and the study of urban political struggles and protests.

In Castells's work, therefore, urban politics is no longer confined to, although it includes, local political institutions. Dunleavy (1980) noted that Castells's content definition of the urban is particularly useful for empirical work dealing with the displacement of urban issues and problems from the local to regional or national level. However, there are also several important difficulties with his analysis. For example, Castells's reluctance to integrate actors' definitions within his theory of system contradictions leads to an unlikely interpretation of the likelihood of widely-based urban movements in response to cuts in collective consumption (Pickvance, 1977). There is little evidence in Britain, for example, of a willingness by the different clients, consumers and employees in different consumption sectors to sink their class and status differences in favour of a radical socialist urban movement

(Saunders, 1980). Recent work on the middle class shows long-established and persisting conflicts, with a well-founded material base, not only between the different groupings comprising the middle class, or between manual and non-manual employees, but also between groups differentially located in the private and public spheres of consumption, especially at the local level (Dunleavy, 1979; King and Nugent, 1979; King and Raynor, 1981). Moreover, the relative non-involvement of trade unions in local issues, despite the growth of the public sector unions, suggests little basis for either working class or broader social movements organised coherently in radical opposition to the different forms of public expenditure cuts.

Pickvance (1977) criticises Marxist urban writers for (1) overemphasising the role of protest movements (as opposed to that of the local authorities) in obtaining change in the urban system; (2) failing to conceptualise adequately local authorities and the social processes within them which affect their response to protest movements; (3) emphasising popular mobilisation to the exclusion of other modes of protest action, such as personal approaches and 'institutional' methods, and reasons for their success or lack of success; and (4) for neglecting the resources available to organisations as a crucial influence on their survival and success. Pickvance develops these criticisms by suggesting that the link between social base and social force can be understood more thoroughly by using concepts developed in non-Marxist sociology. For example, the structure of social relations in a social base will be dependent upon the existence, type and range of formal and informal bodies and groupings in a population. The level of class or community consciousness in a mining village, where work and non-work roles and identities elide, is likely to differ from that in leafier community suburbs. In discussing urban social movements, therefore, there is a need to examine closely alternative forms of consciousness and the availability or otherwise of protest organisations. Similarly, Saunders (1981) suggests that the necessity to adequately encompass actors' definitions in analysis is highlighted by Castells's premise that radicalism declines with political concessions, as there is considerable sociological and comparative data to the contrary.

Three final points are worth making in considering the 'new urban sociology'. First, the tendency to overlook the importance of production as well as consumption in the urban process, especially the securing of the general conditions of capitalist production through the public provision (urban planning) of transport and communication which mainly enhances the profitability of large business. Lojkine's (1977) study of Rennes, for example, indicated that the role of the local municipal apparatus was to facilitate inward investment by big national companies through infrastructural provision and other services and inducements, while at the same time facilitating the interests of large city centre store owners at the expense of small and medium capital. Friedland *et al.*, (1977, p. 499) argue that urban areas are critically important sites at which both economic growth and political integration are organised. 'Government structure in urban areas must therefore perform key functions both to support urban economic processes and to promote the political integration of the urban population.' Others suggest that production and consumption are too closely related in the Marxist labour theory of value to be clearly disentangled in the manner employed by Castells and that the division is largely a fictitious device by the state to ideologically fragment the working class and deflect it from class struggle (Harvey, 1973; Harloe, 1979). However, it is arguable that Castells is concerned with the theoretical specificity of the urban and that his ideal-typical approach does not so much invite empirical disregard for production processes but only their theoretical subordination to collective consumption in defining the 'terrain' for urban sociology.

Secondly, the notion 'collective consumption' is rather elusive, for it could refer to the source of its provision (the state) or the social nature of its direct consumption. Dunleavy (1979) identifies at least twelve different interpretations, but suggests reserving the notion to three types: publicly organised but unsubsidised services with non-market access (e.g. some forms of public housing), publicly organised and subsidised services with market access (such as public transport), and, basically, publicly organised and subsidised services with non-market provision (e.g. education, health). Additionally, it may be possible to distinguish different types of collective consumption based on O'Connor's (1973) delineation between public expenditure as social investment and as social expense. Recipients of the latter will tend to possess collectivist values and have a propensity for political action.

Thirdly, Castells's theory that the state is relatively autonomous from capital in order to act as a more effective guarantor of the longer-term interests of, especially, monopoly capital is largely impervious to empirical analysis, for it is able both to explain those situations where capital benefits from state policies and those where it does not. 'What is necessary, yet lacking, is a counterfactual statement to the effect that, *if* the state necessarily acts in the longer-term interests of monopoly capital (even when it appears to be acting in the interests of other classes), *then* certain types of interventions *cannot* occur' (Saunders 1981, p. 208). Saunders is not suggesting that the state does not safeguard capitalist interests or does not respond to working-class demands but that both theories, separately, are inadequate. Rather than a theory of a monolithic state, a dual-state thesis is proposed which distinguishes between different levels of government, types of expenditure, modes of representation and decision making, and ideology.

Local state, dual state and consumption sectors

Although recognising the difficulties with Castells's analyses a number of writers have drawn on them in developing their own work. In a British context Dunleavy (1979) usefully employs the distinction between individualised and collective forms of consumption to account for the influence of housing and transport locations on political alignment. An additional element in Dunleavy's formulation is the notion of 'consumption sectors' which refers to those areas where consumpton processes are fragmented between individual and collective modes. For example, the existence of an individual/commodity/private mode in housing and transportation provides the basis for electoral cleavages that are relatively independent of occupational class locations. It will be recalled that drawing upon polling data Dunleavy shows a clear tendency for the Conservative lead over Labour to decrease as one moves from the most private to the most public mode of consumption (see Chapter 1).

A further development of the collective consumption approach is found in the dual-state thesis advanced by Cawson and Saunders (1983), and derives from a critical appraisal of Castells. It is an approach to central–local government relations that rejects the notion of the state as a unitary instrument of rule for a particular group or class. Not only is the state divided into different sections, often with conflicting interests, but two different types of political process are associated with central and local levels. These may be characterised in terms of four variables: organisation, function, political and ideological.

i. Organisation One approach to central–local government relations is concerned with the relationship between organisations at the two levels. Rhodes (1981), for example, points to organisational power struggles between central and local government in which each organisation has at its disposal particular resources. Although this struggle generally takes place within certain rules, it is essentially a zero-sum game to change the balance of freedom and influence between the two groups. This 'power-dependence' characterisation of the relationship between Whitehall and the local authorities suggests that both have resources for autonomous action but also that they are dependent on each other for resources outside their own control. For example, central departments tend to have broad-ranging and general financial control over policy, while local authorities possess ground-level operational control and expertise. Multiple conflicts of interest within local government between different tiers and political parties confound simple models of central–local relationships. However, the increasing 'nationalisation' of local politics in a number of countries and indicated in Britain, for example, by the growth of national local authority associations provides a relatively stable and homogenising influence for individual authorities.

The organisational approach has appeared particularly pertinent to analyses of British politics since the return of Conservative administrations determined to tightly control all local authority expenditure, including that which is locally raised, and which has resulted in severe turbulence in central–local relationships. A problem with the organisational approach, however, is that it tends to ignore the substance of central–local relationships and the wider social framework within which they are situated.

ii. Function Saunders (1984) suggests that the increased tension in recent years between central and local government is not simply a reflection of an organisational power struggle but is a product of the deeper tension between production and consumption priorities within the state. Cawson and Saunders's (1983) ideal-typical, dual-state framework associates the requirements for production with policy processes at central and regional level, and those for collective consumption at the local level. Thus, the attempts to control local government from the centre 'has been part and parcel of the attempt to subordinate social to economic priorities in order to restore profitability to private sector investment' (Saunders, 1984, p. 28).

iii. Political Similarly, the central–local division may be regarded as reflecting the different modes of interest intermediation associated with the different tiers and their typical form of expenditure. In this view the investment needs of capital are maintained through largely secretive corporatist policy processes, while local struggles over collective consumption are characterised by a more open or pluralistic politics, but which is subordinated to central, corporatist and investment influence.

iv. Ideological Finally, the ideological principles associated with centrally-located, production-based, corporatism are founded on the market and private property, while those associated with local consumption are characterised by collectivism, civic rights and social welfare.

In this dual-state thesis the typical formation of local interests is based on consumption sectors, between private house owners and council tenants, for example, rather than class divisions. Although some campaigns may draw membership predominantly from one class, they do not constitute class struggles if mobilised in terms of people's relationships to consumption issues as opposed to production. Indeed, the fragility and fragmentation of community responses to public expenditure cuts – typically localised and limited to a narrow range of concerns – is because 'local consumption-based struggles are not class struggles and cannot, therefore, simply be taken under the wing of a socialist movement whose primary concern lies in national questions of economic policy' (Saunders, 1980, p. 551). This view directly challenges one version of the 'local state' thesis put forward by Cockburn (1977), Corrigan (1979), and others, which identifies the function of local government as essentially the same as that for central government, namely pursuing the interests of monopoly capital. It is assumed that local government is merely one branch of the capitalist state and that general theories of the capitalist state can be applied in virtually unmediated fashion to the 'local state'. The function of the local state is, therefore, to facilitate capital accumulation through the provision of infrastructure (e.g. communications, land clearance), helping to maintain the reproduction of labour, and keeping order and generating political legitimacy in responding to working-class demands. In the dual-state view, however, the local level has a specifity, through the provision of collective consumption, that serves to distinguish it from central government.

A problem with the term 'local state' is that it is used to denote two contrary meanings: one in which it has at least relative autonomy from the central state, and the other in which it is simply a local arm of the central state. Duncan and Goodwin (1982) suggest that the local state, like the central state, is a historically-formed social relation and it is constantly being restructured in ways not always functional for capital. Local government develops as part of the conflicts and compromises between different groups and classes in which outcomes, although tending to be functional for capital, have not been guaranteed, not least because social change is not mechanical but the result of people's responses to relations and events. Thus, in Britain, the emergence of local democratic government in the nineteenth century could not be considered a more 'functional' solution for dominant classes than, for example, extending non-electoral institutions to the new industrial towns. Rather, 'the old system was breaking down socially: in many of these towns the working class was developing its own centres of local power . . . [and] the old system was differentially functional for different ruling-class groups' (Duncan and Goodwin, 1982, p. 169). The result was a partial and internally contradictory response by ruling groups to changing social relations and the development of a local–central state system which has been 'a periodic battleground' between the different classes. Consequently, as Dearlove (1979) has indicated, the 'problem' of local government is that it is especially vulnerable to working-class demands. The effect of local reorganisation in Britain in the 1970s – characterised as a response to poor 'councillor calibre' and local 'inefficiency' – was to seek to reduce working-class influence by creating larger authorities and internally reorganising councils with the stamp of corporate management. However, Duncan and Goodwin, and Dearlove, although critical of 'local state' theories that posit too tight a functional fit between state and capital, offer analyses based on the centrality of class relations at the local level rather than the collective consumption approach found in the dual-state thesis. We should note, too, that local government reorganisations in the name of efficiency are also introduced by labour and socialist parties aware of the inaccessibility, bureaucratisation and alienating characteristics of local governments and the often unequal distributive consequences of these features for, particularly, the working class. In Britain, despite recent efforts by socialist councils to protect localities from Conservative public expenditure cuts by arguing for the 'defence of local democracy', there is a long-established suspicion of local government within the Labour Party as a potential obstacle to a reforming central state (Bassett, 1984).

The relative attractiveness of local state theories on the one hand, emphasising the functionality of local government for capital and its role as a branch of a unitary state, and, on the other, the dual-state thesis which focuses on the specificity of collective consumption at the local level and the attendant dangers this poses for the central state and capital, tends to vary on the left with whether a socialist or non-socialist party is in government at the national level. Dual-state theory seems to have great explanatory potential for recent attempts by central governments in many western economies to circumscribe the financial power of local authorities and control levels of collective consumption that threaten both the fiscal base of government and the profitability of capital. Central government has a number of strategies that it can employ for this purpose: organisationally restructuring and subordinating local government; recommodifying or privatising services previously state-provided: 'de-politicising' local decision making by giving more powers to appointed, non-elected regional bodies; and ideologically associating attacks on local government with popular cynicism of local government bureaucracies. These strategies are not without their difficulties, as witnessed by the setbacks experienced in Britain by central government's efforts to abolish the second-tier metropolitan counties. Elected local government has an established democratic legitimacy and attacks on it can attract cross-class and cross-party opposition. On the other hand, however, the pluralistic and fragmented local politics of collective consumption makes united or coherent resistance difficult as groups are affected differently in the different consumption sectors. Nor is there much sign that the public sector unions, strategically located at the interfaces of production and consumption, and national and local politics, are able to cohere local opposition, for example, within local Labour parties.

However, the dual-state thesis has its critics. As we noted previously, Dunleavy (1984) suggests that most spending is capable of multiple classification and that the characterisation of expenditure is determined by the tier of government within which it is located, rather than a particular form of spending being allocated by a particular level of government. Moreover, the fit between social consumption provision and local government varies across countries and is a relatively recent phenomenon in Britain, becoming pre-eminent only in the 1970s. Dunleavy (1984, p. 76) regards as a critical difficulty with the dual-state thesis its poor predictability in comparison with other models over the allocation of social insurance functions between tiers of government. Unlike O'Connor's model, the dual-state thesis does not include these within the collective consumption category, which is limited to specific services supplied by the state apparatus.

Local corporatism and structure

As we have seen, the dual-state model links corporatist forms of interest intermediation and policy implementation to national decision making, with more pluralistic forms at local level. However, the model allows for local corporatist developments, particularly if the local state becomes more involved in production issues. A characteristic of liberal or societal corporatism is that the boundary between the public and private sectors becomes less clearcut, with many 'public' functions provided by ostensibly 'private' associations or by partnerships between public and private agencies. For example, in Britain the development of local enterprise agencies and trusts is an example of private-sector activity specifically related to public services. They provide a broad-based consultancy service to start-up business, with financial and other support from large local companies, local authorities, and the Department of the Environment.

An increasingly key organisation in the enhanced public policy involvement of the private sector at local level in Britain and elsewhere is the chamber of commerce. In the United States the National Chamber of Commerce acted as a valuable source of information and policy dissemination for individual companies involved in Federal Urban Renewal (Friedland, 1982, p. 45), while in a number of American cities they act as co-ordinators of business in advancing interests in local public policy processes. In many European countries, chambers have public law status, with membership compulsory and chambers undertaking a range of public responsibilities, such as industrial training, maintaining registers of companies, the provision of information services, and the administration of airports and other facilities. British chambers of commerce lack the resources of their public law counterparts, but the recent involvement of UK chambers in the New Training Initiative, acting as managing agents for the Youth Training Scheme, has moved them a little closer to the European model. It is one of the developments which indicate the increased 'public' character of locally-organised business in some areas (King, 1985a) and the increased contacts between chambers and local authorities. In part this reflects central government encouragement. Government guidelines on the urban aid programme state that local authorities must consult the private sector on urban programme submissions and that this would normally be through the local chamber of commerce. A study of the Leeds chamber indicates the crucial role that it plays in the discussions with the authority before meetings of the inner-city committee and its influence over particular schemes (King, ibid.).

Increased involvement by local authorities in economic policy making and the encouragement of central government have been instrumental in the development of corporatist tendencies at local level as these have involved the chambers of commerce. It is characterised more by a sharing or devolving of state power than controls on the chambers' autonomy, and a recognition by the state of its relative powerlessness to influence the accumulation of capital. As it is beyond their power to organise or control the process of accumulation, local authorities turn to the organised 'voice of local business' for help in encouraging business to perform. This cuts across party lines. In a study of Leeds, the return of a Labour council, most of whose members are well-acquainted with the public sector but only dimly aware of the private sector, yet committed to promoting industrial expansion, resulted in a strengthening of links between the authority and the chamber (King, ibid.). These public–private initiatives may provide a more flexible form of interventionism and be more finely-tuned to the needs of local small capital than would be provided by more directly statist or bureaucratic prescriptions. However, corporatist developments involving the chamber at local level are dependent on the local authority confining itself largely to infrastructural as opposed to direct financial support or policies that involved a greater 'socialisation' of the accumulation process.

In the manner and type of services that it provides for business, the boundaries between the chamber and the local state often seemed hazy. For example, both sets of officials were involved in offering advice to potential investors, in collecting trade data, in furnishing advice on current legislation to local businessmen. They meet regularly and are found in the same public and social gatherings, and there is a convergence of public and private officialdoms in style, aims and habitat (Lindblom, 1977).

This suggests that the influence of business on local policy making is greater than indicated from studies of the social composition of local councillors. The studies by Hennock (1973), and Morris and Newton (1970), provide a continuous profile of the local political élite in Birmingham from the first town council in 1839 until the mid-1960s, and they are particularly instructive on the role played by business executives as community decision makers. The most general feature in the period up to the First World War is the gradual decline in the number of small businessmen on the council and a steady increase in the number of large businessmen and professionals. Most studies of local politics in the twentieth century indicate a reversal of the process of big business involvement in the council chamber largely as the growth of large concerns predisposed owners and managers to influence national rather than local decision makers. (Bealey *et al.*, 1965; Birch, 1959; Jones, 1969; Lee, 1963). Local politics are thus left to smaller businessmen, primarily in the Conservative Party, and an increasing number of manual and lower professional workers in the Labour Party. However, the pattern of business withdrawal in Birmingham, although steady, appears less rapid than elsewhere, while its control of major committee chairs meant that it was powerful out of all proportion to its numbers.

A similar picture emerges in Elliott *et al.*'s (1978) account of local politics in Edinburgh over the period 1875–1975. They note that the character of property interests changed as local economies came to be dominated by independent small businesses rather than by large firms, often with headquarters many miles away, and that local business councillors were drawn more from the business professions (e.g. solicitors, estate agents) than builders or other direct producers. However, a theme of this and other chapters, is that business exercises its influence over local government less through electoral than administrative or corporatist politics, especially with the more formal and regular involvement of organised business in local policy processes. Local civic networks are also a crucial source of influence, while the private ownership of production in capitalism, and the recognition by local authorities of their dependence on business for employment and investment, provides business with a resource that is more effective than direct lobbying or other forms of direct representation.

Conclusion: public sector unionism and professionalism

An important part of this chapter examines claims about the autonomy of local political processes. Although the realm of urban politics may have a theoretical specificity that derives from local government's role in the provision of services (collective consumption) we have noted the increased external constraints on localities. This involves the power of large business for local policy makers, but also the increasing influence of central government and professional ideologies and interests. Dunleavy's account of high-rise building politics, for example, locates many of the structural influences on local housing decisions as national and professional. Government architects were especially influential for local authority architects' departments through the use of cost controls while the professional architectural and planning associations disseminated an authoritative ideology in which high-rise was a central image of the 'modern movement' and 'urban containment' a crucial planning value. Moreover, communication through the national local government system strongly limited the amount of variation by individual authorities from the general consensus on the desirability and type of high-rise building. Dunleavy and Rhodes (1983, pp. 120–1) refer to the constraints for bi-partisanship and a common view among local authorities as a consequence of the role played by their national associations in consulting with central government and providing information flows on new proposals and policy performances to individual authorities. Joint bodies of the national associations also carry out particular functions for local government as a whole, such as manpower planning, or negotiate national pay settlements with the local government unions. 'Policy communities' or 'issue networks' also exist around specific issues, comprised usually of those drawn from the professions working in local government, the local authority associations, sometimes the trade unions, leading councillors and civil servants (Heclo and Wildavsky, 1974). Both local authority associations and policy communities 'provide a framework within which any individual local authority can situate their own problems, concerns and strategies . . . most of the time local decisions are made within nationally defined parameters of what counts as good policy, rather than helping to redefine those parameters' (Dunleavy and Rhodes, 1983, p. 122).

Dunleavy suggests that these professional decision modes are to be distinguished from bureaucracy or corporatism, even if many professionals are public sector employees. Rather, 'professions have an obvious capacity to generate new initiatives, and they characteristically favour planning-oriented policies stressing rational analysis over simple bureaucratic routines' (Dunleavy, 1984, pp. 76–7). Similarly, in comparison with corporatist modes of interest intermediation, the professions change policy through internal processes of ideological development. In local government, policy in particular areas often seems dominated by professional 'fashions' nationally generated, and adopted almost uniformly by authorities. However, professionalism may fragment general policy within authorities. As Elcock (1982, p. 93) points out, while civil servants tend to be generalist administrators seeking the smooth working of the government machine by generating consensus for policies by, if necessary, watering down and reconciling proposals from different groups of experts 'the highly specialised but narrow professional training most local government officers receive makes co-ordination of proposals or action between departments difficult'. Whereas the professional experts are subordinate to the generalists in central government, they dominate local government. Their professional identification and expertise in particular areas not only makes it difficult to produce general agreement on issues that span several departments, but also inhibits common identification with the local authority service of the sort characteristic of the civil servant's approach to policy making.

However, the development of bureaucratic and corporatist forms of decision making at the local level may be regarded as counter co-ordinating tendencies to the inter-departmental fragmentation induced by professionalism. Mackay and Cox (1979) suggest that land-use planning is the key urban policy with major distributive consequences for social groups, but which is increasingly depoliticised as politicians cease to respond to social classes and groups through competitive party politics and make decisions jointly with officers and co-opted experts. Moreover, power and influence within local authorities has tended to move more firmly into the hands of senior councillors and leading officials, reinforced by corporate management techniques and the creation of general policy and resources committees. Important public–private economic exchanges, for example, involve the more senior and leading councillors, who are increasingly full-time councillors with responsibility allowances and designated office space. Local policy making tends to be the prerogative of a small group of leading councillors and officials, with other councillors confined to peripheral and occasionally oppositional roles (Newton, 1976).

These developments are not necessarily inevitable. The 'bossism' and authoritarian forms of decision making in some Labour groups, for example, has been challenged by councillors with middle-class occupations and high-levels of education (Green, 1981). In the 1980s, as authorities faced public expenditure squeezes from central government, 'backbench' Labour councillors have often rejected both the implementation and type of cuts proposed (e.g. nursery and hospital closures). These councillors generally receive strong support from local public sector unions, and may be associated with them as members or officers, and from district Labour parties who have sought to challenge or limit the control of Labour groups by senior councillors as part of local resistance to monetarist policies. However, there is little evidence as yet of the public sector unions providing a cohering basis for the inherently fragmentary forms of collective consumption protest. Nor does the 'decline of working-class politics' as the middle class take over local Labour wards indicate coherent class struggles developing at local level (Forester, 1976; Hindess, 1971).

Finally, there has been increasing recognition of the part played by interest groups in local politics, largely due to the work by Newton (1976), and given impetus by recent empirical applications of corporatist analysis. However, this is yet to be matched by substantial research on policy processes within local government, on inter-departmental conflicts, professionalism, and central–local relations. Such research would usefully complement both the concern with the 'input' process in policy making (e.g. role of interest groups, parties) and the increased emphasis on the 'outputs' of local government, especially the distributional consequences of policy for different social groups.

8

The State in an International Context

Graham Gibbs

Introduction

Examination of the state in an international context raises questions relevant to the theoretical perspectives outlined in the previous chapters in two major respects. These we may refer to as the internal and external determinants of state relations. Such a distinction is made by Skocpol (1979) and probably originated with the German historian Otto Hintze (Hintze, 1975). Hintze tried to show how two things combine to produce the organisation of the state, first, the structure of social classes, and secondly, the external ordering of states – their position relative to each other, and their overall position in the world. Skocpol argues that the state is 'Janus-faced' with an anchorage both in a class-divided socio-economic structure and in an international system of states. Generalising this distinction, by the internal determinants of state relations we mean all the social, economic and political phenomena affecting the nature of the state which find their origins within the boundaries of the state and which can be analysed predominantly in terms of conditions found within those boundaries. Thus included here will be all the social, cultural, historical, economic and political phenomena which are to be found within the frontiers of a state, and of particular concern will be economic systems, social classes and élites. The external determinants of state relations refer to those relationships in which the state plays a part and which affect the state, and which involve phenomena outside the boundaries of that state. This will obviously include other states, but also will encompass global economic systems and global political and economic agencies for example.

Such a distinction is not absolute. Very few phenomena – if any – can be identified as solely internal or solely external. To take just one example, the political systems in many African countries are the result both of internal factors, such as regionalism, the powers of local élites and the influence of 'charismatic' leaders, but also of external factors such as the political system set up by the colonial authorities, and intervention by the superpowers. However, the distinction is useful for examining the differing perspectives on the state in an international context. Some perspectives lay stress on internal determinants in explanations of the nature of the state while others emphasise the external determinants of state relations. The internal focus for analysis of the state outside the advanced capitalist countries has raised, in particular, the questions of the transition to a stable democratic government (socialist or capitalist, but usually the latter) and of why the transition (if indeed it is properly seen as such) should seem to be lasting so long. The external focus draws attention not only to the way in which states exist in a community of states, but also to how the characteristics of some states are to a large degree created and structured by phenomena and states which lie outside their territorial limits.

Modernisation and modernisation theory

The social sciences first focused their attention on states outside the first world (as opposed to the non-states studied by anthropology) in the period following the end of the Korean war in 1953. The old European colonial empires were beginning to break up, a process which by the end of the decade was to be heralded by the British prime minister of the time, Harold Macmillan, as a 'wind of change' blowing through the African and Asian continents. But at the same time the end of war in Korea saw the beginning of a long slump in world mineral and other commodity prices. The boom in the economies of the advanced capitalist states during the 1950s and 1960s was experienced only as continuing stagnation and impoverishment in the countries of what, in contrast to the first and second worlds of the advanced capitalist and communist states, soon became known as the third world. Sociologists, political scientists and economists found in this third world a 'problem' of development. How could these states get richer, and how could they solve their problems of poverty, hunger, and slow economic growth? In brief, how could they get to be like the countries of the first world, which believed they had eradicated poverty (or were rapidly doing so), had strong manufacturing economies and modern agricultural sectors, and had stable, strong and democratic state systems? As we noted in Chapter 1, a dominant social theory in the 1950s and 1960s was structural functionalism, which initially had little to say about the questions of changing a whole society, but which altered with the development of modernisation theory and a new evolutionary paradigm.

Functionalists for a long time argued for the compatibility of the different institutions of industrial society. For example, between a monetized economy and the legal institutions of private property and contract, between the industrial-organisational complex and both nuclear family patterns and an open (i.e. highly mobile) social structure, between occupational specialisation and formalised education and high literacy rates, between differentiation of the main institutional spheres and competitive pluralism, and between competitive pluralism and democracy and a fully enfranchised citizenry. It was observed that what was happening in the 'developing countries' was the introduction of modern economic and technological complexes. For modernisation theory, as the application of functionalist approaches to development became known, the consequence of introducing these modern economic and technological processes is to generate an inevitable process of transformation in which the necessity for the functional compatibility of the parts of society forces the non-economic aspects to take on their modern form too. The mechanism for this to occur is provided by Parsons's pattern variables (Parsons, 1951). Pattern variables are alternative patterns of value orientations in the role expectations of the actors in any social system. On the basis of compatibility one set of values is to be found particularly associated with modern economic and technological systems. Thus in modern developed societies one finds roles that are functionally specific, achievement-orientated, universalistic and affectively neutral. This means roles where the relations between one person and another are of one kind only, e.g. employer–employee, roles where evaluation of the person depends on what they have achieved, and roles where the standard of behaviour is based on universal principles and roles where rewards are not of an emotional or affective sort but of a neutral or instrumental kind, such as a salary contract. On the other hand, roles which tend to be associated with traditional society are functionally diffuse, ascriptive, particularistic and affectively rewarding.

> The methodological argument of modernisation theories of social change in contemporary developing societies seems to be that these internally consistent action patterns are built into the modern economic/technological institutions which underdeveloped countries so eagerly adopt (or which had been imposed on them during the colonial period) and that these action patterns in turn send their reverberations through the entire social, cultural and political structure of developing societies. (Hoogvelt, 1978, p. 56)

Thus, starting from an economic system based on the universalistic norm of making a profit, where reward is in the form of a money wage paid on the basis of achievement and where people increasingly relate to others as employer–employee, buyer–seller and other functionally specific ways, the rest of society and politics is progressively transformed. Wider kinship groups are replaced by voluntary associations, such as churches, social clubs, trades unions, political parties. The ending of traditional systems of loyalty and security require the creation of a new identity and sense of belonging which is provided by nationalism. Moreover, a consequence of universalistic role behaviour is that relationships in economic settings are based on contract, where the terms and conditions are set down regardless of the individual characteristics of the persons involved. This means that the contracted parties no longer have the trust and security that the contract would be honoured which membership of the same tribe, clan or kin-group would have given them. What is required then, in this view, is for some other body to provide this, and the modern centralised territorial state is regarded as undertaking the task of securing the continuity of economic relationships. To be effective this state requires a legitimate national government, recognised as such by all parties to economic contracts and therefore, modernisation theorists argue, it must be legitimated by a democratic polity.

In summary then, economic development, the adopting of a modern system of production and modern technology, requires a modern political system and state. Such a system is a pluralistic democracy with an enfranchised citizenry, multiple parties and an overall legitimation provided by regular free elections. If such a system is to work properly there has to be a politically sophisticated and mobilised electorate and a group of dedicated, technically competent and trustworthy leaders. A politically sophisticated electorate is created partly by the general economic and social transformations of modernisation, bringing people into cities and into contact with modern factories and modern housing, and partly by the system of education. Educational establishments would teach people about the new issues of a developing nation and an independent state, and this would ensure meaningful and democratic elections and overcome their previous loyalties to kin and tribe (Shils, 1966, 1970).

The new leadership is drawn from the élites in the nation. In the transition from traditional politics they play a crucial role determining how fast and effectively society can move towards national integration and political modernity.

> The characteristics of this modernity are rational and universalistic norms, a consensus of political values and expectations, and viable politial structures that can operate to resolve internal differences and mobilize against external threats; a participant citizenry, holding government responsible and at the same time assuming its own obligations, helps achieve this end. The attitudes and actions of the élites control when, if, or to what degree each characteristic will become part of the operational system. (Scott, 1967, p. 117)

On this view, such élites have the role of leading the nation to development, by providing the political leaders, the technical experts who will run the administration of the new state and the entrepreneurs who will run the businesses. However, as Alavi (1982, pp. 290–1) points out, such an élite perspective visualises necessarily privileged individuals and groups in society and the state. That militates against the pluralist conceptions of politics that are presumed in the functionalist conceptions of modernisation outlined above.

Political development

Although as conceived by Parsons, the introduction of modern economic systems would *inevitably* give rise to modernisation in the political sphere, such are the requirements of what Lerner (1967, p. 24) referred to as 'societies-in-a-hurry' that 'political development' became a concern of social scientists in its own right. Thus proposals were made for promoting political mobilisation, the building of nation states, administration and legal development, and extending secularisation, and especially for the creation of élites with the appropriate skills, knowledge, values and leadership qualities (McLelland, 1966). On this view, élites are important not primarily because of their power or their class backgrounds but because they possess certain personal attributes and social values. A step further away from the idea that change from traditional society is inevitable is represented by the proposal for a general development policy. This shares most of the assumptions of functionalist theory but rather than being content to let society change itself, it gives a role to both the states of the developed countries and to the modernising élites of the developing nations in actively promoting their social, economic and political change (Eisenstadt, 1970).

Despite the recognition in modernisation theory of the external origins of the new economic/technological system and the role of developed countries in promoting development as suggested by development theory, its main thrust in explaining the nature of the state and politics in developing countries is internal. That is, it refers to forces and phenomena *within* national frontiers. This can be seen even more so in those explanations that are put forward as to why the modernisation process seems to be taking so long or why development policies do not seem to be working. For it seemed at one time as if very few of the new states and the developing nations were achieving stable western-style democracies. Many had dictators or one-party systems, and some had communist regimes. Many continued to be divided by 'traditional' ties of kinship and tribe, even to the point of civil war. Nor were their populations being politically mobilised. There seemed to be an enormous divide still, a lack of communications in both directions, between on the one hand the central institutions of the state and on the other the peasants in the countryside and the slum dwellers of the cities. Often all that existed to link the people with power were a series of dyadic patron–client realtionships of a distinctly non-modern kind. Rather than expressing their political views through the democratic process of the secret ballot, peasants and poor town dwellers would seek out political patrons. In return for political support at elections and during other political and power struggles these patrons would dispense administrative favours to their poor clients (Clapham, 1984, pp. 54–9).

On one explanation, these traditional, non-modern phenomena persist merely because of a lag in the way modern values and institutions spread out from the economic/technological complex. Such an explanation of so-called 'breakdowns in modernisation', of course, denies the very imperative for modernisation which underpins modernisation theory. An alternative approach is to regard traditional society as not merely a passive ground upon which the modern society is constructed, but as persisting in a semi-permanent fashion. Modern and traditional thus co-exist in a dual society and aspects of the latter may present 'obstacles' to further development. One part of society rapidly develops as an urbanised monetised, mobile, politically-open, achievement-orientated society. Another part remains separate and traditional, predominantly rural (at least in outlook even if recently migrant to the city), immobile, undemocratic and unaffected by modernisation. The problem for development theory is how to overcome such obstacles and spread modernisation to the traditional sector.

However, there is one 'obstacle' to the development of a democratic state which fits badly with the idea that all obstacles to modernisation are aspects of the pre-existing traditional society. This is the large role played by the military in third world politics. Early views rather optimistically saw military intervention in the state as temporary, an experience that would happen less frequently as modernisation occurred and democracy spread (Leiuwen, 1962). A more common view was that of John J. Johnson (1962), who suggested that the military could have a progressive role in modernisation and nation-state building. In the temporary absence of other more appropriate political élites and of a politically mobilised citizenry, the military could take the leading role in applying development policy to the nation. The military, far from being a traditional leftover, argued Johnson, was a modern institution, a bureaucracy which provided officers with a technical training and in particular an ethos of loyalty to the state and obedience in a hierarchical structure which were sorely needed in the newly independent states and the developing countries.

There was some evidence to support this view. Large numbers of officers in the armies of third world states went to the first world – especially to the USA, UK and France – for their military training, where they obtained 'modern' values and outlooks. Added to that, during the 1960s many military academies began to add the study of the social sciences, especially politics and economics, to their curriculum. Soldiers were thus better prepared for the complexities of running a modern society.

Despite this, the reality was that military regimes rarely governed alone, and even more rarely did so for very long. The economic, social and political problems of third world states were just too complex and intractable. Civilian supporters were needed to run the administration, to give technical advice and to give at least a minimal degree of public support and hence political legitimacy. Third world armies, often already overstretched in undertaking their purely military duties, simply could not provide enough personnel to run the rest of the state apparatus as well. When economic crisis recurred, the military, unable to offer further solutions, had no choice but to return to barracks.

The difficulties of dealing with such events in modernisation theory of the pluralist kind led one commentator, Huntingdon (1968), to reject altogether the concern with political development and to replace it with an investigation of political power and political change, particularly revolutions. For Huntingdon the central political value is the maintenance of order, and its frequent absence in the third world creates major problems for the state. As countries experience development, expectations are raised and the result is an increase in political participation. Sometimes political institutions will be capable of handling the conflict and controlling it, often they will not. The crucial variable is the degree of institutionalisation of the polity. Those states with highly institutionalised political systems will socialise their citizens into what Huntingdon called 'civic' politics, which can take either a western democratic or communist form, but whichever, conflict is contained within the existing system. On the other hand, states that are weakly institutionalised are easily 'overwhelmed' by new political groups; student demonstrators, striking workers, rebelling peasants, or corrupt officials. Such a situation Huntingdon called 'Praetorean politics' and military rule is its normal form (Huntingdon, 1968, pp. 192–263). However, praetorianism is unstable, and often chaos will ensue. In that case a revolution might be the only way of bringing into the political scene new actors who are capable of re-establishing order and producing a durable political system.

Huntingdon, therefore, rejects the distinction in modernisation theory between traditional and modern societies when it comes to politics, and the concern with the establishment of western-style democratic processes. For him the central question in all societies is that of order, and order is not necessarily obtained by democratic means. In doing so he gives a more realistic picture of politics in the third world, although in the end his views do not stray far from the modernisation perspective. His image of politics can be gleaned from the way he defines revolutions as any 'rapid, fundamental and violent domestic change in the dominant values and myths of a society, in its political institutions, social structure, leadership and government activity and politics' (Huntingdon, 1968, p. 264). The picture is of politics divorced from the economic institutions of society and with very little reference to forces external to the third world society, particularly economic forces. Revolutions are to be avoided if possible for they are, as Leys puts it, 'merely pathological modes of restoring order' (Leys, 1982, p. 346). Above all, as Leys points out, Huntingdon rejects the notion of political development only to replace it by its opposite, the equally normative and teleological notion of 'political decay,' a situation characterised by unrest, violence, corruption and coups. The development theorists' concern with promoting modern élites and politically mobilised masses in third world societies is paralleled by Huntingdon's concern to introduce political systems that are highly institutionalised and thus relatively immune to revolutions (Leys, 1982, pp. 335–7).

Criticisms of modernisation theory

Modernisation theory has been tremendously important, both as an academic analysis of the third world and, in the form of development theory, as a policy promoted by governments throughout the world. For many decades modernisation theory influenced American foreign policy and provided the basis for policies of aid both by the developed nations directly, and mediated by international aid agencies (Nafziger, 1979; O'Brien, 1979). Nevertheless, since the mid-1960s it has received increasing criticism on several grounds:

1. It has seen social, economic and political development in the non-advanced nations simply in terms of a transfer from traditional to modern, which is crude and procrustean in the extreme. The theory tends to assume that modernisation is a desirable state and that it is best exemplified in the economy, society and polity of the USA. It assumes that a particular kind of capitalist development, namely that experienced in the USA (and possibly the UK) is one that will be emulated by all developing nations, and has been followed by all the already modernised states. The ethnocentrism of this view is marked, and other development paths e.g. populist and socialist (communist), are ignored, or seen as pathological (Rostow, 1960), or, as in convergence theory, are seen as mere variations on the same development theme. (See Chapter 4.) Moreover, it is false to imagine that all the currently industrialised nations followed the same process of development. In some the state played a major role in promoting industrialisation whereas in others it did not. In some the peasantry disappeared before industrialisation, and in others it remained and quite different political systems and state structures oversaw industrialisation. (See Chapter 2.)

Underlying all this is a teleology that sees the major purpose of all social, political and economic change as bringing about development, modernisation and industrialisation. It is assumed, without evidence, that all states and all peoples want to be modernised. Of course this may well be true for the élites spotlighted by the theory and in many cases indoctrinated with its tenets, but no one has even asked the ordinary people if they want to be modern and, as Moore points out, there is very little evidence from history that they have ever expressed such a wish (Moore, 1968).

2. Following on from this, modernisation theory clearly has a very crude view of the nature of the traditional society. It is

conceptualised mainly in terms of attributes which are the opposite of those said to be found in modern society. Thus Raymond Aron (Aron, 1964, p. 30) has commented that 'All past societies are put into this single category, whether they be the archaic communities of New Guinea, the Negro tribes of Africa, or the old civilisations of India and China. But the only feature they have in common is that they are neither modern nor industrialised.' But, not only does the theory club together radically different societies solely on the basis of the absence of one feature, industrialisation, but it conspicuously ignores another feature which links almost all of the states of the third world, namely their experience at one time or another during the last 500 years of colonisation by the now developed states.

3. As suggested above, despite the fact that the initial 'inoculation' of modern economic/technological institutions must come from outside the society, modernisation theory tends to emphasise internal features in describing the development process and in identifying barriers to this transformation. This internalism affects the conceptionalisation of the state in that almost all its important characteristics are seen as being the result of local phenomena such as the pre-existing traditional society, the degree to which modernisation has occurred and especially the nature of the élites. The major relationship between developed states and states in traditional societies recognised by modernisation theory is that of attempting to promote modernisation, and this is predominantly seen in terms of 'rowing with the tide', hastening a process that is already inevitable. What is almost totally ignored is the past history of relations between third world and developed world, something which has formed the starting point of much analysis of the third world from a Marxist or related standpoint, as we shall see below.

4. Though for development theory the state and the élites who hold power in it are clearly important in promoting modernisation, there is little explicit discussion of the role of the state and its relations with the broader society. The major conception is, as Alavi (1982, p. 289) points out, that 'the state is . . . thought of as an entity that stands outside and above society, an autonomous agency that is invested (potentially) with an independent source of rationality . . . and the capability to initiate and pursue

programmes of development for the benefit of the whole of society'. Modernising élites, charged with the task of dragging their countries into the twentieth century, are seen as using the state as their instrument and claim that what they are doing is ultimately in the national interest. The major role for the state is not so much to control individual interests for the general good, but to oversee the transformation of society to an industrial, modern form which will ultimately be to the general good, or what is usually taken to be the same thing, in the national interest.

Such a view of the state is certainly simplistic, grouping together a whole range of possible and actual arrangements. It is also teleological in the sense outlined above in assuming a certain end point for development, namely a pluralistic, democratic state. However, in getting there, on this view, the state must clearly be undemocratic because in order for it to promote modernisation it must take sides in favour of the modern sector and against the traditional, even if this means favouring a minority. Thus those people whose livelihood depends on the traditional sector or whose culture and society are traditional will not be supported by the state but will be positively discouraged. The claim that this is in the national interest is highly questionable. First, as was argued above, it is not universally agreed that a modern western society is what everyone wants or needs, i.e. there is no uncontested 'national interest'. Secondly, there is considerable evidence that those who run the state apparatus – the élites in modernisation terms – derive a great deal of personal gain from that involvement, often in ways that cannot be seen as to the general national interest. Examples abound, from the personal fortune of President Somoza in Nicaragua before the 1979 revolution to the enormous corrupt payments found throughout the political and administrative system in Nigeria.

Criticisms such as those above led during the late 1960s to what has been termed a paradigm shift in thinking about the third world with consequent changes in the conception of the state. On these new views the external determinants are given much more, and sometimes complete, importance, and one particular aspect of these is stressed, namely the history of the relationship between first world and third.

Imperialism

The one major experience that almost all the countries of the third world have had, which modernisation theory fails to take account of is that they have at one time or another been colonies of European (or North American) states. The modern period of overseas colonisation began in the early sixteenth century when Spanish, Portuguese, English and Dutch (and later French) explorers, traders and settlers began to arrive in the Americas. One immediate effect in many parts, such as the Caribbean, was the virtual elimination of the indigenous Amerindian population. The slave trade from Africa was set up to replace the local population where necessary to ensure labour for the mines and plantations that the colonists set up. In the north of North America and the south of South America European settlers arrived and set up ranches and small farms. Where there had been states, e.g. the Mayas and the Incas, these were totally destroyed and new colonial administrations were established, run from Europe. The main function of the colonies, as seen from Europe, was to provide cheap food, such as sugar and minerals, especially gold and silver, for the colonial powers. The administrations were therefore designed to facilitate this, being controlled mainly by Europeans sent out specially to perform the tasks, rather than local European settlers. Not surprisingly, eventually there was conflict between the American settlers and European states and their administrators, the former wanting to be free of the restrictions on trade, production, politics and power, which the Europeans imposed. The first successful rebellion was that of the North American settlers, who in the late eighteenth century set up the United States of America. This was followed during the first quarter of the nineteenth century by similar revolts in Latin America so that by 1825 only the Caribbean, Canada and a few small enclaves in South America were still under colonial rule.

In Latin America the states which had been set up very much reflected the nature of the victors in the wars of independence. They were either republics from the start, or very soon became so, and they were dominated by the white, Spanish and Portuguese settlers; Indians and Blacks were almost totally excluded from state power (slavery continued in Brazil until 1888, 66 years after independence). They were run by landowners, plantation owners and agricultural traders who constituted the controllers of the bulk of the economy. Aside from the domination by an agricultural ruling class, which is rarely still the case in Latin America, that pattern has continued until today. The major legacy of colonialism was an economy orientated towards producing agricultural and mineral raw materials for European (and later North American) markets, which after independence was run by the local agricultural ruling classes.

In the case of most of Asia and Africa the bulk of colonial expansion did not occur until after most of the American colonies had gained independence. In Africa there had been a European presence since the late sixteenth century, but for a long time contact was concerned mainly with trade, especially the trade of slaves. In Asia trade was also the major link between Europe and the East. But during the nineteenth century (slightly earlier in the case of India), European states began to establish and expand colonies throughout Africa and Asia. This ended with a veritable rush to establish sovereignty over vast tracts of the interior of Africa so that by the end of the nineteenth century there was hardly a single part of Africa or south and south-east Asia that was not a European colony. As in the Americas, there was European settlement, but not on the same scale and restricted predominantly to certain areas, such as Algeria, South Africa, Kenya, Zimbabwe (and Australasia). Local populations were not eliminated in most cases, although the harshness of colonial rule did result in widespread malnutrition and death. In many cases there were existing power structures and even well established states. Rather than being destroyed, these were often incorporated, in part or in whole, into the state structure of the colonies. A *comprador* (Portuguese for go-between or interpreter) class drawn from the indigenous population or from Asian immigrants was established to act as intermediaries between the local people and the new, white, colonial rulers.

However, almost as soon as they had been set up, questions were raised about the wisdom of the creation and continuation of these new imperial realms in Africa and Asia. An early 'classic' discussion of imperialism was that of the English liberal J. A. Hobson. He argued that the new colonies did not provide any economic gains for Britain, on whose empire he focused. They were not good for trade and did not provide jobs for British workers to migrate to, which left the question, why had this phase of colonial expansion taken place? Hobson's answer was that certain sectional interests in Britain, namely industrialist and financiers, had 'usurped control of national resources and used them for their private gain' (Hobson, 1965, p. 46). As a result of insufficient demand at home those with capital to invest had put it into the more profitable colonies and they had used the apparatus of the imperial state to support these investments. For Hobson, the root cause of this was the lack of home demand and the consequent low rates of profit. The cure, he thought, was a redistribution of income to boost home markets.

A writer on imperialism very much influenced by Hobson's arguments was Lenin, who, although he took up much of Hobson's account, rejected the idea that imperialism could be ended merely by a change of government policy in the European states. In his *Imperialism, the Highest Stage of Capitalism*, written in 1916, Lenin argued that while imperialism had happened for economic reasons it was not the result of wrong policy but rather the consequence of an ineluctable process of capitalist development. This is a fundamental point that links Lenin with the underdevelopment and world system theorists whose work will be considered later and separates all these from the modernisation theory writers just considered. The crucial point is that the major relationships between states, and in particular between those of the first world and those of the third, is in the end the result of the inevitable development of capitalist society. There may be different conceptions of what capitalist society is, but all these writers reject the traditional/modern dichotomy which is at the heart of modernisation theory.

For Lenin, at the end of the nineteenth century capitalism passed into a new stage. There had been earlier examples of imperialism, during the early nineteenth century and the sixteenth and seventeenth centuries, and even well before capitalism had existed. It was not so much that capitalism caused imperialism, but rather that modern imperialism took a certain form as the result of the development of capitalism. During the latter part of the nineteenth century, Lenin argued, industrial capital and financial capital had fused. There were now financiers and bankers who lived off the income derived from profit on the shares they owned in industrial companies, and through the new joint stock companies they came to dominate and control industry. As with Hobson, Lenin argued that these financiers exported their capital in order to get the best rate of profit. Capitalism thus changed from a concern with competition and the export of goods to a concern with the export of capital. Thus,

> An enormous 'surplus of capital' has arisen in the advanced countries . . . The need to export capital arises from the fact that in a few countries capitalism has become 'overripe' and (owing to the backward state of agriculture and the poverty of the masses) capital cannot find a field for 'profitable' investment. (Lenin, 1975, p. 59)

A further consequence of the growth of capitalist society, in Lenin's view, was that companies grew in size, amalgamating with other companies, taking them over, or putting them out of business and so monopolising (or oligopolising) markets. These very large companies wanted to dominate markets abroad too, especially where they were investing capital, and so, aided by their own governments, the world was politically and economically divided up. British companies could monopolise the British colonies, French ones the French colonies and so on. But capitalism did not develop evenly in Europe and the USA. In particular, Germany industrialised very rapidly and soon became the most powerful economy in Europe, although comparatively Germany had a small colonial empire. For Lenin, in the absence of further places left to incorporate into imperial empires, conflict over the way world resources were divided was inevitable. The most important characteristic of the First World War was that it was an inter-imperialist war.

Thus Lenin claimed that finance capital was divided into national capitals, British, French, German, etc., and within each nation acts in unison. British capital, for example, dominates the state to such an extent that it will do what is necessary to maximise the profits to be made from investments. That means investing to a large extent outside Europe and especially in Africa and Asia. But here the monopolies encounter two problems. First, they have no monopoly outside their own country. They need to protect their markets, their mineral and agricultural resources from acquisition by competitors, i.e. other national monopolies. And secondly, they need to ensure that normal business conditions are maintained in the areas they are operating, that law and order is maintained, that contracts can be made and enforced, and that there is a communications infrastructure. For both these reasons they will require that their home government establish a colonial state, for, 'colonial possession *alone* gives the monopolies complete guarantee against all contingencies in the struggle against competitors' (Lenin, 1975, p. 77, my emphasis). In other words the colonial state guarantees the conditions necessary for capitalist accumulation and hence the further growth of the monopolies.

There are several consequences of Lenin's argument. First, in the industrial countries he implicitly uses an instrumentalist explanation of the relationship between the monopolies or finance capital and the state, for capital and state are almost one and the state simply does what capital requires. The state cannot act in any independent way. Moreover, finance capital is assumed to speak with one voice, otherwise the state would need to act in contradictory ways. At the same time, the unanimity of finance capital operates only within nations; between national monopolies there is the usual capitalist competition and conflict. Even here, however, as Lenin discusses, the monopolies attempted to negotiate agreements with other companies to divide up the world into exclusive spheres of operation. To the extent they achieved this they partly rendered redundant the need for colonialism. As we shall see later, the activities of modern transnational corporations have not required colonialism and nor have they usually been able to make such exclusive agreements amongst themselves, but normally they have required the existence of capitalist state. Secondly, in the non-industrialised countries, Lenin stresses the desire for control of territory. He saw growth under imperialism as coming from ever greater exploitation of resources, rather than from, say, technological innovation. Of course, not every non-industrialised country was a colony, and almost none of Latin America was. But Lenin saw the colonial empire as the model for the future.

Imperialism today?

The strengths of Lenin's arguments are that he highlights a particularly important stage in the history of the third world, namely imperialism. He suggests that at root there was an economic motivation to colonial expansion that essentially consisted of the expansion of the capitalist system. The state at home and the colonial state both had a role in facilitating this expansion. It thus becomes clear just how simplified is the modernisation theory view of the traditional society. Society in the third world was affected in a most profound way by imperialism which means that colonial and post-colonial societies cannot accurately be described as traditional, and which establishes that there is a major relationship between first world states and third world.

However, in the years since the publication of Lenin's work on imperialism there have been many changes in the world which have raised questions about some aspects of his theory. Most importantly, almost all the countries that were once colonies are now independent states. As far as the third world is concerned it is the states of Latin America rather than the European colonies which turned out to be the pattern for the future. In fact even during the colonial period finance capital from London reached far higher levels in independent Latin America than it did in many of the colonial possessions in Africa. For example, in 1848 the government of Peru agreed to place half the state's annual income from guano (bird dung fertilizer and Peru's major export at that time) in the Bank of England to pay Peru's outstanding national debt, then £4.5 million. London merchant houses already controlled all the guano trade, but eventually under pressure from local merchants the government was forced to let them take over. However, massive borrowing in the late 1860s rapidly increased Peru's foreign debt. In 1872 it was £35 million, and Peru was then the largest debtor on the London money market. This forced Peru to hand the guano trade back into foreign hands, and the government granted a monopoly to a French merchant house, Dreyfus, which in return serviced the national debt. Finance capital in Europe, it seems, found no need for the states of Latin America to become colonies in European empires.

What is significant in this example is that in Peru there was already a state which, as Lenin suggested, could guarantee the general conditions for capitalist enterprise, and which was tied into the international capitalist system. In Africa and some parts of Asia this was not so. Therefore, as Elson points out, there was a need for direct territorial control;

> precisely because of the absence of the capitalist system of economic and political relationships . . . direct control of land was essential where a capitalist system of land ownership and economic contrasts did not exist. An important function of the colonial state was indeed to impose capitalist property relations. (Elson, 1984, p. 167)

The argument here is very similar to that of modernisation theory which recognises that the state performs the function of enabling modern systems of contract, exchange, employment of wage labour – in other words capitalist relations – to operate when older (traditional, i.e. non-capitalist) systems and their built-in guarantees no longer suffice.

Lenin erred in thinking that direct territorial control was a permanent necessity, for once the state had been established and once capitalist economic relations were operating, there was no longer any need for continued imperial control. Companies operating from the industrialised countries have found it perfectly possible and very profitable to operate in the independent states of the third world. Furthermore, in addition to guaranteeing the general conditions for the operation of capitalism and creating and controlling a workforce of wage labourers, the third world state plays a role in negotiating and contracting with overseas companies (as the Peru example shows) and also polices a system of patents and licensing that enables companies to keep control over their technology. The latter two functions have been particularly important in the last fifty years and consequently it appears that Elson's argument underemphasises the importance of resource agreements between states and companies. There are many examples of states making direct agreements with companies, usually to the mutual benefit of those in the state apparatus and the companies. For example, in Liberia overseas companies like the Bethlehem Steel Corporation are involved in very advantageous operations with the government which guarantee iron ore at a set price and very low rates of taxation (Lanning and Mueller, 1979, pp. 257–73). Here we have examples of independent states co-operating with overseas companies in capitalist expansion rather than just simply clearing the ground and oiling the wheels.

A second criticism is aimed at Lenin's argument that with the growth of monopolies at home, companies would have capital to invest but a lack of profitable domestic outlets for it. Therefore, they would export their capital. The overall consequence would be accelerated industrial growth in the areas capital was exported to, the colonies, and retarded growth in the industrial centres. However, firstly, the evidence that the export of capital was peculiar to the late nineteenth century, the period of major colonial expansion, is lacking. As Warren points out there does not seem to be a sudden leap in foreign investment to coincide with the 'scramble for Africa'. Export of capital was important in the UK from 1820 onwards and if anything its rate of growth up to 1870 was greater than after that year. In addition, several leading imperialist powers such as the USA, Japan and Italy were net importers of capital, yet they, with Germany, led the late nineteenth-century outburst of colonialism (Warren, 1980, pp. 57–70). There is also debate about what one should properly understand by foreign investment. Emmanuel suggests that Lenin mistook foreign assets for export of capital. Because overseas assets were owned by a European company does not mean that all that amount of capital was exported from Europe, for assets can grow from reinvestment (Emmanuel, 1982). For example, Emmanuel points out that over the period 1870–1914, UK investments abroad grew from about £1 billion to about £4 billion. This looks like export of capital, but £1 billion invested in 1870, and earning a profit of just over 3 per cent would, if the profits were reinvested be worth £4 billion 44 years later. In fact the best estimates of profit on such investments during this period are between 4 and 5 per cent, so the UK could have *imported* capital – about £1.5 billion – during this time and still seen investment grow to about £4 billion by 1914. Emmanuel presents some evidence for thinking that the UK did in fact import capital during this period. If any period was characterised by the export of capital, argues Emmanuel, it was the first half of the nineteenth century rather than 1870 to 1914, the period with which Lenin was concerned.

Looking to the industrialised countries, Warren suggests little evidence for a superabundance of capital. Germany even had to restrict foreign investment for a while because of a lack of domestic investment (Warren, 1980, p. 63), while the growth of monopoly was not connected with investments abroad. Moreover, there has, of course, been no noticeable slowdown in the growth of the industrialised economies which can be attributed to an export of capital. In fact the late nineteenth-century imperial period was a time of the fastest growth in the economies of Germany, France and the USA and of continuing fast growth in the UK (Warren, 1980, pp. 70–1).

In conclusion, the central thrust of imperialism and colonialism was not so much directly economic, such as to control markets and resources, but to establish capitalist societies and capitalist states where none existed. Lenin's belief in the instrumental nature of the state in the industrialised countries led him to believe that the best form of environment for monopolies abroad was one that was similarly instrumental, namely the colonial state directly controlled by the imperial power. In fact the motives for imperialism were much more diverse, for the role of colonial settlers was very important as was the continuing importance of trade. Moreover, we have to be clear about the difference between the actual export of capital – capital from the industrialised countries invested abroad – and the expansion of overseas investments which may be achieved by using large amounts of local capital.

Underdevelopment and world systems

As was suggested above, a corollary of Lenin's claim that there was an export of capital to the colonies was their rapid development. Certainly ports were constructed, and roads and railways were built, with European and North American capital and expertise and local labour – often at great cost in terms of loss of life. But the rest of society did not develop and there was no significant industrial manufacturing sector in most of the colonies. They were predominantly export economies, exporting primary goods, mineral and agricultural produce, which the ports, roads and railways greatly facilitated. In order to attempt to accommodate these facts, by the late 1960s there developed a new school of social thought. This tried to explain the apparent continued lack of industrial development and with it the continuing poverty of the mass of people in the third world, yet at the same time it rejected the emphasis in modernisation theory on traditional barriers to change and its lack of reference to the external, international relations between first world and third. This school thus took on board Lenin's emphasis on the historical experience and effects of colonialism and his concern with the links between first world and third, but at the same time was greatly concerned to explain why the third world had not experienced industrial development up to the level found in North America and Europe.

The original leading figure and great polemicist of this view is A. G. Frank. He was mainly concerned to counter what he saw as the simplistic and ideological views of modernisation theory on the third world. Basically he argued that it was quite wrong to see the lack of development in the third world as a result of failure to change from a traditional form of society as a result of the resistance of that traditional sector to the imperatives of modern social institutions. In particular, he wanted to challenge the idea that lack of development in the third world is unconnected with the extent of development in the first world. Rather, Europe developed at the expense of other societies, especially the colonies, and it achieved this by incorporating them into a social, economic and cultural system on a world scale dominated by the West. In developing themselves, the countries of Europe and North America systematically underdeveloped the third world. The third world is not traditional but has already been transformed in the main by the process of colonisation. In that sense, the third world now is not in the same situation as that of countries of the developed world before they developed. 'The now developed countries were never *under*developed, though they may have been *un*developed' (Frank, 1969, p. 4).

The establishing of third world countries as colonies of European and North American states achieved a transformation of the economy and society in these countries and it began the process of underdevelopment. Economies were shaped to fit into the requirements of the imperial powers, beginning a process which continues to the present. The new colonial states were tied into a world capitalist system which even independence did not allow them to escape. Colonial conquest was the moment of incorporation into the world capitalist system, and the 'development of capitalism throughout the world has simultaneously generated – and continues to generate – both economic development and structural underdevelopment' (Frank, 1967, p. 13).

This is a complete change of vision from that of both modernisation theory and Lenin's views on imperialism. Far from the spread of modern – i.e. capitalist – institutions bringing about development, Frank believes that it will merely achieve greater underdevelopment. This is so because, argues Frank, the capitalist system has three essential interlinked characteristics. It is hierarchical, monopolistic and exploitative. Relations between the parts of the world capitalist system can be seen as links in a chain of what he calls satellite–metropolis relationships. At any one level, one can identify a metropolis which exercises a monopoly on some aspects of the economy and society. This enables it to exploit other lower levels of the world system, which Frank calls the satellites. Exploitation consists of the transfer of surplus to the metropolis. Typically each satellite will act as metropolis too, and exploit its own satellites, keeping part of what it extracts and passing part up the chain to the higher levels. In this way every part of the world economy is linked through a chain of satellite–metropolis relations to the central metropolis, the commercial and industrial centres of the first world, London, New York, Paris, Tokyo; and surplus is extracted at each level and progressively passed up the chain so that it ends up in the first world. Countries that were colonised in the sixteenth century have been linked into this system ever since. Any changes that have since occurred, notably independence, have been changes in the mode of domination only, not changes in the economic system (Frank, 1969).

Frank thus attacks two aspects of modernisation theory. First, he rejects the idea of dualistic societies; the notion that third world countries typically consist of a dynamic, modern, industrial sector and a static, traditional, predominantly rural sector, which have very little contact with each other. For him, as O'Brien puts it, 'even the most remote Bolivian peasant is linked in an unbroken chain to the rich New York capitalist' (O'Brien, 1975, p. 27, fn.). It might seem that some sectors, like the self-sufficient farming area of north-east Brazil, are backwaters of traditional society. But even here, says Frank, society is the product of the decay of earlier export industries and the peasants are not as self-sufficient as they appear. Local markets link them with the world market and the money they make selling their produce depends more and more on world prices, and the things they buy with that money are more often the creation of industrial production. Secondly, Frank attacks the trickle down theory of economic development. This is the idea that the poor of the third world will gradually become better off as the wealth created and owned by the élites of the modern sector 'trickles down' to them as the élites buy produce in local shops, use local services and employ local people. The situation is more aptly described as 'trickle up'. The rulers of third world states will use their relatively powerful position to extract surplus from those lower down the chain, some of which they pass on up the chain, but some of which they will keep for themselves.

In contrast with Lenin, it is not actual colonial control which is important so much as the incorporation into a world system of satellite–metropolis relations which was inaugurated by colonialism. Independence may change the mode of domination, but it basically consists simply of a change in the personnel who are involved in the chain of relationships. Even in independent nations in the third world, the ruling classes owe their positions – their wealth and power – to their positions in the 'chain'. Frank therefore expects the local bourgeoisie to use the state to further a policy of underdevelopment, i.e. of ever greater integration into the world capitalist system (Frank, 1972, p. 13). As evidence Frank here gives the example of Latin America following independence. The rupture that independence represented set in motion a debate between what became known as the 'European' and 'American' factions of politicians. 'Europeans' were supporters of free trade especially with Europe, hence their name, while the 'Americans' wanted protection for domestic industries. The Europeans were led by the local merchants, who, argues Frank, were strong because of the nature of the export economy which had been inherited. The 'European' faction eventually won the day, and the Latin American states have remained linked in to the world capitalist system as dependent economies. Frank uses the term 'lumpenbourgeoisie' to refer to these ruling factions. They are not a true bourgeoisie because they owe their position as much to their place in the hierarchy of satellite–metropolis relations as to the ownership of capital (Frank, 1972, pp. 58–61). As de Souza puts it, these minor partners in the dependent state (bourgeoisie, bureaucrats, technocrats) are 'in the government but do not have political power' (quoted in Jenkins, 1984, p. 179).

An approach which in many ways is similar to that of Frank, especially in the reference to a world economic system, but which gives much more emphasis to the role of the state is that of Wallerstein. Both would agree that since about the sixteenth century there has been a capitalist world system in existence which incorporates many different independent political entities. However, where Frank sees a chain of satellite–metropolis relationships running throughout this economic system, Wallerstein recognises a tripartite division of the world into core, periphery and semi-periphery. As we described in Chapter 2, this division reflects a world division of labour. The core consists of the industrialised countries, where economic activities concentrate on manufacturing and animal rearing with a relatively highly skilled, well-paid and free workforce. The periphery is the underdeveloped world where economies are characterised by mineral and other primary goods production using low skilled, forced or semi-free labour. The semi-periphery stands as a kind of half-way category partly industrialised, partly not, both exploiter and exploited. States enter into this model as the basic units which may move up or down the hierarchy of core, semi-periphery and periphery. For Wallerstein, the nation-state does not exist outside of the world system, for it is the creation of the capitalist world economic system. Its function is to reduce the freedom of the world system, to intervene into the economic system so that some are favoured rather than others.

> Normal market considerations may account for recurring initial thrusts to specialization (natural or socio-historical advantages in the production of one or another commodity), but it is the state system which encrusts, enforces, and exaggerates the patterns, and it has regularly required the use of state machinery to revise the pattern of the world wide division of labour. (Wallerstein, 1979, p. 292)

But in the end, for Wallerstein, the explanation of the activities of the states, and in particular the strengths of the various state machineries cannot make reference to their internal, cultural features, but can only be given in terms of 'the structural role a country plays in the world-economy at that moment in time' (Wallerstein, 1979, p. 21). For Wallerstein too, then, the characteristics and activities of the state are determined by forces external to its frontiers.

Two points follow from this. First, that a study of the relation between states and their particular societies is insufficient and secondly, that because all states coexist in the single capitalist world system, the division between capitalist and socialist states is more apparent than real.

Criticisms of world systems approaches

Given the central place accorded to the notion of the capitalist world economy in the approaches of Wallerstein and Frank, it is not surprising that appraisal of their views has often focused on their conception of capitalism. One question that has been raised concerns the time at which the capitalist world system was established. Frank suggests that there was capitalism in South America in the sixteenth century. The consequences for the colonial powers, Spain and Portugal, are that either their colonies were capitalist before they were or that these two countries were capitalist in the sixteenth century too. Whilst some might baulk at this idea, for Frank and Wallerstein what distinguishes capitalism is the existence of a certain kind of exploitative exchange relationship. Thus for Wallerstein the essential nature of the capitalist system is that there are market relations – that is production for sale in a market in order to make a profit. The capitalist world system can be said to have started in the sixteenth century not because it was then worldwide, but because from that time it existed at a higher level than the single state. Exploitation exists in this system because producers receive less than they produce. For both Frank and Wallerstein the different forms that such exploitation may take, wage labour, slavery, feudal serfdom, sharecropping and so on are not of any central importance. Much criticism of these two writers has centred on whether it is valid to characterise capitalism in terms of relations of exchange rather than focusing on how production is carried out. Laclau, for example, believes only the latter is valid. For him, 'the fundamental economic relationship of capitalism is constituted by the free labourer's sale of his labour power, whose necessary precondition is the loss by the direct producer of ownership of the means of production' (Laclau, 1977, p. 23). The central problem is to know *how* the surplus that is transferred is produced and whether there are any specific features of the productive system that limit its development. In contrast with Frank's claim that even the remotest parts of the third world are capitalist, Laclau argues that the development of capitalism across the world is uneven. Some parts of societies do not exhibit fully developed capitalist relations. In fact Laclau suggests that many societies, in the third world in particular, may contain non-capitalist forms of production coexisting with capitalist ones. In the language of recent Marxist scholarship, peripheral social formations contain capitalist and non-capitalist modes of production articulated together. Wallerstein is clear in his rejection of this view. It is not the case that each state has its own mode(s) of production but that the world economy has only one mode of production, capitalism.

As Worsley points out, there is more at fault with Wallerstein's view than improper interpretation of Marx (Worsley, 1983). First, the role of the state is restricted to certain areas only. For Wallerstein, the state intervenes at the level of the market and the development of trade, especially at the international level. He pays little attention to the state's role in production or to the role of the state in creating the general inputs needed for production, such as raw materials, technology, workers and legal and political institutions. A consequence of Wallerstein's view for Worsley is that he does not understand that a precursor to the development of an economy is the establishment of political power, especially at the level of the state. This omission by Wallerstein of any consideration of the 'internal' activities of states is reflected in his treatment of exploitation. As we have seen, exploitation for world systems theorists is seen simply in terms of producers receiving less than they produce. The great differences in the mode of social control and the different legitimating ideologies that go with them, plus the relative extent of reliance on force and the varying ways in which the state is involved in these are all played down or ignored.

As a result the position of the world systems' theorists is both over-deterministic and arbitrary. The arbitrariness of the model is a consequence of defining capitalism in terms of exchange. This exchange is unequal or exploitative, but the model cannot explain the need for such inequality. The rich states are seen as lucky beneficiaries, the poor as unlucky victims. The situation is the result of a natural accident, in Wallerstein's terms, namely the initial natural advantages of Europe. World systems' theorists 'cannot see the exploitation of overseas countries as systematic, i.e. as a requirement of the continued expansion and reproduction of centre capitalism' (Hoogvelt, 1982, p. 181). At the same time the possibility of escaping the system is virtually ruled out. Skocpol points out that the model rests on 'the teleological assertion . . . that things at a certain time and place had to be a certain way in order to bring about later states or development that accord (or seem to accord) with what his system model of the world capitalist economy required or predicts' (Skocpol, 1976–7, p. 1088). The system is so powerful that attempts by states or others to break out are impossible unless brought about by accidental, external features, such as the 1930s recession and subsequent world war which Frank suggests broke the metropolis–satellite chain for a while and enabled Latin America to industrialise by import substitution. 'It is a picture of a world *so* determined by capitalism, and particularly by those who control the core capitalist states, that it leads logically to fatalism and resignation, for it becomes difficult to see how any part of such a tightly-knit system can possibly break away' (Worsley, 1983, p. 512). The ability of ruling classes to manipulate the system is overemphasised. The model underemphasises agency, especially on the part of those who resist domination, and as Worsley suggests, the success of liberation movements, revolutionary movements and of the communist states suggests that an important question in social science is the examination of the conditions under which resistance to the capitalist world system occurs and is successful.

As we have seen, one of the initial motives behind the formulation of underdevelopment theory and the world systems approach was to explain the lack of the kind of development in third world countries expected by the supporters of modernisation theory. Frank replaces the idea of modernisation by that of the development of underdevelopment. Frank does not deny that change will occur, only that this change cannot be independent development. There is always the possibility of dependent industrialisation, but this would be unlikely to have much impact on the poverty of the masses, and rather make matters worse. Third world states are dependent states, and their local capitalists are a lumpenbourgeoisie or dependent bourgeoisie, ruling locally only to the extent that they support the continued incorporation of their countries into a capitalist world system. There is some evidence for such an outlook on the part of local ruling classes. Studies of Latin American businessmen during the 1970s showed that they were not opposed to foreign and transnational corporate investment

(Johnson, 1972; Petras and Cook, 1973). For underdevelopment theorists, this suggested the continued support by local ruling classes for the external domination of third world economies and the continuing penetration of economies by foreign capital, entailing the transfer of ownership and decision making abroad, and they concluded that nationalist capitalist development was not viable in the third world. The only alternative was revolution and socialist development outside the world capitalist system, although as suggested above, Frank and Wallerstein have little to say about what kind of political struggles might bring this about.

However, during the 1970s several third world countries experienced considerable industrial development of a kind that could not be dismissed as mere underdevelopment. Countries such as Brazil, South Korea, Taiwan, Argentina and Singapore achieved industrialisation and impressive growth rates without breaking their ties with the international capitalist system. This has lead some dependency writers such as Cardoso and Falletto to be less pessimistic about the possibilities of development (Cardoso and Falletto, 1979; Cardoso, 1982). Dependency and development are not necessarily incompatible, they suggest, for dependency does not always lead to stagnation. There can be what Evans has called 'dependent development' (Evans, 1979). This development is real in the sense that the productive forces in the nation are developed and increased. Society becomes increasingly industrialised and urban. At the same time it is still dependent because much technological development, especially in industries making the means of production, remains outside the third world. Third world industry remains dependent on the first in this respect. However, Cardoso and Falletto do not expect this development to 'solve' the problems of third world countries. It will not do anything about inequality but will tend to marginalise the mass of the people and often as a result require authoritarian government. But dependent development is important in one respect, argue Cardoso and Falletto. External domination, of a kind envisaged in Lenin's theory of imperialism or Frank's development of underdevelopment will come to be replaced by internal domination. New local groups and classes created by development will be formed and the state will in part reflect their interests. At the same time, development will create other groups and classes who will oppose the form of development. Thus development opens up the possibility of new internal conflicts in third world societies. The example of Brazil during the period 1968–74 will serve to illustrate this. Such rapid growth was experienced that it was dubbed the 'Brazilian Miracle'. Industrialisation strategy was based on the *Tri pe*, the three feet of international capital, indigenous local capital, and state-owned enterprises (Evans, 1979, pp. 268–70). By the mid-1970s, local businessmen were beginning to feel that they had not derived sufficient benefit from the miracle. Their resentment was directed at the increasingly large state-owned sector, and they demanded substantial privatisation. Because state-owned meant run by an authoritarian, military state, such requests soon turned into demands for greater democratisation and liberalisation of all decision-making processes. At the same time, industrialisation had brought into existence a large urban proletariat and by the late 1970s they too were voicing demands for greater participation in government, and for a greater share of the material benefits of the miracle. If Brazil is an example of dependent development then it is certainly showing all the signs of the growth of new locally dominant classes attempting to bend the state to their will, and the emergence of groups and classes who are opposed to the inegalitarian and authoritarian form that the development has taken.

The possibility that the third world could experience real industrial development is argued even more forcefully by Warren (1980, pp. 186–255). He rejects Cardoso and Falletto's argument that development in the third world will entail technological dependency, the marginalisation of the masses, growing inequalities and diminishing conditions of life for the majority. His is a trenchant restatement of Lenin's optimistic view that imperialism will in the end bring about the industrial development of the third world. At some length Warren shows how as a whole there has been an improvement of living conditions in the third world, evidenced not least by the rapidly growing populations, and that the masses brought into the cities by industrial growth are not marginalised. The informal economy is intimately linked with the formal industrial and commercial economy and is itself to a large extent part of the real industrial growth of the economy. Even foreign technology, while perhaps expensive to acquire in the first place, can in the long run produce positive benefits.

One must not lose sight of the time element, for as Japan has

> shown, initial acquisition of foreign technology, however costly, can lead eventually to great economic power, itself the basis for substantial independent technological innovation. The process of borrowing technology can be regarded as creating dependence only if it is viewed statically. (Warren, 1980, p. 181)

The debates about the societies of the third world are not settled. Whether they are dependent or not, whether industrial development is real, sustained and independent, how the world capitalist system should be understood (relations of production or relations of exchange) and what the role of the state is, are all questions about which there is continuing disagreement. But what can be usefully concluded from such debates is that the state is a key institution in the explanation of development or lack of development. Moreover, they show the crucial importance of integrating an understanding of the state into an adequate conceptualisation of the operations of the worldwide economy.

Relative autonomy in the world economy

The writers just considered, from Lenin and Warren to Frank and Wallerstein, have in common the belief that the relationships between states in the world, and in particular between those of the first world and the third are inseparable from the operations of the capitalist economic system at an international level. Lenin argued that these relationships took the form of colonial empires established to facilitate the international export of capital. The role of the state in this process was subservient to the needs of the dominant national bourgeoisies of the imperial nations. The relationship between state and society is an instrumentalist one, not going much further than Marx and Engels' conception of the state as 'a committee for managing the common affairs of the whole bourgeoisie' (Marx and Engels, 1968, p. 37), with in this case the relevant bourgeoisies being those of the imperial powers. In one sense Wallerstein's conception of the state is not very much different. As Worsley suggests, it is a common feature of world systems' theories that the role of the state is almost entirely subsumed into the requirements of the economic system. In fact for Wallerstein the modern nation-state is the *creation* of the world capitalist system. Such a view of the state's total subservience to the world economic system, to external domination was criticised above for being both over-deterministic and arbitrary. If we reject the argument in its extreme form, then several questions about the interaction of the state and international economic system can be posed in both theoretical and empirical senses. In particular we can ask what has been the different impact of capitalist development on different states, and to what extent can the state act in ways that are independent of the constraints of the capitalist economy, and how is the impact of the international capitalist system mediated to individual countries?

State and international economic system

Much of the writing on the development of the capitalist system would seem to suggest that there is a strengthening tendency for the economic system to have a homogenising effect on the states of the world. The only major and continuing difference allowed is that between developed and underdeveloped (or core, semi-periphery and periphery, in Wallerstein's terms). For example, one of the more recent views on the development of capitalism is the internationalisation of capital thesis associated with the work of Palloix (1975). He sees internationalisation as a three stage process. First, there is internationalisation of commodity-capital (the development of international trade), then of money-capital (export of capital as in Lenin), finally of productive capital (the transnational corporation). The last stage makes the world economy the basic arena for capital and thus also the only adequate level for its analysis. Throughout the world, production becomes more homogeneous, the same products are made using the same techniques, and advertised in the same way. Patterns of consumption too, especially in terms of the products used, are homogenised. There is a continuing process of concentration and centralisation of capital with more and more branches of industry and agriculture becoming dominated by oligopolistic corporations. Transnational corporations are key agents in this process, but other companies are subject to the same process. However, despite giving the impression that it is an ineluctable and ubiquitous force, the internationalisation of capital is only a process and a tendency. Its development will be uneven, and we could therefore expect to find different state forms indicating the unevenness of its development, reflecting the extent to which pre-capitalist economies and non-economic factors continued to have effect. Such a point is made by Hamza Alavi in his analysis of the state in the third world (Alavi, 1982). His approach is based on three ideas. First, that economies in the third world are a form of peripheral capitalism, which he defines as a form of society where there are several dominant classes, each associated with a different mode of production. Secondly, all state actions occur within the limits set by the structural imperatives of capitalism. Alavi argues that this does not determine the state's behaviour, but it does lay down the consequences of certain state actions; for example, if the state ignores the imperative it may bring on an economic crisis. Third, typically, in the third world state there will be competition between classes within the state apparatus. Such classes will include the national or local bourgeoisie and what Alavi calls the metropolitan bourgeoisie, by which he means the owners of capital external to the third world society, and usually situated in the developed countries. These factors, combined with the differing historical experiences of third world countries, will produce, says Alavi, two basic types of society.

The first is found in those countries where there is a plurality of 'fundamental classes', and none of them can be unambiguously designated as the ruling class. There are what Alavi calls a comprador bourgeoisie and an industrial (local or national) bourgeoisie, as well as a capitalist land-owning class. The metropolitan bourgeoisie is also present, both by virtue of the local operations of transnational corporations and 'through the mediation on its behalf of the respective metropolitan states in their dealings with states in peripheral capitalist societies' (Alavi, 1982, p. 298). These are factors we shall return to in more detail later. The second kind of society is found in some parts of Africa, where the indigenous population has consisted mainly of peasant communities without large landowning classes. After independence a 'class vacuum' was created when the colonial rulers and Asian traders (expatriate bourgeoisies) were expelled. Some writers have argued that this left the way clear for the 'new petty bourgeoisie' of the salaried middle class to dominate the state (Saul, 1979; Hein and Stenzel, 1979). Alavi rejects this view because of the over-riding role and structural presence of the metropolitan bourgeoisie as a 'fundamental class'. Nevertheless, the educated salaried middle class is important because it occupies the upper echelons of the bureaucracy and the military and hence holds a place of strategic importance, particularly for the metropolitan powers. However, its role is not that of mere capitalist functionaries because, Alavi suggests, its members inhabit more than one cultural domain. Although imbued with Western culture and the logic of capitalist rationality it also tends to fracture on the basis of ethnic, regional, linguistic or sectarian loyalties (Alavi, 1982, pp. 299–300). Indigenous culture has a tendency to 'break through'.

Both these models or ideal types of 'peripheral capitalist society' raise problems for the application of theories of the state derived from experience of the advanced capitalist countries. Purely instrumentalist views, that the state acts simply at the behest of the ruling class, and functionalist views, that it acts in the national interest, cannot be sustained because there is no unambiguous ruling class or 'nation'. The existence on a semi-permanent basis of such a bonapartist situation (see the discussion in Chapter 3) raises the question as to the degree to which the state in the third world possesses relative autonomy of action *vis-à-vis* society and economy, both national and international. Anglade and Fortin (1985, pp. 24–6) suggest three ways in which issues of relative autonomy can be raised in the context of what Alavi calls peripheral capitalist societies. The first is the notion, common to much debate about the state in the first world, that the state managers, bureaucrats, technicians, politicians and so on need to have a degree of autonomy from the social bases of the state. They need this because there are conflicting interests that have to be reconciled. There are competing dominant classes, and fractions of these classes may have needs which conflict with those of what Anglade and Fortin call the 'pact of domination'. Moreover, the legitimacy of the state can in some instances only be maintained by meeting to some extent the demands of subordinate classes. The second dimension to the notion of relative autonomy concerns the relationship between economy, state and regime. By regime, Anglade and Fortine follow Poulantzas's notion of the formal links between the various structures of the state and the mediations and representations provided by political parties (see Chapter 3). Examples of regimes are the various democratic systems (constitutional monarchy, republic, presidentalism, parliamentary system, two party, multi-party, etc.) and politically exclusionary regimes such as authoritarian, corporatist and fascist. The issue of autonomy here is the extent to which there can be different forms of regime given the constraint of a particular kind of economy, state and society.

Thirdly, Anglade and Fortin suggest that we have to raise the question of the state's autonomy in an external sense, that is its room for manœuvre in the world system. There are important differences here between states in their ability to act with regard to each other and with regard to international organisations. It is necessary to remember too that the state occupies an ambiguous fulcrum between its own society and the international economic and political sphere. So, in the case of external autonomy there is a 'need to avoid conceptualising inter-state relations as if states were homogeneous and self-contained actors. The class nature of the state must be integrated dialectically with the insertion of the nation-state into the world system' (Anglade and Fortin, 1985, p. 26).

Transnational corporations and the state

The third dimension of autonomy identified by Anglade and Fortin suggests that an important area of inquiry concerns exactly how the impact of capitalist world economy – particularly if understood in the dynamic sense of the internationalisation of capital – and of the state found within that economy is *mediated* to individual countries, and how states react to that mediation. Study of states' reactions to various mediations will entail an examination of relative autonomy in each of the three senses distinguished above. One form of mediation is that of international and transnational organisations. Major examples of such organisations are the World Bank, UN, IMF, UNESCO, the International Labour Organisation and the EEC. But perhaps the pre-eminent form of mediation in the modern world is the operation of transnational corporations. These are also referred to as multinational corporations or international firms, and here will be abbreviated to TNC. The importance of TNCs derives in part from the sheer size of their operations. In 1971 they are said to have produced commodities worth $300 thousand million outside their home territories, which was more than the total value of world trade (Tugendhat, 1973, p. 21). In 1974 the turnover of each of the ten largest TNCs in the world was greater than the gross national product of 153 different countries, and by 1976 the total sales of the seven largest TNCs was greater than the gross national product of Britain (Smith, 1980, p. 236). But the impact of TNCs in the world is also significant because they usually constitute the most dynamic sector of the economy. They use the most modern technology, are the most capital intensive and tend to show the highest rates of profit. For these reasons it is worth looking in more detail at the relationships between TNCs and state throughout the world.

The TNC today has a truly international character. Employment, production and capital invested are spread throughout the world, and it has been argued that one consequence is the weakening of the nation-state. That is, to use Mandel's phrase, the TNCs are becoming 'state indifferent' (Mandel, 1978, p. 328). Such an argument is made by Robin Murray, who suggests a growing divergence between the activities of nation-states and those of TNCs. On the one hand, he argues, the economic functions of the state need not always be performed by a TNC's 'own' nation-state and are in fact progressively less so performed, and on the other, the increasing operational divergence of TNC and nation-state significantly weakens the state and reduces its ability to control the major TNCs and the economy in general (Murray, 1971). However, as Mandel points out, those TNCs which fail to get the backing of either their 'home' state or of the state within whose frontiers the bulk of their operations take place will lose in competition with those TNCs that do (Mandel, 1978, p. 329). There is, says Mandel, a continuing need for economic programming by the state involving various monetary, credit, budgetary, tax and tariff devices to overcome the recurrent crises which afflict the world capitalist economy. In fact, he predicts that TNCs 'will not only need a state, but a state which is actually stronger than the "classical" nation state, to enable them, at least in part, to overcome the economic and social contradictions which periodically threaten their gigantic capitals' (Mandel, 1978, p. 330). There is, however, in Mandel's argument something akin to Miliband's view of the state (see Chapter 3), but in this case rather than a national state acting on behalf of the national bourgeoisie, the world community of states acts on behalf of the TNCs. This is clearly a very optimistic picture of state co-operation. The tendency will be for states, by using economic policies, to try to protect the interests of what they perceive as their 'own' TNCs at the cost of overseas competitors, whilst at the same time co-operating with other states to ensure the continued existence of the overall capitalist system. The difficulty states have in reconciling these two needs is evidenced by the continuation of the inter-state rivalry even within co-operative arrangements like the EEC. Moreover, bearing in mind Anglade and Fortin's stricture to avoid assuming that the states are homogeneous and self-contained actors, states may be persuaded or forced to act in ways that are contrary to those desired by TNCs. Examples are states which impose a ban on investments in South Africa because of political pressure against apartheid, or states which place restrictions on companies wishing to sell advanced electronic and military equipment to the USSR. There is a sense, though in which Mandel is right. The TNC does rely in the last instance on its 'own' state to guarantee the conditions under which it is operating in other countries. In cases where these conditions are under threat, because of economic crisis, military defeat, revolution or other political upheaval the 'home' state can act, by diplomatic pressure if possible, but by the use of military force if not. British government actions in Iran and Egypt and the many interventions of American troops in Latin America to protect business interests show this very clearly. The point is that states have armies, TNCs do not.

The discussion so far of the mediating role of TNCs has concentrated very much upon the role of the state in the developed capitalist countries. After all, they will tend to have TNCs they may wish to defend. In the case of the third world, however, the issue is very much more one of whether TNCs should be encouraged into the country or not, and if so under what kind of conditions, and what kind of economic, social and political system will be attractive to them. On the more simplistic modernisation theory views, the TNC is the embodiment of the most modern of industrial institutions. Therefore, any country which wishes to achieve rapid modernisation will be keen to encourage the development of TNC operations inside their frontiers. There may of course be conflict involved in this, but modernisation theorists will see this as the result of the resistance of the backward, traditional sectors of the developing society. So far as the modern élites and the national state which they run on the one hand and the TNCs on the other are concerned, there is a mutual interest in expanding TNC activities in the third world. However, reality is rather different. Although there are many examples of mutuality of interest (the example of Liberia given above is one such) there are also many examples of conflict between the state in the developing nation and the TNCs.

Such a conflict tends to be based around the evidence that TNCs act in ways that may be harmful to the third world country in which they are operating. For example, there is now much research showing the way in which TNCs syphon profits from their subsidiaries back to the first world through the use of transfer pricing, excessive charges for licences and patents, and trading through 'free ports' (Vaitsos, 1973, 1975). As a result many states in the third world during the 1970s introduced measures to control the operation and financial dealings of TNCs (Jenkins, 1984, pp. 191–3; Vaitsos, 1975, pp. 199–201). Many introduced constraints on ownership of companies within their frontiers such that new enterprises had to have a certain degree of local ownership, usually a majority (Jenkins, 1984, pp. 189–91). One suggested explanation for this shift is that during this period the state became more powerful and more knowledgeable with regard to the TNCs. Thus as European TNCs entered the third world there was much greater competition between TNCs and this gave the state more power to pick and choose and to impose tighter controls on whichever companies it did allow to operate. Moreover, it is suggested that the experience of operating with TNCs for some years meant that states now had an increased knowledge of their activities and hence became aware of the ways in which their country might be losing out.

There are several problems with these explanations. First, the timing of events is inaccurate. Competition between American and European TNCs began in the 1950s, well before state policies changed, and the knowledge about the running of these companies came not so much from their having operated for some time, but from the very attempts that were made to regulate these operations. In addition, as events turned out, in the late 1970s state policies changed yet again to one of encouraging TNCs, and removing many of the restrictions that had been applied to them. Secondly, these explanations share with the modernisation approach several dubious assumptions. Both tend to assume that there is a single or unified national interest which the state, or the élites which run that state, naturally represent. For example there is no room for any class conflict within the state apparatus, nor for contradictory state actions which reflect the differing interests of different class fractions within a ruling class. Nor is there any possibility of analysing the way in which states at times seem to operate independently of civil society and class forces (Jenkins, 1984, pp. 178–9).

Turning to underdevelopment and dependency theories, the problems faced by these approaches in explaining state–TNC relatons in the third world are in some ways similar to those of modernisation theory. As we have seen, a major characteristic of most of these approaches is that the internal social and political structure tends to be ignored, and in particular the state is undertheoretised. There are dominant classes, but they are only locally dominant and they owe this solely to their position in the chain of relationships running throughout the capitalist world economy. The state is unproblematic because there is simply an alliance of the locally dominant classes with international capital, and the nature of the state can therefore be derived from the needs of international capital. This, for example, is the explanation given for the emergence of repressive regimes in Latin America since the mid 1960s (Frank, 1981, p. 10). The problem, then, for this approach is to explain the periods when third world states act in ways which are not in the interests of international capital, for example when they regulate the activities of TNCs or when they favour national enterprises rather than foreign ones.

It is clear then that an explanation of the relationship of third world states to the activities of TNCs requires a conception of the state that takes account of the balance of class forces in the society in question, the degree to which the state can act in an independent fashion and to what extent transnational economic and political forces have effect. A recent work that goes some way towards meeting these requirements is Jenkins' study of the operation of the TNCs in Latin America. He argues that the oscillation of state policies towards TNCs requires a more sophisticated analysis of the state. Drawing upon ideas about the internationalisation of capital, the relationship between class conflict and the state, and the independent activities of the state and state enterprises Jenkins provides a case study which illustrates very well Anglade and Fortin's three dimensions of relative autonomy outlined above.

In the period up to 1950 several Latin American states had populist governments which tended to be hostile to foreign capital, at that time still mainly concentrated in extractive industries and public utilities, and a few states nationalised some foreign-owned industry. In the late 1950s, though, many states changed approach and introduced laws that positively encouraged foreign investment. Foreign firms were granted preferential treatment compared with local ones. Investors were given protected markets and guarantees of repatriation of profits. Jenkins suggests this change was connected with two factors (Jenkins, 1984, pp. 183–5; Cardoso and Falletto, 1979, pp. 150–9 give a similar argument). First, the policy of promoting import substitution industries which most countries had been following had reached its limits. In a world market where the terms of trade had turned against the third world (low prices for raw materials and high prices for manufactured goods), the current wisdom of development theory was that states needed to encourage foreign investment in order to develop new industries. Secondly, there were political changes which had enabled a change of approach. Populism in Argentina and Brazil came to an end, and the working class suffered defeats; unions came under tighter state controls and there were reductions in real wages. States turned from a policy of *nationalism* with respect to development to one based on *developmentalism*. The shift of foreign investment away from the extractive and export sectors was encouraged because it was seen to be developing the manufacturing base of the economy and thus serving the national interest. 'The contradiction between the "national" and the "international" was thus conveniently swept away' (Jenkins, 1984, p. 185). But the late 1960s and early 1970s saw a shift back again to stricter control over foreign capital. Perhaps most significant among the actions taken by Latin American states – which in many ways mirrored those of the pre-1950s – was Decision 24 of the Andean Pact. This agreement between Chile, Bolivia, Peru, Ecuador and Colombia set up a range of controls on foreign capital, trademarks, patents, licensing agreements and royalties.

Jenkins suggests several reasons for this turnaround. First, there were factors associated with the overall capital accumulation in the countries in question. In particular there was a conflict between TNC capital and general capitalist expansion, which manifest itself as a balance of payments crisis. The outflow of royalties, profits and so on associated with TNCs and their reliance on imported inputs, came increasingly to be seen as the cause of the payments crisis. In both Mexico and Brazil in the early 1970s, for example, almost half the total trade deficit was accounted for by the trade undertaken by TNC subsidiaries. Secondly, local businessmen increasingly wished to enter the most dynamic and most profitable parts of the market, then dominated by TNCs. In combination with the sectors of the state apparatus which favoured nationalism they pushed for a shift to policies more favourable to national capital. Thirdly, the left in politics had grown in importance and power. Development theory had been rejected in favour of dependency theory. States which took a nationalistic position against TNCs could appear to be supporting the tenets of dependency theory and in doing so further enhance their legitimacy.

The authoritarian state

In Latin America the attempts by states to control TNC came to an end in most cases when the governments were overthrown by military coups. The first was in 1964 in Brazil, and it was soon followed by others in Chile, Uruguay and Argentina. As well as having a much more open attitude towards foreign capital and foreign companies these new regimes were distinguished by a new kind of repressive and authoritarian rule. The phenomenon, sometimes called bureaucratic authoritarianism, was not limited to Latin America and many states in Asia acquired such military authoritarian regimes as well. As we have seen, modernisation theorists held the view, perhaps rather optimistically, that with economic development would come democracy. This was shown to be false in the light of the experience of many of these authoritarian states, such as Singapore, South Korea and Brazil, when they managed remarkable economic growth and showed no signs of giving way to democracy. Besides, this did not answer the question why these governments became authoritarian in the first place. One suggested answer is that there are tensions and frustrations involved in economic growth which can only be managed by the exercise of state authority. In the absence of any windfall of capital such as was experienced by Britain with the influx of wealth from the third world, states which wish to industrialise must ensure that a significant proportion of the wealth created by the economy is not distributed in the form of, for example, more equitable income distributions, but goes towards investment for industry. Under either capitalism or communism, this requires a strong, authoritarian state to keep in check any demands for the distribution of wealth. Certainly, the authoritarian governments involved have used the full force of repression to ensure that they are 'containing the thrust from below' as Alavi puts it (Alavi, 1982, p. 301), and these regimes have usually overseen an increase in social inequalities.

As was mentioned above, in his more recent works, Frank has abandoned his earlier view that capitalism in the third world is unable to produce development (Frank, 1981, p. 10). He now argues that there can be some development, but that it requires the repression of wages to make production profitable and competitive exports possible. Such repression is achieved by authoritarian, and often military, regimes. Industrial development along these lines depends upon the existence of an international division of labour in which the labour intensive stages of production are transferred to those third world countries which can provide a cheap, pliable and 'disciplined' workforce. Such an explanation is further extended by Roberts (1978, pp. 175–7) by linking it to the existence of the informal economy in third world countries. He argues that informal production helps to cheapen the cost of labour in large-scale industry and commerce. Informal production is the term used to describe a host of different activities undertaken on a small scale, including craft production and repair, transport, commercial and personal services. It is informal because it usually escapes government legislation about minimum wages, vehicle maintenance standards, safety at work, social security provisions and so on. Roberts suggests that the existence of informal production is convenient for the dominant classes since it permits economic growth while maintaining high levels of consumption among the wealthy. But crucially this depends on a political context where the population has no effective means of influencing the allocation of resources which might lead to an increase in their standard of living. 'This political context is partly produced by authoritarian government and partly by the weak development of political labour organisation amongst the urban working class, under social and economic conditions that tend to divide and isolate the members of this class from each other' (Roberts, 1978, p. 175).

However, evidence that Roberts himself presents suggests that this argument should not be taken too far. Examination of the consumption pattern of the urban workers in Latin America shows an increasing tendency for them to purchase goods from the large-scale, capitalist, formal sector, and less and less from informal and craft production (Roberts, 1978, p. 113). Informal production is therefore becoming less significant in cheapening labour costs. Moreover, as Jenkins points out, government subsidies are probably even more important than low wages in making exports from third world countries internationally competitive (Jenkins, 1984, p. 199). Above all explanations such as those of Frank and Roberts for the appearance of authoritarianism focus too much upon the repression and control of one class, the workers. They tend to see the state acting merely to meet the needs of the internationalisation of capital and thus deny the state any relative autonomy.

Alavi in his discussion of authoritarianism not only suggests the state has a good deal more ability to act on its own account, but points out that in many third world countries it is not just the subordinate classes which confront the authoritarian or military state. The 'dominant' classes too do not have full control over the state, and in fact are to a considerable extent in the hands of a powerful and centralised state apparatus (Alavi, 1982, pp. 301–2). This comes about because the state in question is an 'overdeveloped' state. Under colonialism the state developed powers beyond what were actually needed after independence for the orderly regulation of society (Alavi, 1972). Such 'overdeveloped' states may also perform several useful functions. They suppress any attempts at revolution, insurrection or even at building up independent working class movements, and unpopular administrative decisions may be made without reference to the populace. In several cases, the state acquires extra legitimacy because in the past the military which is in charge has acted as national saviours. Alavi is wrong to put so much stress on the post-colonial nature of authoritarianism since such rule in Latin America generally followed relatively democratic republics rather than colonial authorities. But it is important to recognise, as Alavi does, that the extent to which authoritarian states are able to operate autonomously of national dominant classes can only be determined by empirical investigation of particular examples.

The case of Brazil is interesting here because, at least on the surface, the authoritarian state established in 1964 seemed to combine pro-international capital policy with a very large increase in state-owned capital, especially in manufacturing, a situation which might suggest it had a high degree of autonomy. By 1974, 19 out of the largest 20 Brazilian corporations were state owned, and some 60 per cent of all investment during 1967–73 was carried out by the state (Munck, 1984, p. 223). One Brazilian politician was moved to remark in 1977 that 'Great Britain is a crypto-capitalist country, with socialist rhetoric, and Brazil a crypto-socialist country with capitalist rhetoric' (Roberto Campos, quoted in Munck, 1984, p. 224). Does this indicate a significant growth in the autonomy of the state in Brazil, especially *vis-à-vis* the international economy and the local bourgeoisie, and, more particularly, did state forms develop their own independent interests? Certainly a great deal of state investment continues to be in the infrastructure, transport, communications and so on. This can be seen as providing essential support for industrial investment by TNCs. But in Brazil the state also became significantly involved in manufacturing, to the extent that some have argued that state enterprises were a countervailing force to TNC penetration of the economy (Newfarmer and Mueller, 1975). However, it is important to separate ideology from actuality in this case. As Anglade and Fortin point out, the presence of the state in manufacturing in Brazil does not imply so much genuine state accumulation but more the subsidisation of private enterprise. State firms underpriced the inputs provided to private enterprises and consequently they made low profits or even losses (Anglade and Fortin, 1985, p. 42). Nor do the bureaucrats and technocrats who run the state-owned enterprises show the ideological cohesiveness which the remark by Campos above might indicate. As Evans points out, to constitute a class in their own right state executives would need an ideology that goes beyond seeing themselves as skilled technocrats implementing a general project (Evans, 1979, p. 268). The evidence is that they continue to see local private capital as the most appropriate for Brazil's development, and as the discussion above of *Tri pé* showed, local private business has been successful in its demands for a privatisation of the state sector.

Even in the case of Brazil then, where substantial state manufacturing was developed, the state maintained only limited autonomy *vis-à-vis* both the local bourgeoisie and international capital. On the other hand, although such state policies were greatly facilitated by authoritarian repression of working class political organisations this is no reason for treating the state as a mere bureaucratic administration of the affairs of the ruling classes. It also has a public face, the arena of state politics, where questions of legitimacy, development, nationalism and independence are uppermost. As Jenkins put it, the state has a

> dual and contradictory role as both a *national* state, whose legitimacy is posed largely in national terms and, simultaneously, as a partner in the promotion of the internationalisation of capital . . . To put it another way, the role of the state in presenting the interest of capital as the national interest is rendered particularly problematic where a large section of that capital is foreign owned. (Jenkins, 1984, p. 181)

It is a recognition of the importance of the political role of the state as well as its economic one that is perhaps O'Donnell's most important contribution in his discussion of what he calls bureaucratic authoritarianism (O'Donnell, 1979). He too accepts that authoritarianism was a response by the state to the need to carry out economic policies which would attract foreign investment but which entailed an increase in social inequalities. Such policies were challenged by the powerful working class movements which had developed during the previous populist period of import-substitution led growth. Authoritarian rule put an end to such political and economic 'instability'. But there is no inevitable economic logic in this 'solution'. The particular state of the class struggle and the peculiarities of other political and historical conditions are crucial in determining the possibilities and course of authoritarian rule. A particular problem here for the bureaucratic authoritarian state is its claim to be the national state since authoritarianism entails a 'drastic contraction of the nation' (O'Donnell, 1979, p. 294), as citizenship is suppressed and appeals to the needs of the people are no longer a basis for demands for substantive justice. The response of the regime is to redefine the idea of the nation so that those who do not fit into the socially harmonious and technocratic design are left out. The consequence is a 'statisation' of the meaning of the nation, which 'implies that its general interest be identified with the success of state institutions in their quest to establish a particular order in society and to normalise the economy' (O'Donnell, 1979, p. 295). However, this means that state institutions lose any external basis of legitimation, the serving of interests superior and external to themselves. Institutions serve the nation because they serve themselves. Domination becomes naked. Ideological appeals in the media and the like to ideas of 'national security', 'order and progress' and national pride and success, will succeed only so long as for all levels of society there *is* national success and progress. Brazil achieved this in 1968–74, during the so-called miracle, but since then the grip of bureaucratic authoritarianism has become less and less sure. In particular, the economic crisis of the late 1970s and 1980s has affected the middle sectors of society, such as the salaried middle classes and the small local businessmen, as well as the poor. Problems for the bureaucratic authoritarian state come when appeals to national interest fail and all the excluded sectors come together in an alliance against the regime in power.

The signs now are that authoritarian regimes throughout the world are experiencing such problems. In Latin America several authoritarian states have reverted to at least some degree of democratic rule, and in Asia states like the Philippines seem to be experiencing great pressure to 'open up' the political apparatus. It remains to be seen, though, whether democratic regimes can be any more successful than the authoritarian in dealing with the acute economic crises that they face – in particular the problem of external debt – and in dealing with the conflicting aspirations of the classes within their societies. As Anglade and Fortin note,

> the contemporary Latin American state might be acquiring an increasing degree of autonomy *vis-à-vis* the dominant classes in civil society but . . . at the same time – it is facing growing external constraints as a result of foreign indebtedness and the operation of the world financial system, which reduces its capacity for autonomous decision making. (Anglade and Fortin, 1985, p. 26).

Conclusion

We began this chapter by making a distinction between the internal and external determinants of the nature of the state and its activities. We have seen that the view of modernisation theory is one that concentrates its attention very much on internal factors which affect the state and politics. This approach was rejected by those who wrote from an underdevelopment or world systems perspective, and who gave much more attention to international factors. Although these views gave a more realistic picture of the history of states – especially in the third world – we criticised them, amongst other reasons, because they tended to view the state as something that could be 'read off' from the operational necessities of the capitalist world economy. The error here is failing to see that the existence of an economic system at any point throughout the world depends on the prior acquisition of political power, especially at the level of the state. In order to analyse this political struggle at the level of the state we need to go beyond the problematic of dependency theory, namely the concept of 'internal' and 'external' determinants. As Bernstein suggests, there is a need to transcend this more or less static dichotomy and 'within the framework of a theory of world economy . . . analyse *any* social formation in its specificity – as a complex ensemble of class relations and contradictions, of the economic, political and ideological conditions and forms of class struggle' (Bernstein, 1982, p. 232). In the last three sections some of the ways this could be done were examined.

The internationalisation of capital imposes structural imperatives on states which lay down the limits within which they can act. States which either deliberately act in ways which contravene these structural limits or which allow things in their societies or economies to get so out of hand that the limits are exceeded run the risk either of intervention by some more powerful state to rectify things or of proceeding to a revolutionary transformation of their society. The important point is that the economy does not determine the outcome. The state can have a great deal of autonomy, from society and from the world economy. One way of analysing, in particular, the ways in which the state as an institution stands between on the one hand the world economy and world community of states and on the other its own society, economy and polity, is by examining key mediating institutions, such as the TNCs. What such an analysis shows is that there is no consistent relationship between state and TNC. Whether relations are hostile or, as is more usual, harmonious, depends upon a whole host of particular, social, historical and cultural factors. There is no typical state reaction because in the end there is no typical state.

9

Postscript: The State and the New Cold War

Imperialism and the superpowers

When Lenin wrote his polemical summary of radical thinking on the nature of imperialism it was 1916 and the imperialist powers were engaged in a catastrophic world war. The empires were real, as was the conflict between them. Today, however, those empires are no more, the colonial possessions are independent states, and perhaps just as important, although there is commercial rivalry between corporations based in different national territories, there is no inter-imperialist rivalry between the European states of the kind that concerned Lenin. There is, however, another conflict which has come to be of central importance to world peace, that is the conflict between the superpowers, the USA and the USSR. How is this conflict to be explained, especially the recent development of what has become known as the new cold war, and is it properly described as inter-imperialist rivalry? Moreover, what can the ideas about the state we have discussed in the previous chapters contribute to our understanding of this conflict?

In Chapter 8, we discussed some of the theories which suggest a link between commercial interests, such as the activities of the transnational corporations, and the actions of states, especially those which act as 'home' state to particular transnationals. It is in this sense that the USA could be called an imperialist power today. Since 1945 it has been the single predominant power in the world outside the communist bloc. While there may be academic debate about whether or not the USA gains from the operation of its commercial interests throughout the world, American policy makers and governments have no doubt where their interests lie. USA dominance in many parts of the world predates the Second

World War. From the establishment of the Monroe doctrine in 1823, which declared that the Americas were a USA sphere of influence, to the post-war interventions of USA troops in Lebanon (1958), Vietnam and Grenada, USA governments have used diplomacy, cajouling, bullying, threats, and in the end military force to defend commercial interests. Since 1850 the USA military has intervened in Latin America some 70 times (including Grenada) (Lernoux, 1982, p. 173), in many cases at the request of USA companies whose assets or conditions of operation were seen as 'under threat'. In this sense then, there are reasons for thinking of the USA as an imperialist state, even though clearly not one of the 'classic' kind, with formal colonies and dependencies.

In using the theory of imperialism to explain current superpower conflict, problems occur over why it is not the other capitalist states (with their rival transnational corporations) with which the USA is in conflict, but the Soviet Union and its communist allies, which have no transnationals and virtually no commercial interests in the third world. This is not to say that there may not be conflict between the USA and other capitalist states over commercial interest. Several authors have noted the development of three capitalist power centres (Halliday, 1982, 1983; Chomsky, 1982c; Mandel, 1975; Wallerstein, 1984). As well as the USA, these authors suggest Western Europe and Japan have now developed to a degree where they have become economic rivals to the USA. The EEC is now a larger economic unit (larger gross national product) than the USA, and although it has only about half the gross national product of these two units, Japan has a very large trade surplus with the USA. However, the important difference between this inter-state competition and nineteenth-century imperialism is that it is restricted mainly to trade. In military terms the USA is still the hegemonic power, so much so that some Americans have been concerned that Western Europe and Japan should spend a larger portion of their budgets on the military and hence relieve the USA of some of its 'burden'.

Turning to the Soviet bloc, how far can we say that the USSR rules politically and economically as an imperial power? In a political sense the answer seems clear. The USSR has a sphere of influence, so that Eastern Europe, Afghanistan, Cuba, Vietnam and a few other states come under its domination. Since 1945 it has used troops on several occasions to impose its will in these states, in particular to ensure the continuation of its kind of communist system. But it tends to view its activities in these states as an aspect of domestic policy rather than as elements in a strategy of global imperialism. Since 1945 it has not generally used its military power to extend its influence to new areas, only to protect already existing communist governments. This is a contentious point though. Current USA leaders believe the USSR has been continuously trying to extend its domain. As we shall see, whether this is truth or USA ideology is a matter of current debate. Without doubt, however, the USSR exerts political dominance within its sphere, particularly in Europe and the states on its Asian border, Afghanistan and Mongolia. But how far can this domination be seen as an economic one too? Barratt Brown (1974, pp. 294–304) suggests there are three ways in which the Soviet Union could be seen to be extracting economic gain from its sphere. First, the mixed Russian–East European enterprises set up after the Second World War were used by the USSR to monopolise markets and restrict local development. Secondly, it was argued that the USSR charged East Europe more for goods and materials it sold to them than it charged the West and paid them less for what they produced than it paid the West for similar goods. However, neither of these is of continuing economic importance, and should perhaps be seen very much as part of Soviet war reparations policy. In fact, since 1960, the trade balance with East Europe has not been in favour of the Soviet Union. The third suggestion that Barratt Brown makes is that trade within COMECON, the communist bloc trading zone, is unequal, since the less developed countries such as Cuba and south east Europe lose out because they are paid world market prices. If such prices in the capitalist world market are unequal or unfair – as the Soviet Union (as well as dependency theorists) suggests – then they must also be unfair within COMECON. This situation has come about because the Soviet economists have not developed any non-monetary basis for calculating prices. However, with perhaps the exception of Cuba, Vietnam and the ex-Portuguese colonies in Africa, such trade is not the same as the dominant form of trade between capitalist developed and underdeveloped countries. 'There is no evidence of the division of labour, typical of the capitalist world, between capital goods and other finished manufactured exports from the developed countries in exchange for raw materials from the underdeveloped' (Barratt Brown, 1974,

p. 297). If the USSR does operate economic imperialism within its bloc, then it is not the kind that perpetuates underdevelopment. In fact several countries in the communist bloc have industrialised since 1945, most notably North Korea. When it is involved in buying raw materials from underdeveloped countries (such as sugar from Cuba) the USSR is usually doing it to provide support for the communist state concerned, rather than for commercial gain.

In fact the USSR relationship with other states in its sphere of influence is not generally one based on the attempt to make economic gain, or to make a profit. Soviet overseas investments are negligible. The main Soviet interest in its sphere is political, and to some extent parallels that of the USA in maintaining the capitalist system as a whole. The aim of the USSR is to preserve and strengthen the Soviet bloc as a whole, and whereas American actions can be seen as preserving the privilege of capital throughout the capitalist world, it can be argued that the political power of the party and the preservation of central planning seem to be features that the Soviets will use any means to preserve. As Westoby puts it, 'Soviet control is a continuous system of guidance–suggestion–intervention through the upper reaches of the party apparatuses. It depends, thus, on the party and the state's internal cohesion, and the authority of the state; it is when this is threatened that the Soviet leadership intervenes most directly' (Westoby, 1983, p. 235).

As we noted in Chapter 4, others would disagree with this description of the Soviet state, and hence with its role internationally. Tony Cliff, for example, takes the view that capitalism was *restored* in the Soviet Union in about 1928, only not in the form of private capital but as state capital (Cliff, 1974). In this 'state capitalism', state bureaucracy and the development of an authoritarian leadership were necessary in order to substitute state coercion rather than market forces in extracting a surplus for industrialisation. For Cliff, the Russian state is an imperialist 'state capitalist' state which colonised eastern Europe and imposed a similar social and political system and similar programmes for industrialisation. The problem about such views, in so far as they claim to be Marxist, is how they explain the process of accumulation given that the major capitalist mechanisms such as profit and competition are absent. This is a particularly important question if the USSR is to be seen as a capitalist imperialist state because there is a need to explain the driving force behind its imperialist expansion. As the discussion above showed the usual economic relationship found between a capitalist state and in colonies (or neo-colonies) is absent. Kidron, who generally follows Cliff's argument, gives an answer by suggesting that the force for economic development in the USSR is its involvement in the 'permanent arms economy' (Kidron, 1970, Chapter 3). Military–political competition replaces economic competition. In the USSR, in the absence of internal competition, it is the arms race that pushes bureaucrats and workers to greater productivity. Presumably the 'colonisation of eastern Europe' simply provides the state-capitalist USSR with a larger workforce and raw materials base in the international arms race.

Not all writers are so orthodox about Marx. As we saw in Chapter 8, Wallerstein takes the view that it is in the spirit of Marx to define capitalism by relations of exchange rather than production. Thus for Wallerstein there is only one world-economy, capitalism, and the superpower conflict is not of two different economic systems, but of different political ideologies. Socialism or communism as a world system does not exist (although it might in the future). The communist state is just a 'collective capitalist firm so long as it remains a participant in the market of the capitalist world-economy' (Wallerstein, 1979, p. 35), a view very close to that of Cliff. The role of the state in this system is to reduce the freedom of operation of the world-economy. Communist states do this in part by excluding the USA (and most other capitalist operations) from areas of the world. But the major effect of the existence of the USSR and other communist states is not to offer an alternative economic system to capitalism but rather to show how state intervention can bring about rapid expansion of industrial productivity without private ownership. Communist states thus pose a threat to the ideological justification of capitalism. Overall, though, Wallerstein plays down the importance of East–West conflict. Far more important is the division of the world into core, semi-periphery and periphery, where both the USA and the USSR are core powers, and above all, the growth and then decay of American hegemony and the development of West–West conflict – conflict between Europe, Japan and the USA (Wallerstein, 1984, p. 63). Wallerstein suggests that from 1873 British dominance in the world steadily declined and was replaced by that of the USA, which took over the hegemonic role, with clear primacy after the Second World War. Following this war, the USA saw the need for new markets, not least because the Soviet bloc, which was closed to American exports, had now expanded to include China and East Europe. Consequently, says Wallerstein, the USA embarked on three developments. First, recovery in Europe under American leadership was promoted by the Marshall plan. Secondly, the USA tightened its political and commercial hold on Latin America, and third, it set about ensuring that all the European colonies attained independence. Thus American commercial interest replaced European ones, first in the Middle East and then later in Asia and Africa. However, the contradictions involved in these processes came to a head around 1967 (Wallerstein, 1984, p. 40). By that year Europe and Japan had both grown as economic units to such a size that the USA could no longer claim hegemony over the world-economy.

We saw in Chapter 8 how Worsley criticised Wallerstein's views on the state in the world system because the idea of a world system was over-deterministic and gave illicit priority to the economic. Worsley also disagrees with Wallerstein over the importance of East–West differences. Worsley rejects Wallerstein's monistic view 'there is only one world system, capitalism', and instead argues that there are several worlds. First, for Worsley there is an important difference between capitalism and communism. This follows from his rejection of Wallerstein's 'exchange' notion of capitalism and his counterposing of a 'production' notion. Capitalist and communist states *are* based on fundamentally different economic systems because they produce goods under different social relations and fundamentally different political systems. Second, there is a difference in levels of development or industrialisation, which Worsley argues is real in its effect, with the massive migration of workers from underdeveloped to developed countries just one example (Worsley 1983). Put together these distinctions produce four worlds; the developed capitalist first world, the developed communist second world, the underdeveloped capitalist third world, and a fourth category of underdeveloped communist, often put into the second world category but perhaps deserving its own. The disagreement with Wallerstein is particularly strong over the communist countries. Worsley rejects what he calls Wallerstein's 'neo-Trotskyist view' that institutionalised state socialism is not socialist at all. On Wallerstein's model, says Worsley,

> communist countries do not constitute a distinct type of society: the Second World is decomposed and divided into one or other of the three categories, the Soviet Union, for example, being a core country and Cuba a peripheral one. Since the model is predominantly an economic one, it ignores such institutions as the Warsaw Pact or the military assistance given by the USSR to Cuba, Vietnam and other regimes and movements. Yet paradoxically, it ignores the existence of such economic institutional realities as COMECON, or the post-revolutionary aid supplied by the USSR to Cuba and Vietnam. (Worsley, 1984, p. 313)

Thus whereas for Wallerstein the USA–USSR conflict is mainly important because of the ideological challenge the Soviet bloc poses, showing the possibility of a future 'anti-systemic' socialist movement, for Worsley the clash is economic and political.

Let us summarise the discussion so far. Both the superpowers have their respective sphere of influence. The USA, once predominant in the capitalist sphere is now challenged commercially, but not politically, by Europe and Japan. In the communist bloc there is a split into Soviet Union-dominated and Chinese-dominated spheres, but without doubt the Soviet Union is the foremost military power. Both superpowers intervene in their spheres, using military force where necessary, to preserve and strengthen their overall continuity. The American intervention is very often directly linked to supporting its commercial interests. However, given the lack of such interests in the Soviet sphere, their interventions must have a different origin. There are conflicting views about this. Cliff argues for a state capitalist interpretation with the USSR colonising East Europe and imposing communism on it, which following Kidron, is based on the competitive need to keep up in the international arms race, an argument which can of course be applied to the USA too. Wallerstein takes a similar view about the Soviet state, but also significantly sees it providing an alternative model for the development of productivity, thus undermining capitalist ideological justification. However, for Worsley, the superpower conflict is not just a clash of ideologies within a capitalist system. He argues that East–West conflict is based on real differences of political and economic system, and is thus importantly different from the classical imperialism of the nineteenth and early twentieth centuries, when imperialist competition was between capitalist state and capitalist state.

The new cold war

What this indicates is that however we interpret the superpower conflict, theories of the classical imperialism kind need considerable modification. This is especially true if we try to explain a recent phenomenon, namely the development of what has been called the 'new cold war' between the USA and the USSR (Chomsky, 1982b). Two recent writers on this development have been particularly enlightening, and, moreover, their respective positions echo several of the arguments already outlined. Those writers are Noam Chomsky (1982a, 1982b, 1982c) and Fred Halliday (1982, 1983, 1984).

Chomsky suggests that the new cold war, the increase in hostile relations between the superpowers and the accompanying build up of nuclear and other weapons, is merely the most recent of three major periods of American military expansion (Chomsky, 1982c, p. 57). The first started in 1950, just before the Korean war, the second in 1961 and the last in about 1980. However, behind these expansions is a consistent foreign policy that the USA has operated since 1945. During the Second World War, says Chomsky, American State Department planners developed the concept of Grand Area Planning. The Grand Area is that which the USA thought necessary for world control. 'Their geo-political analysis attempted to determine which areas of the world would have to be "open" – open to investment, the repatriation of profits, access to resources and so on – and dominated by the United States' (Chomsky, 1982c, p. 25; and see Chomsky, 1982a, p. 227). In 1945 there were still some major impediments to the operation of such a Grand Area, in particular the remaining colonial empires of the European states. The USA used its overriding economic power, including the Marshall plan and the manipulation of lend-lease, to bring to an end these restrictions to American commercial penetration. Attempts by the European states to resist this were soon stopped, such as in the case of the British and French invasion of Egypt in 1956. The USA also successfully managed to block the development of national capitalism in Europe of the kind that had existed before the

Second World War. In the Far East, the entire Japanese empire was incorporated into the Grand Area. The one part of the world left out was the communist states. For some years the USA had been trying to penetrate the Soviet Union by means of trade and commerce, but despite lend-lease treaties with the USSR during the Second World War they had been unsuccessful. Planners in the USA turned from what Chomsky calls the 'trader' approach, to the 'Prussian' tactic, namely the threat and use of military force.

It was not long before the USA began to see challenges to the Grand Area. In the late 1940s Greek communists, the backbone of the Greek resistance against the German occupation, were opposing British attempts to reinstate the Greek monarchy and a capitalist system. The USA stepped in to assist Britain and the monarchists not because a communist government in Greece was a direct threat to the USA, nor because the USSR was actively supporting the communists in Greece, although this was the claim of American propaganda at the time, but because communist success might 'infect' neighbouring states like Turkey and then the middle east, where America now had vital oil interests. This argument later became known as the domino theory, and was used to justify many subsequent American interventions in far-flung parts of the Grand Area, most notably of course, in south-east Asia. Within such an attempt at 'policing the globe', the cold war, says Chomsky, is highly functional, both for the USA and the USSR.

> The cold war provides a framework within which each of the superpowers can use force and violence to control its own domains, against those who seek a degree of independence within the blocs themselves – by appealing to the threat of the superpower enemy to mobilise its own population and that of its allies. (Chomsky, 1982a, p. 224)

Such an ideological framework is necessary because the control of states and liberation movements by the superpowers in their respective blocs requires 'the application of very ugly measures which are morally difficult for people to accept' (Chomsky, 1982a, p. 226), and some of those measures may be very costly both in money terms and in loss of life. Thus for Chomsky the key to American actions in the cold war, and for the USSR to a lesser extent, is not, despite the propaganda, the increasing military and nuclear threat of the other superpower, nor the possibility of the 'enemy' actually undermining the system in either bloc, but the control by each power of the states within their respective spheres of influence. Chomsky points to the fact that despite the huge build-up of the nuclear arsenals of both the USA and the USSR, they still spend by far the majority of their military budgets on conventional weapons of the kind that can be used in action against third world countries and liberation movements. On no occasion since the Second World War have the troops of the USA or the USSR been in action directly against each other, but they have both been used many times in countries within their spheres of influence. Chomsky notes that in the American 1985 fiscal year, defence budget plans are for a 13 per cent rise in spending overall, but a 34 per cent increase in expenditure in 'force projection' – intervention and aggression – because of, in the words of Defence Secretary Caspar Weinberger, 'both an expansion of US interests in the third world and an increase in third world conflicts' (Chomsky, 1982c, p. 57).

Expenditure on military equipment is very important in Chomsky's view in explaining why against the constant background of policy to control the Grand Area (and the USSR equivalent in its bloc) the USA should have entered into a new period of military expansion in around 1980. The reason is that the increased level of international tension and the mood of crisis at home and abroad justify the American response to the economic recession, which was a 'vast increase in the state sector of the economy in the familiar mode: by subsidising and providing a guaranteed market for high-technology production, namely, military production' (Chomsky, 1982b, p. 17). Military expenditure fits the needs of such a Keynsian stimulation of the American economy, says Chomsky, because it is high-technology, rapidly becomes obsolescent, and the tax-payer has to foot the bill. Nor is this economic stimulation confined to military weapons. Japan has recently announced a large government supported research programme into what has been called the 'fifth generation' of computers. In the USA, to meet this challenge, funding for supercomputer development is coming from the Pentagon, the Department of Energy (largely concerned with producing nuclear weapons) and from NASA (also in the main a military organisation). So the USA's response to Japan's fifth generation project is largely contained within the proposed military expansion. This kind of military Keynsianism may also be functional for the USSR too. As Chomsky puts it, in an argument that echos that of Kidron, 'the domestic power of the military-bureaucratic élite that rules the Soviet Union is enhanced by the diversion of resources to military production' (Chomsky, 1982b, p. 194).

While Chomsky pictures the new cold war largely in terms of the continuities of American policy, there are, in his view, also some significant changes (Chomsky, 1982a, pp. 229–32). Military expenditure was used during the cold wars of the 1950s and 1960s too, but then the diversion of large parts of American economic capacity to 'waste' production did not seriously affect its dominance because there were not any significant economic rivals in the Grand Area. Now things are different. Both Europe and Japan are important commercial rivals of the USA, and, Chomsky argues, the ideology of the cold war has the further benefit, so far as the USA is concerned, of providing a reason why Europe and Japan should also divert their productive capital from useful things to military waste. That the Europeans and the Japanese have so far largely resisted American prompting is perhaps indicative of the degree to which the interests of these powerful capitalist rivals conflict with those of the USA. This is particularly so, says Chomsky, in the case of raw materials, another new factor in the cold war. Whereas in the past imperialist conflict was often prompted by the fear of losing control of scarce resources, now there is a real scarcity. Chomsky expects there to be increased divergence of interests between the USA and Europe as Europe increasingly takes an independent line to protect its access to resources, particularly oil in the middle east.

In many ways the account of the origins of the second cold war given by Halliday is similar to Chomsky's. He agrees about the importance of the new militarism in the USA and the connected state support for military industries, and he agrees about the sharpening of 'inter-capitalist' contradictions such as the development of strong competing economies in Europe and Japan, and the difficulties that creates for American strategy in the new cold war. He too emphasises the fact that although the Soviet Union is in most respects considerably less powerful than the USA, 'the ideology [of Soviet superiority] serves to legitimate an American quest for strategic ascendancy' (Halliday, 1982, p. 298). But crucially, Halliday's view of the new cold war is not primarily of an ideological conflict whose function is to enable the USA to control the Grand Area, but rather a real conflict between two competing and radically different political, social and economic systems. Halliday therefore stresses two factors in recent world history, which amongst the many recent developments such as those Chomsky has mentioned, are indicative of a real and important conflict between the USA and Soviet blocs. These are the erosion of American nuclear superiority by the USSR and the new wave of third world revolutions between 1974 and 1980.

With regard to the first of these points, it is important to put things into context. The USSR has not gained nuclear superiority, argues Halliday. It has a slightly higher megatonnage of nuclear weapons, but fewer of these are mounted on multiple re-entry warheads, so their destructive capacity is much less. Moreover, the supposed Soviet 'first-strike' capacity ignores the American Poseidon submarine force which the USSR is unable to destroy but which can deliver nuclear warheads in the USSR. Nevertheless, the Soviet Union has advanced, the USA no longer has overwhelming superiority, and there is something akin to nuclear parity. The new cold war then involves an attempt by the USA to regain an overwhelming superiority so that once again, in the eyes of American military planners who believe such things, it becomes possible for the USA to win a nuclear exchange.

However, says Halliday, it was not the effect of nuclear parity on bilateral relations that most worried the USA. What was more important was that 'it reduced the ability of the USA to intervene and manage the Third World, and to contain social revolution there' (Halliday, 1983, p. 78). It is in the third world, in Halliday's view, that one finds the 'sharp end' of conflict between the USA and the USSR. The USA thought that the countries there could be stabilised with sympathetic, capitalist regimes, and it thought that the USSR would, as a trade-off for nuclear parity, agree to cease giving assistance to states and movements which were hostile to the USA. In both cases it was wrong. Although from 1962 to 1974 its policy in containing revolutionary movements in the third world was successful, in 1974, to use Halliday's phrase, the dykes burst. In the following six years there were 14 seizures of power by insurrectionary movements which produced a range of governments that often looked to Moscow for support rather than to Washington and the capitalist world. These include, in Africa, the two former Portuguese colonies, Angola and Mozambique, and

Ethiopia, the third most populous country on the continent; in Asia, Iran, Afghanistan and above all Vietnam; and in what the USA likes to think of as its own backyard, Nicaragua in Central America. In many of these revolutions the USSR, or its surrogates such as Cuba, gave economic and military assistance. In Vietnam it was Soviet tanks that allowed the North Vietnamese army to defeat the south, while Soviet airlifts of Cuban forces to Angola and Ethiopia were vital in preserving their respective revolutions, and the USSR itself sent 85 000 troops to Afghanistan to prevent the overthrow of the communist government there. It is in this way, Halliday suggests, that the USSR constituted a real threat to American dominance in the Grand Area. Certainly the American response contains a great deal that is false and ideological, but behind it is the real threat to American interests that Soviet support for these revolutions and the near parity in nuclear weapons represent. 'The result of the combination of these factors is that the third world has now come to occupy a central place in the anxieties of NATO councils and constitutes one of the major spurs for the unleashing of a New Cold War in the west' (Halliday, 1982, p. 300).

The respective arguments of Chomsky and Halliday parallel the positions of Wallerstein and Worsley already outlined. In particular the disagreement as to whether there is a significant and fundamental divide between the capitalist and communist spheres, or whether the difference is only of ideological importance. Both Worsley and Halliday argue that there is a reality to the political and economic divide in the world. There are different systems each of which believes the other should one day cease to exist, and while there may be ideological aspects to the conflict, that ideology is based in the end in reality. The Soviet Union really has gained in strength, it has supported insurrectionary movements throughout the world, the USA really does use its economic and political muscle to promote counter-revolution where it can, and above all, the nuclear weapons are real. On the other hand, both Wallerstein and Chomsky stress the way that each superpower is concerned with maintaining its supremacy within its sphere of influence, and, as Chomsky stresses, uses the threat of the other to justify military build-up and armed intervention. But Chomsky gives the impression that despite his clear dislike for the Soviet system, the USSR is not a real threat to the USA. Both may have nuclear weapons, but if one of them is going to use them for first strike, then it will be the one that has already done so at Hiroshima and Nagasaki, namely the USA.

The differences can be seen clearly in the way that Halliday and Chomsky interpret the events in southeast Asia in the 1970s. For Halliday, the American defeat in Vietnam is one of the significant 14 revolutions of the 1970s. Not only was the most powerful state in the world defeated, but socialist regimes were established in Laos, Vietnam and Cambodia. The war weakened the USA *vis-à-vis* its capitalist competitors (Japan did particularly well), and it also sent a signal to other revolutionary movements that the USA could be defeated. It lent support to the revolutionaries in Central America, it greatly encouraged the defeat of Portuguese forces in their colonies in Africa and made possible the Cuban intervention in Angola – not least because the American public, 'suffering' from the 'Vietnam syndrome', was unwilling for the USA to become involved in another war. The Vietnamese defeat of the USA was a global defeat, and the new American arms build-up and the new aggressive posture in the world is, for Halliday, an attempt by the USA to make good that defeat. None of this is denied by Chomsky, although his emphasis differs. Vietnam was not important in itself – there were little or no American interests in Indo-China. Its significance is in terms of the domino theory. If there had been an independent communist South Vietnam able to carry out some degree of modernisation and industrialisation it would have had a demonstration effect elsewhere in south-east and south Asia. This part of the world might have been extracted from the Grand Area. While the USA did not succeed in defeating the communists in Vietnam, they were successful in ensuring that the rest of the region remained under American domination, and open to American commercial interests.

However, perhaps the disagreement is not as great as it seems. Both Chomsky and Halliday agree that successful revolutions in the third world do have a demonstration effect. As we have just seen, for Chomsky this is what constitutes the domino effect. Halliday takes the point a stage further. Many of the revolutions in the period he is concerned with, and many before that, were specifically anti-colonial, and there would certainly have been a domino effect in encouraging further colonies to seek independence. However, the revolutions of the late 1970s were of a different kind. For a long time, argues Halliday, the USA had left the control of most of the

Grand Area to individual states with only advice and economic support from the USA. In the late 1970s, that policy of 'delegation of counter-revolutionary responsibility to local regimes and ruling classes, epitomised in Vietnam and Iran' (Halliday, 1983, p. 83), was defeated. The revolts of the late 1970s, in Iran, Afghanistan and Nicaragua for example, were against local ruling classes. The distinction is similar to one made by Roxborough, when he suggests that in the underdeveloped countries two sets of struggles are present, 'the struggle against dependency and for national liberation and development; and the class struggle against the local ruling class' (Roxborough, 1979, p. 159). The first struggle is associated with the local bourgeoisie or capitalists, the second with the working class. Halliday suggests that two things follow from the occurrence of these revolts. First, the USA is being forced to play a much more direct role in the management of the Grand Area, although it does not have a completely free hand here. For example, public pressure at home was such that it had to withdraw its forces from Lebanon in 1984, and so far it has had to carry out most of its 'policing' role in Central America through local intermediaries like the Contras. Secondly, the recent third world revolutions may have an even wider domino effect. 'Precisely because they are directed against the indigenous ruling classes, they presage the revolutions of the future and they serve, more than the anti-colonial victories, to reinforce the challenge to imperialism' (Halliday, 1983, p. 82).

Without doubt, the issues of the superpower conflict are as vital to us as any that affect us in the world today. It is therefore important that we have as clear as possible an understanding of the processes that lie behind that conflict. The examination of the state undertaken in this book may go some way to providing such an understanding. Once we begin to know something of the workings of the capitalist or communist state, of the importance of bureaucratic structures, of the relationship of the state apparatus with the economy, of the role of social classes and of the behaviour of states in an international context, then we can be more certain of our understanding of the superpower conflict. And with understanding comes the hope of control and the hope of continued existence.

Bibliography

Abercrombie, N., Hill, S. and Turner, B. (1980), *The Dominant Ideology Thesis*, London, Allen & Unwin.
Alavi, Hamza (1972), 'The state in post-colonial societies; Pakistan and Bangladesh', *New Left Review* 74 (July/August 1972), 59–81. Reprinted in Harry Gouldbourne (ed.) (1979), pp. 38–69.
Alavi, Hamza (1982), 'State and class under peripheral capitalism' in Alavi and Shanin (eds) (1982), 289–307.
Alavi, Hamza and Shanin, Teodor (eds) (1982), *An Introduction to the Sociology of 'Developing Societies'*, London, Macmillan.
Alford, R. (1963), *Party and Society*, Chicago, Rand McNally.
Almond, G. and Verba, S. (1963), *The Civic Culture*, New Jersey, Princetown University Press.
Almond, G. (1980), 'The intellectual history of the civic culture concept', in Almond, G. and Verba, S. (eds), *The Civic Culture Revisited*, Boston, Little, Brown.
Altvater, E. (1973), 'Notes on some problems of state intervention', *Kapitaliste*, 1.
Anderson, P. (1974), *Lineages of the Absolutist State*, London, New Left Books.
Anglade, Christian and Fortin, Carlos (eds) (1985), *The State and Capital Accumulation in Latin America, Vol 1 Brazil, Chile, Mexico*, London, Macmillan.
Aron, R. (1964), *Industrial Society*, London, Weidenfeld & Nicolson.
Ashford, D. (1981), *Politics and Policy in Britain*, Oxford, Blackwell.
Bachrach, P. and Baratz, M. (1962), 'Two faces of power', *American Political Science Review*, 56, 947–52.
Bachrach, P. and Baratz, M. (1970), *Power and Poverty*, New York, Oxford University Press.
Badie, B. and Birnbaum, P. (1983), *The Sociology of the State*, Chicago, University of Chicago Press.
Barratt Brown, Michael (1974), *The Economics of Imperialism*, Harmondsworth, Penguin.
Barry, B. (1970), *Sociologists, Economists and Democracy*, London, Collier Macmillan.
Bassett, K. (1984), 'Labour, socialism and local democracy', in Boddy, M. and Fudge, C. (eds), *Local Socialism?*, London, Macmillan.
Bealey, F. *et al.* (1965), *Constituency Politics*, London, Faber.

Beer, S. (1965), *Modern British Politics*, London, Faber.
Bendix, R. (1964), *Nation-Building and Citizenship*, New York, Wiley.
Berelson, B. (1954), *Voting*, Chicago, University of Chicago Press.
Berger, S. (1981), *Organising Interests in Western Europe*, Cambridge, Cambridge University Press.
Bernstein, Henry (1982), 'Industrialisation, development and dependence' in Alavi, H. and Shanin, T. (eds) (1982), 218–35.
Birch, A. (1959), *Small Town Politics*, London, Oxford University Press.
Blank, S. (1973), *Industry and Government in Britain*, Farnborough, Saxon House.
Bracher, K. (1973), *The German Dictatorship*, London, Penguin.
Bradshaw, A. (1976), 'A critique of Steven Lukes', *Sociology*, 10, 121–7.
Brown, A. (1974), *Soviet Politics and Political Science*, London, Macmillan.
Butler, D. and Stokes, D. (1974), *Political Change in Britain*, London, Macmillan.
Cardoso, F. H. and Falletton, E. (1979), *Dependency and Development in Latin America*, London, University of California Press.
Cardoso, F. H. (1982) 'Dependency and development in Latin America' in Alavi, H. and Shanin T. (eds) (1982), 112–27.
Castells, M. (1977), *The Urban Question*, London, Edward Arnold.
Castells, M. (1978), *City, Class and Power*, London, Macmillan.
Cawson, A. (1982), *Corporatism and Welfare*, London, Heinemann.
Cawson, A. (1985), 'Corporatism & Local Politics' in Grant, W. (ed.), *The Political Economy of Corporatism*, London, Macmillan.
Cawson, A. and Saunders, P. (1983), 'Corporatism, competitive politics and class struggle', in King, R. (ed.), *Capital and Politics*, London, Routledge & Kegan Paul.
Chomsky, Noam (1982a), 'Strategic arms, the cold war and the third world' in *New Left Review* (eds) (1982), 223–36.
Chomsky, Noam (1982b), *Towards a New Cold War. Essays on the Current Crisis and How We Got There*, London, Sinclair Browne.
Chomsky, Noam (1982c), 'The United States: from Greece to El Salvador' in Chomsky, N., Steel, J., and Gittings, J. (1982), *Superpowers in Collision: The New Cold War of the 1980s*, London, Penguin, 24–58.
Clapham, Christopher (1985), *Third World Politics, An Introduction*, London, Croom Helm.
Clark, G. and Dear, M. (1984), *State Apparatus*, Boston, Allen & Unwin.
Clarke, S. (1977), 'Marxism, Sociology and Poulantzas's theory of the state', *Capital and Class*, 2, 1–31.
Cliff, Tony (1974), *State Capitalism in Russia*, London, Pluto Press.
Cockburn, C. (1977), *The Local State*, London, Pluto Press.
Cohen, J. (1983), *Class and Civil Society*, Oxford, Martin Robertson.
Corrigan, P. (1979), 'The local state', *Marxism Today*, July, 203–9.
Crenson, M. (1971), *The Unpolitics of Air Pollution*, Baltimore, John Hopkins Press.
Crewe, I. *et al.* (1977), 'Partisan de-alignment in Britain, 1964–1974', *British Journal of Political Science*, 7, 129–31.

Crouch, C. (1979), *State and Economy in Contemporary Capitalism*, London, Croom Helm.
Crouch, C. (1983), 'Pluralism and the new corporatism: a rejoinder', *Political Studies*, 31, 3, 452–60.
Dahl, R. (1956), *A Preface to Democratic Theory*, London, University of Chicago Press.
Dahl, R. (1961), *Who Governs?*, New Haven, Yale University Press.
Dearlove, J. (1973), *The Politics of Policy in Local Government*, London, Cambridge University Press.
Dearlove, J. (1979), *The Re-organisation of British Local Government*, London, Cambridge University Press.
Dearlove, J. and Saunders, P. (1984), *Introduction to British Politics*, Cambridge, Polity Press, and Oxford, Blackwell.
Dennis, N. (1972), *Public Participation and Planners Blight*, London, Faber.
Downs, A. (1957), *An Economic Theory of Democracy*, New York, Harper & Row.
Dowse, R. and Hughes, J. (1972), *Political Sociology*, London, Wiley.
Duby, G. (1962), *L'Economie Rurale*, Paris.
Duncan, G. and Lukes, S. (1963), 'The new democracy', *Political Studies*, 11, 156–77.
Duncan, S. and Goodwin, M. (1982), 'The local state and restructuring social relations', *International Journal of Urban and Regional Research*, 6, 157–86.
Dunleavy, P. (1979), 'The urban bases of political alignment', *British Journal of Political Science*, 9, 409–43.
Dunleavy, P. (1980), *Urban Political Analysis*, London, Macmillan.
Dunleavy, P. (1981), *The Politics of Mass Housing in Britain*, Oxford, Clarendon Press.
Dunleavy, P. (1983), 'Voting and the Electorate', in Drucker, H. *et al.* (eds), *Developments in British Politics*, London, Macmillan, 30–58.
Dunleavy, P. and Rhodes, R. (1983), 'Beyond Whitehall', in Drucker, H. *et al.* ibid., 106–33.
Dunleavy, P. (1984), 'The limits to local government', in Boddy, M. and Fudge, C. (eds), *Local Socialism?*, London, Macmillan, 49–81.
Durkheim, E. (1933), *The Division of Labour in Society*, Toronto, Macmillan.
Dyson, K. (1980), *The State Tradition in Western Europe*, Oxford, Martin Robertson.
Easton, D. (1965), *A Systems Analysis of Political Life*, New York, Wiley.
Eisenstadt, S. N. (1966), *Modernisation: Protest and Change*, New Jersey, Prentice-Hall.
Eisenstadt, S. N. (ed.) (1970), *Readings in Social Evolution and Development*, Oxford, Pergamon.
Elcock, H. (1982), *Local Government*, London, Methuen.
Elliott, B, *et al.* (1978), 'Property and political power: Edinburgh 1875–1975', in Garrard, J. *et al.*, *The Middle Class in Politics*, Farnborough, Saxon House.

Elson, Dianne (1984), 'Imperialism' in Gregor McLennan, Held, D. and Hall, S. (eds), (1984), *The Idea of the Modern State*, Milton Keynes, Open University Press, 154–82.
Emmanuel, Arguiri (1983), 'White-settler colonialism and the myth of investment imperialism' in Alavi, H. and Shanin, T. (eds) (1982), 88–106.
Evans, Peter (1979), *Dependent Development*, New Jersey, Princetown, University Press.
Flynn, R. (1983), 'Co-optation and strategic planning in the local state', in King, R. (ed.), *Capital and Politics*, London, Routledge & Kegan Paul.
Forester, T. (1976), *The Labour Party and the Working Class*, London, Heinemann.
Frank, A. Gunder (1967), *Capitalism and Underdevelopment in Latin America*, New York, Monthly Review Press.
Frank, A. Gunder (1969), *Latin America: Underdevelopment or Revolution*, New York, Monthly Review Press.
Frank, A. Gunder (1972), *Lumpenbourgeoisie, Lumpendevelopment*, New York, Monthly Review Press.
Frank, A. Gunder (1981), *Crisis in the Third World*, London, Heinemann.
Friedland, R., Piven, F. and Alford, R. (1977), 'Political conflict, urban structure and the fiscal crisis', *International Journal of Urban and Regional Research*, 1, 3, 447–51.
Friedland, R. (1982), *Power and Crisis in the City*, London, Macmillan.
Friedrich, C. and Brzezinski, Z. (1956), *Totalitarian Dictatorship and Autocracy*, Cambridge (Mass), Cambridge University Press.
Galbraith, J. (1967), *The New Industrial State*, London, Hamilton.
Gamble, A. (1981a), *An Introduction to Modern Social and Political Thought*, London, Macmillan.
Gamble, A. (1981b), *Britain in Decline*, London, Macmillan.
Gerth, H. and Mills, C. (1948), *From Max Weber*, London, Routledge & Kegan Paul.
Giddens, A. (1981), *A Contemporary Critique of Historical Materialism*, London, Macmillan.
Goldthorpe, J. *et al.* (1978), 'Trends in class mobility', *Sociology*, 12, 441–68.
Gouldbourne, Harry (ed.) (1979), *Politics and State in the Third World*, London, Macmillan.
Gouldner, A. (1979), *The Future of the Intellectuals and the Rise of the New Class*, London, Macmillan.
Gramsci, A. (1971), *Selections from the Prison Notebooks*, London, Lawrence & Wishart.
Gramsci, A. (1978), *Selections from Political Writings 1921–6*, London, Lawrence & Wishart.
Grant, W. and Marsh, D. (1977), *The CBI*, London, Hodder and Stoughton.
Grant, W. (1985), 'Introduction' in Grant, W. *The Political Economy of Corporatism*, London, Macmillan.

Green, D. (1981), *Power and Party in an English City*, London, Allen & Unwin.
Habermas, J. (1971), *Towards a Rational Society*, London, Heinemann.
Habermas, J. (1976), *Legitimation Crisis*, London, Heinemann.
Halliday, Fred (1982), 'The sources of the new cold war' in *New Left Review* (eds) (1982), 289–328.
Halliday, Fred (1983), *The Making of the Second Cold War*, London, Verso/NLB.
Halliday, Fred (1984), 'The conjuncture of the seventies and after: a reply to Ougaar', *New Left Review* 147 (Sept/Oct 1984), 76–83.
Harding, N. (1984), 'Socialism, society, and the organic labour state', in Harding, N. (ed.), *The State in Socialist Society*, London, Macmillan.
Harloe, M. (1979), 'Marxism, the state and the urban question, in Crouch, C. (ed.), *State and Economy in Contemporary Capitalism*, London, Croom Helm.
Harris, N. (1972), *Competition and the Corporate Society*, London, Methuen.
Harrison, M. (1984), 'Corporatism, incorporatism and the welfare state', in Harrison, M. (ed.), *Corporatism and the Welfare State*, Aldershot, Gower.
Harvey, C. (1973), *Social Justice and the City*, London, Edward Arnold.
Heclo, H. and Wildavsky, A. (1974), *The Private Government of Public Money*, London, Macmillan.
Hein, Wolfgang and Stenzel, Konrad (1979), 'The capitalist state and underdevelopment in Latin America: the case of Venezuela' in Gouldbourne, Harry (ed.) (1979), 92–116.
Held, David (ed.) (1983), *States and Society*, London, Martin Robertson.
Held, David (1984), 'Power and legitimacy in contemporary Britain' in McLennan, G., Held, D. and Hall, S. (eds), *State and Society in Contemporary Britain*, Cambridge, Polity Press; Oxford, Basil Blackwell.
Held, D. and Kreiger, J. (1984), 'Theories of the state', in Bornstein, S. *et al.* (eds), *The State In Capitalist Europe*, London, Allen & Unwin.
Hindess, B. (1971), *The Decline of Working Class Politics*, McGibbon & Kee, London.
Hindess, B. (1983), *Parliamentary Democracy and Socialist Politics*, London, Routledge & Kegan Paul.
Hintz, O. (1962), 'Wesen und Wandlung des Modernen Staates', in Oestreich, G. (ed.), *Staat und Verfassung*, Goltingen, Vandenhoeck & Ruprecht.
Hintz, O. (1975), *Historical Essays* (ed.), Gilbert, Felix and Berdhal, Robert, M., New York, Oxford University Press.
Hirst, P. (1977), 'Economic classes and politics', in Hunt, A. (ed.), *Class and Class Structure*, London, Lawrence & Wishart.
Hobsbawm, E. (1969), *Bandits*, London, Weidenfeld & Nicolson.
Hobson, J. A. (1965), *Imperialism: A Study*, Ann Arbor, University of Michigan Press (first published 1902).

Holloway, J. and Picciotto, S. (1978), 'Introduction: towards a Marxist theory of the state', in Holloway, J., and Picciotto, S. (eds), *State and Capital*, London, Edward Arnold.
Hoogvelt, Ankie M. (1978), *The Sociology of Developing Societies*, 2nd edn, London, Macmillan.
Hoogvelt, Ankie M. (1982), *The Third World in Global Development*, London, Macmillan.
Hunter, F. (1953), *Community Power Structure*, North Carolina, Chapel Hill Books.
Huntingdon, S. P. (1968), *Political Order in Changing Societies*, New Haven, Yale University Press.
Jenkins, Rhys (1984), *Transnational Corporations and Industrial Transformation in Latin America*, London, Macmillan.
Jessop, B. (1978), 'Capitalism and democracy: the best possible political shell?' in Littlejohn, G. *et al.* (eds), *Power and the State*, London, Croom Helm.
Jessop, B. (1979), 'Corporatism, parliamentarism and social democracy', in Schmitter, P. and Lehmbruch, G. (eds), *Trends Towards Corporatist Intermediation*, London, Sage.
Jessop, B. (1982), *The Capitalist State*, London, Martin Robertson.
Johnson, D. L. (1972), 'The national and progressive bourgeoisie in Chile' in Cockroft, J. D., Frank, A. G. and Johnson, D. L., *Dependence and Underdevelopment*, New York, Anchor.
Johnson, J. J. (ed.) (1962), *The Role of the Military in the Underdeveloped Societies*, New Jersey, Princetown University Press.
Jones, G. (1969), *Borough Politics*, London, Macmillan.
Kavanagh, D. (1983), *Political Science and Political Behaviour*, London, Allen & Unwin.
Kerr, C. *et al.* (1973), *Industrialism and Industrial Man*, London, Penguin.
Key, V. (1961), *Public Opinion and American Democracy*, New York, Knopf.
Kidron, Michael (1970), *Western Capitalism Since the War*, Harmondsworth, Penguin.
King, R. (1982), 'Political Sociology', *Teaching Politics*, 11, 1, 71–85.
King, R. (ed.), (1983), *Capital and Politics*, London, Routledge and Kegan Paul.
King, R. (1985a), 'Sociological approaches to power and decisions', in Wright, G. (ed.), *Behavioral Decision Making*, New York, Plenum Press.
King, R. (1985b), 'Urban politics and markets', *British Journal of Political Science*, 15, 255–68.
King, R. (1985c), 'Corporatism and the local economy', in Grant, W. (ed.), *The Political Economy of Corporatism*, London, Macmillan.
King, R. and Nugent, N. (eds) (1979), *Respectable Rebels*, London, Hodder & Stoughton.
King, R. and Raynor, J. (1981), *The Middle Class*, London, Longman.
Kornhauser, W. (1960), *The Politics of Mass Society*, Glencoe, Free Press.

Laclau, Ernesto (1977), *Politics and Ideology in Marxist Theory: Capitalism, Fascism, Populism*, London, Verso/NLB.

Lane, D. (1985) *State and Politics in the USSR*, London, Blackwell.

Lanning, Greg with Mueller, Marti (1979), *Africa Undermined. Mining Companies and the Underdevelopment of Africa*, Harmondsworth, Penguin.

Lasswell, H. (1949), *Power and Personality*, New York, Norton.

Lazarsfield, P. *et al.* (1948), *The People's Choice*, New York, Columbia University Press.

Lee, J. (1963), *Social Leaders and Public Persons*, Oxford, Oxford University Press.

Leiuwen, E. (1962), 'Militarism and politics in Latin America', in Johnson, J. J. (ed.) (1962).

Lehmbruch, G. (1979), 'Consociational democracy, class conflict, and the new corporatism', in Schmitter, P. and Lehmbruch, G. (eds), *Trends Towards Corporatist Intermediation*, London, Sage.

Lenin, V. (1917), *State and Revolution*, Collected Works, London.

Lenin, V. I. (1975), *Imperialism, The Highest Stage of Capitalism*, Moscow Progress Publishers (first published 1917).

Lerner, D. (1967), 'Comparative analysis of processes of modernisation' in Milner, H. (ed.) (1967), *The City in Modern Africa*, London.

Lernoux, Penny (1982), *Cry of the People. The Struggle for Human Rights in Latin America – The Catholic Church in Conflict with US Policy*, Harmondsworth, Penguin.

Leys, Colin (1982), 'Samuel Huntingdon and the end of classical modernisation theory', in Alavi, H. and Shanin, T. (eds) (1982), 332–49.

Lindblom, C. (1977), *Politics and Markets*, New York, Basic Books.

Lipset, S. (1960), *Political Man*, London, Heinemann.

Lipset, S. and Rokkan, S. (1967), *Party Systems and Voter Alignment*, New York, Free Press.

Longstreth, F. (1979), 'The City, Industry and the State' in Crouch, C. (ed.), *State and Economy in Contemporary Capitalism*, London, Croom Helm.

Lojkine, J. (1977), 'Big firm's strategies, urban policy and urban social movements', in Harlow, M. (ed.), *Captive Cities*, London, Wiley.

Lukes, S. (1974), *Power: A Radical View*, London, Macmillan.

McClelland, David, C. (1966), 'The impulse to modernisation' in Myron Weiner (ed.), (1966), 28–39.

McKay, D. and Cox, A. (1979), *The Politics of Urban Change*, London, Croom Helm.

Macpherson, C. (1966), *The Real World of Democracy*, Oxford, Clarendon Press.

Mandel, E. (1975), *Late Capitalism*, London, New Left Books.

Mandel, E. (1979), *From Class Society to Communism*, London, Ink Links Limited.

Mann, M. (1970), 'The social cohesion of liberal democracy', *American Sociological Review*, 35, 423–39.

Marcuse, H. (1964), *One-Dimensional Man*, London, Routledge & Kegan Paul.

Margolis, M. (1983), 'Democracy: American style', in Duncan, G. (ed.), *Democratic Theory and Practice*, Cambridge, Cambridge University Press.

Martin, R. (1983), 'Pluralism and the new corporatism', *Political Studies*, 31, 1, 86–102.

Marx, K. and Engels, F. (1968), 'Manifesto of the Communist Party' in Marx, K. and Engels F. (1968), *Selected Works, In One Column*, London, Lawrence & Wishart, 35–63.

Merriam, C. (1925), *New Aspects of Politics*, Chicago, University of Chicago Press.

Michels, R. (1915), *Political Parties*, New York, Hearst's International Library, reprinted New York, Dover Publications, 1959.

Middlemas, K. (1979), *Politics in Industrial Society*, London, Deutsch.

Miliband, R. (1969), *The State in Capitalist Society*, London, Weidenfeld & Nicolson.

Miliband, R. (1977), *Marxism and Politics*, London, Oxford University Press.

Miliband, R. (1982), *Capitalist Democracy in Britain*, London, Oxford University Press.

Mills, C. (1956), *The Power Elite*, New York, Oxford University Press.

Moe, T. (1980), *The Organisation of Interests*, Chicago, University of Chicago Press.

Moore, B. (1968), *The Social Origins of Dictatorship and Democracy*, London, Penguin.

Munck, Ronaldo (1984), *Politics and Dependency in the Third World. The Case of Latin America*, London, Zed Books and Newtonabbey, Ulster Polytechnic.

Murray, Robin (1971), 'The internationalisation of capital and the nation state', *New Left Review* 67, May–June 1971, 84–109. Reprinted in Radice, H. (ed.) (1975), 107–34.

Nafziger, E. Wayne (1979), 'A critique of development economics in the US' in Seers, D. (ed.) (1979), 32–48.

Nedelmann, B. and Meier, K. (1979), 'Theories of contemporary corporatism', in Schmitter, P. and Lehmbruch, G. (eds), *Trends Towards Corporatist Intermediation*, London, Sage.

Neumann, G. (1944), *Behemoth: The Structure and Practice of National Socialism 1933–44*, New York.

New Left Review (eds) (1982), *Exterminism and Cold War*, London, Verso/NLB.

Newfarmer, R. and Mueller, L. (1975), *Multinational Corporations in Brazil and Mexico: Structural Sources of Economic and Non-Economic Power*, Report to the Subcommittee on Multinational Corporations of the Committee on Foreign Relations, United States Senate, Washington, US Government Printing Office.

Newman, O. (1981), *The Challenge of Corporatism*, London, Macmillan.

Newton, K. (1976), *Second City Politics*, London, Oxford University Press.

O'Brien, Donal Cruise (1979), 'Modernisation, order and the erosion of a democratic ideal' in Seers, D. (ed.) (1979), 49–76.

O'Brien, Phillip (1975), 'A critique of Latin American theories of dependency' in Oxaal, Ivar, Barnett, Tony and Booth, David (eds) (1975), *Beyond the Sociology of Development. Economy and Society in Latin America and Africa*, London, Routledge & Kegan Paul, 7–27.

O'Connor, J. (1973), *The Fiscal Crisis of the State*, London, St James Press.

O'Donnell, Guillermo (1979), 'Tensions in the bureaucratic–authoritarian state and the question of democracy' in Collier, David (ed.) (1979), *The New Authoritarianism in Latin America*, New Jersey, Princetown, University Press, 285–318.

Offe, C. (1975), 'The theory of the capitalist state and the problem of policy formulation', in Lindberg *et al.* (ed.), *Stress and Contradiction in Modern Capitalism*, Lexington, D. C. Heath.

Offe, C. (1981), 'The attribution of public status to interest groups' in Berger, S. (ed.), *Organising Interests in Western Europe*, London, Cambridge University Press.

Offe, C. (1984), *Contradictions of the Welfare State*, London, Hutchinson.

Offe, C. and Ronge, V. (1975), 'Theses on the theory of the state', reprinted in Giddens, A. and Held, D. (eds), *Classes, Power and Conflict*, London, Macmillan, 249–56.

Offe, C. and Weisenthal, H. (1980), 'Two logics of collective action', in Zeitlin, M. (ed.), *Political Power and Social Theory*, New York, JAI Press.

Olson, M. (1965), *The Logic of Collective Action*, Cambridge, Mass, Harvard University Press.

Pahl, R. and Winkler, J. (1974), 'The coming corporatism', *New Society*, 10 October, 72–6.

Palloix, Christian (1975), 'The internationalisation of capital and the circuit of social capital' in Radice, H. (ed.) (1975), 63–88.

Panitch, L. (1980), 'Recent theorisations of corporatism', *British Journal of Sociology*, 31, 159–87.

Parkin, F. (1968), *Middle-Class Radicalism*, Manchester, Manchester University Press.

Parkin, F. (1969), 'Class stratification in socialist societies', *British Journal of Sociology*, xx, 4, 1969, 355–74.

Pateman, C. (1970), *Participation and Democratic Theory*, Cambridge, Cambridge University Press.

Pateman, C. (1980), 'The civic culture: a philosophical critique', in Almond, G. and Verba, S. (eds), *The Civic Culture Revisited*, Boston, Little, Brown, 57–102.

Parry, G. (1969), *Political Elites*, London, Allen & Unwin.

Parry, G. and Morriss, P. (1974), 'When is a decision not a decision?', in Crewe, I. (ed.), *British Political Sociology Yearbook*, London, Croom Helm.

Parsons, T. (1937), *The Structure of Social Action*, New York, Free Press.

Parsons, T. (1951), *The Social System*, Glencoe, The Free Press.

Parsons, T. (1966), *Societies: An Evolutionary Approach*, New Jersey, Prentice-Hall.

Parsons, T. (1967), 'On the concept of political power', in Parsons, T., *Sociological Theory and Modern Society*, New York, Free Press.

Petras, J. and Cook, T. (1973), 'Dependency and the industrial bourgeoisie: attitudes of Argentine executives toward foreign economic investments and US policy', in Petras, J. (ed.), *Latin America: From Dependence to Revolution*, New York, John Wiley & Sons.

Pickvance, C. (1977), 'From social base to social force', in Harloe, M. (ed.), *Capital Cities*, London, Wiley.

Pierson, C. (1984), 'New theories of state and civil society', *British Journal of Sociology*, 18, 4, 563–71.

Poggi, G. (1978), *The Development of the Modern State*, Hutchinson, London.

Polsby, N. (1963), *Community Power and Political Theory*, New Haven, Yale University Press.

Poulantzas, N. (1973), *Political Power and Social Classes*, London, New Left Books.

Poulantzas, N. (1974), *Fascism and Dictatorship*, London, New Left Books.

Poulantzas, N. (1978), *State, Power, Socialism*, London, New Left Books.

Radice, Hugo (ed.) (1975), *International Firms and Modern Imperialism*, Harmondsworth, Penguin.

Rhodes, R. (1981), *Control and Power in Central–Local Relations*, Farnborough, Gower.

Richardson, J. (1982), 'Tripartism and the new technology', *Policy and Politics*, 10, 3, 343–61.

Roberts, Bryan (1978), *Cities of Peasants*, London, Edward Arnold.

Rose, R. (1976), 'Social structure and party differences', in Rose, R. (ed.), *Studies in British Politics*, London, Macmillan.

Rostow, W. W. (1960), *The Stages of Economic Growth*, Cambridge, Cambridge University Press.

Roxborough, Ian (1979), *Theories of Underdevelopment*, London, Macmillan.

Saul, John, S. (1979), 'The state in post-colonial societies: Tanzania', in Gouldbourne, H. (ed.) (1979), 70–91.

Saunders, P. (1979), *Urban Politics*, London, Hutchinson.

Saunders, P. (1980), 'Local government and the state', *New Society*, 51, 550–1.

Saunders, P. (1981), *Social Theory and the Urban Question*, London, Hutchinson.

Saunders, P. (1984), 'Rethinking local politics', in Boddy, M. and Fudge, C. (eds), *Local Socialism?*, London, Macmillan.

Schumpeter, J. (1943), *Capitalism, Socialism and Democracy*, London, Allen & Unwin.

Scott, Robert, E. (1967), 'Political élites and political modernisation: the crisis of transition', in Lipset, S. M. and Solari, A. (eds) (1967), *Elites in Latin America*, Oxford, Oxford University Press.

Seers, D. (ed.) (1979), *Development Theory. Four Critical Studies*, London, Frank Cass.

Sharpe, I. (1982), 'The Labour Party and the geography of inequality', in Kavanagh, D. (ed.), *The Politics of the Labour Party*, London, Allen & Unwin.
Shils, E. (1966), 'Modernisation and higher education' in Myron Weiner (ed.) (1966), 81–97.
Shils, E. (1970), 'Political development in the new states – alternative courses of political development', in Eisenstadt, S. N. (ed.) (1970), 291–311.
Simmie, J. (1981), *Power, Property and Corporatism*, London, Macmillan.
Skocpol, Theda (1976–7), 'Wallerstein's world capitalist system: a theoretical and historical critique', *American Journal of Sociology*, 82, 5, 1075–90.
Skocpol, Theda (1979), *States and Revolutions: A Comparative Analysis of France, Russia and China*, Cambridge, Cambridge University Press.
Smelser, N. (1963), 'Mechanisms of change and adjustment to change' in Hoselitz, B. and Moore, W. (eds), *Industrialisation and Society*, New York, Mouton.
Smith, Sheila (1980), 'Multinationals and the Third World', *Politics and Power*, 2, 235–50.
Streeck, W. (1982), 'Between pluralism and corporatism', *Journal of Public Policy*, 3, 3, 265–84.
Therborn, G. (1977), 'The rule of capital and the rise of democracy', London, *New Left Books*, 103, May–June.
Thompson, G. (1984), 'Economic intervention in the post-war economy', in McClennan, G. *et al.* (eds), *State and Society in Contemporary Britain*, Cambridge, Polity Press; Oxford, Blackwell.
Truman, D. (1951), *The Governmental Process*, New York, Knopf.
Tugendhat, C. (1973), *The Multinationals*, Harmondsworth, Penguin.
Vaitsos, Constantine (1973), 'Bargaining and the distribution of returns in the purchase of technology by developing countries' in Bernstein, H. (ed.) (1973), *Underdevelopment and Development: The Third World Today*, Harmondsworth, Penguin, 315–22.
Vaitsos, Constantine (1975), 'The process of commercialisation of technology in the Andean Pact' in Radice, H. (ed.) (1975), 183–214.
Vogel, D. (1983), 'The power of business in America: a re-appraisal', *British Journal of Political Science*, 13, 19–43.
Wallerstein, Immanuel (1974), *The Modern World System*, New York, Academic Press.
Wallerstein, Immanuel (1979), *The Capitalist World Economy*, Cambridge, Cambridge University Press.
Wallerstein, Immanuel (1984), *The Politics of the World Economy. The States, The Movements and the Civilizations*, Cambridge, Cambridge University Press.
Warren, Bill (1980), *Imperialism, Pioneer of Capitalism*, London, Verso/NLB.
Weber, M. (1968), *Economy and Society*, New York, Bedminster Press.
Weiner Myron (ed.) (1966), *Modernisation: The Dynamics of Growth*, London, Basic Books.

Westergaard, J. (1977), 'Class, inequality, and corporatism', in Hunt, A. (ed.), *Class and Class Structure*, London, Lawrence & Wishart.
Westergaard, J. and Resler, H. (1975), *Class in a Capitalist Society*, London, Penguin.
Westoby, Adam (1983), 'Conceptions of communist states' in Held, D. *et al*. (eds) (1983), 219–40.
Wolfe, A. (1977), *The Limits of Legitimacy*, New York, Free Press.
Wolfinger, R. (1971), 'Non-decisions and the study of local politics', *American Political Science Review*, 65, 1063–80.
Worsley, Peter (1983), 'One world or three? A critique of the world-system theory of Immanuel Wallerstein' in Held, D. *et al.* (eds) (1983), 504–25. First published in Miliband, R. and Saville, J. (eds) (1980), *Socialist Register*, London, Merlin Press, 298–338.
Worsley, Peter (1984), *The Three Worlds: Culture and World Development*, London, Weidenfeld & Nicolson.

Index